Shaping China's Future
in World Affairs: The Role
of the United States

Shaping China's Future in World Affairs: The Role of the United States

Robert G. Sutter
with the assistance of Seong-Eun Choi

WestviewPress

A Division of HarperCollins*Publishers*

Copyright © 1996 by Westview Press, Inc., A Division of HarperCollins Publishers, Inc.

Published in 1996 in the United States of America by Westview Press, Inc., 5500 Central Avenue, Boulder, Colorado 80301-2877, and in the United Kingdom by Westview Press, 12 Hid's Copse Road, Cumnor Hill, Oxford OX2 9JJ

A CIP catalog record for this book is available from the Library of Congress.
ISBN 0-8133-2957-4 (HC)

The paper used in this publication meets the requirements of the American National Standard for Permanence of Paper for Printed Library Materials Z39.48-1984.

10   9   8   7   6   5   4   3   2   1

Contents

1

Shaping China's Future in World Affairs: The Role of the United States

Introduction

China has often been seen as a challenge or an opportunity to the prevailing international system. The victory of communist forces in China in 1949 was followed in 1950 by the signing of the Sino-Soviet alliance, the start of the Korean War, and Chinese military force intervention in the Korean conflict. Chinese actions prompted a reconfiguration of world politics. The United States and its allies and associates felt compelled to broaden the emerging international containment system from Europe and the Middle East to East Asia. The result was twenty years of military confrontation, economic isolation, and political stalemate.

China's break with the Soviet Union in the 1960s provided a basis for the realignment of Asian politics carried out by Richard Nixon and Mao Zedong in the early 1970s. Cooperation with China was now seen as an important strategic opportunity for the West in its continuing competition with expanding Soviet power. China too saw its interests directed against Moscow and sided with the United States and its allies and associates for mainly strategic reasons.

As Americans and other outsiders observed firsthand the conditions prevailing in China, they often reevaluated their past, sometimes exaggerated views of China's power and influence. Nevertheless, most thought well of the Chinese leaders' efforts after the death of Mao Zedong in 1976 to revitalize China's stagnating economy through reforms that gave freer rein to Chinese private enterprise and to Chinese economic interaction with the developed countries of Asia and the West.

As the East-West conflict declined in the 1980s as a result of Mikhail

Gorbachev's playing down of military expansion and his renewed emphasis on international détente, China's strategic importance as a counterweight to Soviet expansion declined to some degree in world opinion. But this appeared to be more than compensated for by the strong positive interest seen in the developed countries regarding China's steady progress toward economic reform and outreach to foreign economic powers, and by Beijing's concurrent interest in complementary political change.

The prevailing international view of China's power and influence took a radical turn downward in 1989. In the period immediately following the June 1989 Tiananmen incident and subsequent collapse of communist regimes in Europe and elsewhere, it was common for journalists, analysts, and other observers outside China to judge that the communist regime in China was destined for collapse. Observers also sometimes warned of major retrogression in Chinese economic reforms, speculating that Beijing would feel compelled in the face of domestic and foreign pressure to revert to autarchic development policies of the Maoist past. These would reduce Chinese interdependence with other countries and substantially reduce China's incentive to avoid disruptive behavior in interaction with its neighbors and other world powers.[1]

On balance, China's record in recent years has undercut the more extreme near-term predictions of collapse or retrogression. The regime in Beijing has presided over a period of unprecedented growth in the Chinese economy. This growth has not only benefitted many in China, but has come at a time of general lackluster growth in other parts of the world. The result has been a period of unprecedented international investment in and interaction with the Chinese economy. When combined with Beijing's careful avoidance of major controversy and generally accommodating posture in world affairs in recent years, the result has been to erode foreign sanctions and to enhance the international legitimacy of the Chinese leaders. The success of China's continued economic reform also has undermined the arguments of those conservative Chinese leaders who might be inclined to press for a more autarchic development strategy and a more assertive, less flexible posture in world affairs.

Nevertheless, analysis of key determinants of China's future shows a wide range of possible outcomes for China over the next decade. In particular, a good deal of the success of Beijing's efforts in recent years came under the leadership of senior leader Deng Xiaoping. Deng's demise means that a vacuum at the center of political power in China could lead to political struggles with possibly adverse outcomes for the country. The leadership transition is likely to complicate an already difficult set of problems of governance caused by dynamic economic growth, rapid social change, a realignment of central and local power arrangements, and other factors.

A positive scenario for China's future posits an effective administration and greater political reform along with powerful economic modernization. More negative scenarios fall into two categories. The first sees a series of developments leading to degeneration of government effectiveness and authority with a range of negative effects on China's economic and social development. The second envisions China developing formidable economic power while retaining strong authoritarian political control. This raises the possibility of an emerging Chinese economic and military superpower, less interested in accommodation with the outside world and unfettered by the political checks and balances that accompany less authoritarian political structures.

U.S. Interests in and Influence on China

The United States has a lot at stake in China's future. China lies at the center of the world's most dynamic economic region. Disruption in China not only would have a major impact on U.S. investment (over $7 billion utilized since 1979) and trade (over $40 billion annually) with China, but also would have a serious effect on U.S. trade, investment, and other commercial interaction throughout East Asia. Strategically, cooperation from China is central to U.S. efforts to maintain peace on the Korean peninsula, the Taiwan Strait, and the South China Sea; curb the spread of nuclear weapons and related delivery systems; and create a cooperative atmosphere among the great powers in the UN Security Council in order to deal effectively with international trouble-spots. Because of its size, economic growth, and location, China is having an increasingly important impact on U.S. interests in curbing environmental pollution and promoting sustainable development internationally. Over the longer term, China is one of the few world actors capable of creating economic, political, and military power sufficient to pose a strategic danger to the United States.

The United States also exerts important influence on China.[2] Beijing recognizes that the United States still exerts predominant strategic influence in East Asia and the Western Pacific; is a leading economic power in the region, surpassed locally only by Japan; and is one of only two world powers capable of exerting sufficient power around China's periphery to pose a tangible danger to Chinese security and development. As the world's only superpower, the United States also exerts strong influence in international financial and political institutions (e.g., the World Bank and the UN) that are very important to Beijing, and its role in particular areas sensitive to Beijing–notably policy regarding Taiwan and international human rights–is second to none.

As a result, Beijing sees the United States as the key link in the international balance of power affecting Chinese interests. This judgment goes far toward explaining why Chinese leaders so avidly sought a visit to China by President Clinton. It would signal to all at home and abroad that the United States has muffled its opposition to and endorses cooperation with the Beijing government. Of course, there is ample evidence that some Chinese leaders remain deeply suspicious of U.S. motives. They believe the U.S. government is conspiring to weaken and undermine the Chinese leadership and "hold back" China from a more prominent position in world affairs.

There is general agreement in the United States that Washington should use its influence in order to have Beijing conform to international norms and over time to foster changes in China's political, economic, and security systems compatible with American interests. At the same time, there is little agreement in Washington on how the United States should achieve these objectives. At present, the United States and China have a mixed relationship, cooperative on some issues (Cambodia, Korea, anti-drug efforts, anti-crime efforts, trade promotion) and contentious on others (intellectual property rights, market access, missile proliferation, Taiwan, human rights). As China undergoes its post-Deng Xiaoping leadership transition, U.S. officials will be called upon to decide how to position U.S. policy toward China's future government.[3]

Post-Cold War International Conditions

The interaction of China's uncertain future with the sometimes confused U.S. policy toward China will have a significant impact on the international environment. If the two powers are able to achieve cooperation and close interaction on the basis of common interests in peace and development, this presumably would be advantageous for most world people. At the same time, there is plenty of opportunity for friction and conflict in future U.S.-Chinese relations. Given the size and importance of both countries, such frictions will probably have a serious impact on a wide range of people and nations positioned between the United States and China.

Prevailing conditions in international affairs give U.S. observes little clue as to which of many possible outcomes ranging from confrontation to cooperation is more likely in U.S.-China relations over the next decade. The rapid change from the collapse of the cold war bipolar order has seen several trends emerge. But few are in a position to judge how long these trends will last and what effect they will have on international affairs, including those of China and the United States, over the next decade. The trends include the following:[4]

- *Multipolarity.* The nation state is still a dominant actor in world politics. With the demise of the cold war order, these states have broken out of some of the constraints imposed by the alliance politics of that era. Allies now argue and compete with one another more openly. Other "nonaligned" power centers (e.g., China, India, and Indonesia) have also emerged as important world actors;

- *Distribution of power.* Reflecting the more fluid multipolar post-cold war order, one is hard put to determine a stable balance of power in many world regions. More common is a distribution of power, which is fluid and subject to change. The rigid alliance-based, balance of power is a thing of the past;

- *Democracy, free markets, interdependence.* Post-cold war economic and political trends have been dominated by the prominence of powerful free market economies promoting economic interaction and interdependence throughout the developed and developing world. There have been few notable exceptions to this trend, although many countries have not done well economically or politically as they have adjusted to the prevailing free market ways of the world. Less universal but still important is the spread of democratic ideas and practices among many of the previously authoritarian regimes of the Soviet bloc and similar regimes in parts of the third world and elsewhere. The transitions toward democracy have been most dramatic in places like South Africa, Russia, and South Korea, but examples abound in all regions. Of course, there remain plenty of examples of politically authoritarian leaders who are determined to hold on to their power and resist popular pressure for change;

- *Domestic-centered politics.* As they have pulled back from the life-and-death struggle of the cold war, politicians from Moscow to Washington and from Tokyo to Berlin have been compelled to focus on domestic problems. Gorbachev and George Bush were replaced by the much more domestically oriented Boris Yeltsin and Bill Clinton. Expectations that Germany and Japan would use their large economic power to greatly influence the post-cold war world have been dampened by the needs of leaders in both countries to deal with pressing political, economic, and other domestic problems. Other power centers like China, India, and Brazil also have remained focused on internal issues in the current period;

- *Primacy of economics over politics.* The political ideologies that dominated debate in the cold war are a thing of the past. Increasingly leaders throughout the world are basing their political standing on their ability to meet the needs and improve the material conditions of their people. This trend inclines states and peoples to cooperate for economic advantage and helps to promote greater international interdependence. Nevertheless, counter currents remain. Nationalism and religious fundamentalism are used by leaders, often in areas without good prospects for economic advantage in the current world order. They can provide a core for conflict and disruption of the main trend toward economic development;

- *Transnational issues.* With the decline of the importance of security and strategic issues following the end of the cold war, so-called transnational issues have achieved new importance. In general these issues reflect international concerns that cross national boundaries and challenge traditional views of state sovereignty. They require leaders to adjust their views of national power in order to deal with them effectively. Notable examples include international pressures to promote better human rights conditions; to improve environmental quality; to discourage unfair trade or economic practices; to curb the proliferation of weapons of mass destruction; to deal effectively with mass migrations of suffering peoples; to curb the spread of highly infectious diseases; and to suppress international terrorist, drug, or criminal activities; and

- *Influence of technology.* Peoples throughout the world are increasingly aware of events in other areas that have an effect on their lives. The so-called communications revolution includes mass media and personal channels that challenge governments anxious to control access to sensitive information by their peoples. The prime minister of Vanuatu tried in vain in mid-1995 to blackout news in his country of France's decision to resume nuclear testing in nearby French Polynesia. The prime minister presumably wanted to avoid the disturbances and anti-French feelings such news would likely engender. Nevertheless, most nations are too interconnected with world information systems–needed for effective economic policies and growth–to allow such an isolationist stance to succeed.

Scope of this study

In making a case for the importance of Chinese-U.S. interaction for the future international order, this study adheres to the following steps:

- It first examines China's record in world affairs, assesses China's growing role today, and determines what trends and influences are likely to be most prominent in the decade ahead;
- It then examines conditions inside and outside China that are likely to affect China's policy and practice abroad;
- Making a case that the U.S. policy and behavior toward China may be the most important and unpredictable variable determining China's future approach to world affairs, the study examines why the United States has so much influence on China today and why U.S. policy toward China is so hard to predict; and
- The study concludes with an evaluation of three possible outcomes for China in the next decade, what they would mean for the international order, and what, if anything, the United States can do about them.

Notes

1. For background on this period, see among others, Kerry Dumbaugh, *China and Congress in 1992*, Congressional Research Service (CRS) Report 93-894F, October 12, 1993. These and other CRS products referred to in this book have been reprinted in and are available to the general public in *What Should be the Policy of the United States Government Toward the People's Republic of China*, compiled by the Congressional Research Service, Library of Congress, 104th Congress, 1st Session, Senate Document 104-3, (Washington, DC: U.S. Government Printing Office, 1995).

2. For background, see Robert Sutter, *China In World Affairs–U.S. Policy Choices*, CRS Report 95-265S, January 31, 1995, pp. 15-19.

3. For a review of U.S. policy options and approaches toward China, see *China-U.S. Relations*, CRS Issue Brief 94002 by Kerry Dumbaugh, Washington, DC (updated regularly).

4. This discussion benefitted greatly from consultations with Thomas Robinson, Washington, D.C., June 1995.

2

China's Foreign Policy in Historical Perspective

China says it pursues an independent foreign policy. The goals of this policy are safeguarding world peace, opposing all forms of hegemonism, and achieving economic modernization. China repeatedly emphasizes that it needs a peaceful international environment so that it can devote resources to its ambitious development plans. The goal of economic modernization has long been a driving force behind China's increasingly active participation in world affairs, exemplified by its greatly expanded economic relations with foreign countries since the late-1970s. As part of what it calls an "independent foreign policy of peace," Beijing has joined numerous international organizations and maintains diplomatic relations with more nations than at any time since the founding of the People's Republic in 1949. By the mid-1990s, China had diplomatic relations with more than 150 nations, and–in contrast to earlier periods–was willing to interact with governments of different social systems or ideologies on a basis of peaceful coexistence and mutual respect.[1]

Many of Beijing's overall foreign policy goals and the forces that shape its policy have been similar to those of other nations. China has sought to protect its sovereignty and territorial integrity and to achieve independence of action. Its foreign relations have been conditioned by its historical experiences, nationalism, ideology, and the world view of its leaders, as well as by the governmental structure and decision-making process. At times, its domestic policies have had wide-ranging ramifications for its foreign policy.[2]

This section draws heavily from the author's chapter in the forthcoming country study on China to be published under the direction of Robert Worden of The Federal Research Division of the Library of Congress. It is used here with permission.

As with most nations, China's actual conduct of foreign relations sometimes has been at odds with official policy. Beijing's stress on ideology and principles in its official statements at times makes the contrast between statements and actions particularly noticeable. In addition, the need of its leaders to react to changing events and circumstances has added an element of unpredictability to its foreign policy decisions at several crucial junctures since 1949.[3]

China's foreign policy since 1949 also has had several rather unique tensions: between practicality and adherence to principles, between militancy and peacefulness, between an ideologically based self-reliance and a necessity-based dependence on other nations and their economies, and between China's actual and potential capabilities. These contradictory characteristics have created a sometimes confusing picture of Chinese foreign policy. Has Chinese foreign policy basically been pragmatic or primarily based on principles and ideology? Has China been peace-loving or intent on fomenting world revolution? Is China's ultimate goal to be self-sufficient or economically interdependent with the rest of the world? And, is China basically still a poor developing country that is, at most, a regional power, or is it actually a nascent economic and military giant deserving of superpower status?[4]

Since 1949, Chinese foreign policy has exhibited all of these contrasting features. Beijing has emphasized principles and ideology above everything else in foreign relations, especially during the 1950s and 1960s, but China's leaders have also shown a practical side that gave them the flexibility to change policies, sometimes drastically, when they deemed it in China's best interest. One of the most dramatic changes was the shift from an alliance with the Soviet Union against the United States and Japan in the 1950s to an explicitly anti-Soviet policy and rapprochement with the United States and Japan in the 1970s. Since 1949, Chinese foreign policy has fluctuated between periods of militancy–for example during the Cultural Revolution (1966-1976), when China called for worldwide revolution–and periods when Beijing has been a chief proponent of peaceful coexistence among nations, such as during the mid-1950s and again during the 1980s and 1990s. How self-reliant or dependent on others China should become in order to modernize has been a constant dilemma in Chinese policy since the nineteenth century. As this policy fluctuated, Chinese foreign relations have alternated between a tendency toward isolation and periods of openness to foreign assistance and influence. Finally, the contradiction between China's actual capabilities since 1949 and its perceived future potential has been another salient and distinctive feature of its foreign relations. China's tremendous size, population, natural resources, military strength, and sense of history have placed it in the unusual position of being a poor developing country that has often been treated as a major global power having a special relationship with the United States and the Soviet Union and, since 1991, with Russia.

Development of China's Foreign Policy

Understanding the origins and forces shaping China's foreign policy provides a framework within which to view both the changes and the continuities in Chinese foreign policy since 1949. The origins of China's foreign policy can be found in its size and population, historical legacy, world view, nationalism, and Marxist-Leninist-Maoist ideology. These factors have combined with China's economic and military capabilities, governmental structure, and decision-making processes to make certain foreign policy goals prominent: security, sovereignty and independence, territorial integrity and reunification, and economic development.[5]

Historical Legacy and World View

China's long and rich history as the world's oldest continuous civilization has affected its foreign relations in various ways. For centuries, the Chinese empire enjoyed basically unchallenged greatness and self-sufficiency. China saw itself as the cultural center of the universe, a view reflected in the concept of the "Middle Kingdom" (zhongguo, the Chinese word for China). For the most part, it viewed non-Chinese as uncivilized barbarians. Although China was occasionally overrun and ruled by these "barbarians," as during the Yuan (1229-1368) and Qing (1644-1922) Dynasties, the non-Chinese usually retained enough Chinese institutions to maintain a continuity of tradition.

Over time, the Chinese developed a world view that their emperor was the ruler of all humankind by virtue of his innate superiority and that relations with other states or entities were tributary, rather than state-to-state relations between equals. Traditionally, there was no equivalent of a foreign ministry; foreign relations included such activities as receiving tributary missions to the imperial court by countries seeking trade with China and military expeditions to keep neighboring peoples outside China's borders. The first Europeans who sought trade with

China, beginning in the sixteenth century, were received as tributary missions and had to conform to the formalities and rituals of the tribute system at the Chinese court. China's view of itself as the undisputed center of civilization remained basically unchanged until the nineteenth century, when the Qing Dynasty began to deteriorate under Western pressure and internal upheaval.[6]

A traditional concept related to China's view of itself as the Middle Kingdom that continues to have relevance is the idea of "using barbarians to control barbarians." In modern times, this practice has taken the form of using relations with one foreign power as a counterweight to relations with another. Two salient examples are China's policy of "leaning to one side" in the alliance between China and the Soviet Union during the 1950s for support against the United States and its rapprochement with the United States in the 1970s to counteract the Soviet threat China perceived at the time. China's strong desire for sovereignty and independence of action, however, seems to have made Chinese alliances or quasi-alliances short-lived. Throughout its history, the People's Republic of China has developed close or alliance-like relations with several nations, only to draw apart. Only China's relationship with Pakistan has remained close throughout the twists and turns of Chinese foreign relations since 1949.[7]

China's historical legacy includes a tendency toward isolationism and an ambivalence about opening up to the outside world. In imperial times, China's foreign relations varied from cosmopolitan periods, such as the Tang, to isolationist periods, such as the Ming, when few foreigners were allowed in the country. China's inward-looking world view and its centuries of self-sufficiency and isolation contributed to the country's difficulty when confronted by expansionist Western powers in the nineteenth century. The debate over remaining self-reliant and hence avoiding possible corruption by foreign influences or opening up to the outside world in order to modernize more quickly has continued for over a century. Post-Mao economic development since the late 1970s has been based on an "open door" to advantageous economic, technical, and scientific interchange with the outside world. Foreign trade and outside investment in China have grown far faster than the overall economy. Yet many in China remain deeply suspicious that the United States and others will use this economic interchange to undermine communist rule and to press China to conform to norms of international behavior established by the United States, its allies, and its associates.[8]

Nationalism

Nationalism was a natural outgrowth of China's long and rich historical tradition. It also arose from the injustices China suffered in more recent history–in particular, China's domination by foreign powers from the nineteenth century until the end of World War II. During this time, which China refers to as "the century of shame and humiliation," the formerly powerful imperial government devolved to what China calls "semi-colonial" status, as it was forced to sign unequal treaties and grant foreigners extraterritorial privileges. Foreign powers divided China into spheres of influence. Most debilitating and humiliating was the foreign military pressure that overpowered China, culminating in Japan's invasion and occupation of parts of China in the late 1930s. The bitter recollection of China's suffering at the hands of foreign powers has continued to be a wellspring of Chinese nationalistic sentiment since 1949. The suspicion of foreign powers, opposition to any implication of inferior status, and a desire to reassert sovereignty and independence have strongly influenced Chinese foreign policy. Examples of this attitude are Mao Zedong's 1949 declaration that "the Chinese people have stood up" and Deng Xiaoping's 1982 pronouncement that "no foreign country can expect China to be its vassal or expect it to swallow any bitter fruit detrimental to its interests."

In the 1990s, China's leaders use nationalistic sentiment to offset outside criticism of Chinese policies and behavior on a range of issues, including its trading practices, proliferation of weapons of mass destruction and related technology, and human right violations. Many Chinese leaders portray criticism on these issues as reminiscent of the imperialist demands on China in the past and as reflective of an underlying desire by the United States and other nations to use such pressures to keep China weak and to "hold back" its development as a major world power.[9]

Nationalism fuels China's desire to achieve territorial integrity and to restore its sovereignty over areas previously considered a part of China. Although China has not fully resolved border disputes with India, Russia, and Vietnam (and other nations with which it has a dispute over the South China Sea islands), Beijing had concluded boundary settlements with Pakistan, Burma, Nepal, Afghanistan, the Democratic People's Republic of Korea (North Korea), and Mongolia. Negotiations on border issues were held intermittently with the Soviet Union from 1949 to 1991 and with Russia since 1991, and with India since the early

1980s. The difficulty of resolving these issues seems to reflect nationalistic pride both in China and in the other countries concerned.[10]

The restoration of sovereignty over certain areas previously under Chinese control was complicated by special circumstances. For example, Qing Dynasty control over Outer Mongolia (now the Mongolian Republic) had been supplanted by Russian and later Soviet influence for several decades before 1949. Although it was most likely with reluctance and regret, Chinese leaders generally conceded independence to Ulaanbaatar, and China recognized the Mongolian People's Republic (as it was known from 1924 to 1992) as a separate nation in 1949. By contrast, asserting sovereignty over another outlying area, Tibet (called Xizang–western frontier–by China), was considered such an important strategic goal that military force was used to gain control there in 1950, to reassert it in 1959, and reinforce central control over dissidents in the late 1980s.[11]

Two other Chinese areas under the control of foreign powers in the mid-1990s were Hong Kong and Macao. According to Chinese statements, these "problems left over from history" were the result of imperialist aggression and the incompetence of Chinese rulers. Macao, the first European enclave on the Chinese coast, was occupied by Portugal in 1557 and ceded to Portugal under an 1887 treaty. Britain gained control of Hong Kong island and adjacent territory through three treaties with China in the nineteenth century. In the mid-1980s, China concluded formal arrangements with Britain and Portugal for the return of Hong Kong to Chinese sovereignty in 1997 and Macao in 1999. Both agreements were made under a policy of "one country, two systems," which is supposed to allow the areas a high degree of autonomy as "special administrative regions" of China. From the Chinese perspective, negotiating the return of both Hong Kong and Macao to Chinese sovereignty before the end of the twentieth century was undoubtedly one of the major foreign policy accomplishments of Chinese leaders in the twentieth century.[12]

The most crucial issue of national reunification, however, remained unresolved in the mid-1990s: Taiwan. Chiang Kai-shek and his Republic of China forces fled to Taiwan after the founding of the People's Republic in 1949. The government they established there continues to claim authority as the government of the Chinese nation. Although China continues to seek to reunify Taiwan with the mainland, in the 1980s it replaced its previous militant goal of "liberating Taiwan" with the idea of reunification under the "one country, two systems" policy. Some observers consider the joint declarations on Hong Kong (with Britain in 1984) and Macao (with Portugal in 1987) as possible precedents for reunifying Taiwan. Because of the legacy of mistrust between the leaders of the two sides and other complex factors, however, this difficult and long-standing problem did not appear close to resolution in the mid-1990s. Indeed, the rise in the Taiwan government and its main opposition party of forces favoring formal political separation from the mainland poses a major challenge to Beijing's efforts to achieve reunification.[13]

Influence of Ideology

Marxist-Leninist and Maoist ideological components of China's foreign policy, varying in significance over time, have included a belief that conflict and struggle are inevitable, a focus on opposing imperialism, and the determination to advance communism throughout the world–especially through the Chinese model. Maoist thinking has added the concept of flexibility while adhering to fundamental principles.[14]

One of the most basic aspects of China's ideological world view has been the assumption that conflict, although not necessarily military conflict, is omnipresent in the world. According to Marxist-Leninist analysis, all historical development is the result of a process of struggle between classes within a nation, between nations themselves, or between broader forces such as socialism and imperialism. A basic tenet of Chinese leaders holds that the international situation is best understood in terms of the "principal contradictions" of the time. Once these contradictions are understood, they can be exploited in order to, as Mao said, "win over the many, oppose the few, and crush our enemies one by one." China has amplified the Leninist policy of uniting with some forces in order to oppose others more effectively in a "united front." Chinese leaders have urged the formation of various united fronts as they have perceived the contradictions in the world as changing over time.[15]

Perhaps because of the belief that struggle is necessary for progress, China considered world war inevitable for much of its history since 1949. This changed in the 1980s, when Chinese leaders began to say that the forces for peace had become greater than the forces for war. One reason for growing world stability was seen in "multipolarization," that is, the growth of additional forces, such as the third world and Europe, to counterbalance the bipolar tension between the United States and the Soviet Union. Even after the demise of the Soviet Union in 1991, China's interpretation of world events still focused on the perceived struggle between opposing forces, notably competing nation-states in a multipolar international system.[16]

Opposition to imperialism is another major ideological component of Chinese foreign policy. The Leninist emphasis on the struggle against imperialism made sense to Chinese leaders, whose nationalism had evolved in part in reaction to China's exploitation by foreign powers during the nineteenth century. Although opposition to imperialism and hegemonism has remained a constant, the specific target of the opposition has changed since 1949. Viewing world affairs in somewhat oversimplified terms, China focused on opposing U.S. imperialism in the 1950s; on opposing collusion between U.S. "imperialism" and Soviet "revisionism" in the 1960s; on combating Soviet social-imperialism or hegemony in the 1970s; and on opposing hegemony by either superpower in the 1980s. With the end of the cold war and the demise of the Soviet Union by the early 1990s, China still sees signs of "hegemonism" in the efforts of the United States and other large powers to press weaker countries, including China, to conform to international norms supported by the United States and other developed nations.[17]

The extent of China's determination to advance communism throughout the world has fluctuated since 1949. In the early 1950s and during the 1960s, Chinese leaders called for worldwide armed struggle against colonialism and "reactionary" governments. China supplied revolutionary groups with rhetorical and, in some cases, material support. Central to its support for leftist movements was the idea that they should take China as a model in their struggle for national liberation. While stressing that its experience was directly applicable to many other countries, China suggested that each country should adapt its revolution to its own conditions–creating ambiguity about China's position on "exporting" revolution. For the most part, however, since 1949, China's encouragement of revolution abroad appeared to receive a lower priority than other foreign policy goals.[18]

Militancy and support for worldwide revolution peaked during the Cultural Revolution, when China's outlook on liberation struggles seemed to take its cue from Minister of National Defense Lin Biao's famous 1965 essay "Long Live the Victory of People's War!" This essay by Mao's heir apparent predicted that the underdeveloped countries of the world would surround and overpower the industrial nations and create a new communist world order. Alleged Chinese involvement in subversive activities led Indonesia and several African countries to break off diplomatic relations with Beijing in the mid- and late 1960s.

In the mid-1970s, China reduced or discontinued its support for most revolutionary and liberation movements around the world. It shifted toward cultivating state-to-state relations with established governments, seeking economic and other advantages from dealing with the world as it is, rather than pushing for revolutionary change. Some countries continued to be suspicious of China's intentions, however. Especially in Southeast Asia, where Beijing had supported local communist insurgencies, China's image as an unpredictable, sometimes radical power intent on fomenting world change continued to affect its foreign relations.[19]

One of the most salient characteristics of Chinese foreign policy since 1949 has been its claim that it consistently adheres to principles even though particular interpretations and policies have changed dramatically. A statement by Mao Zedong seems to summarize this apparent contradiction: "We should be firm in principle; we should also have all flexibility permissible and necessary for carrying out our principles." Although claiming that China has never deviated from such underlying principles as opposition to imperialism and safeguarding peace, Chinese leaders have made major shifts in foreign policy based on their pragmatic assessment of the international situation. According to Chinese leaders, China has pursued a long-term strategy and is not influenced by expediency. In keeping with the view of its foreign policy as constant and unvarying, Chinese pronouncements often describe their policy with words such as "always" and "never."[20]

The Five Principles of Peaceful Coexistence embodied in an agreement signed by China and India in 1954 illustrate how certain principles have provided a framework for both continuity and change in post-1949 Chinese foreign policy. The Five Principles played an important ideological role in the mid-1950s, when China began to cultivate the friendship of the newly independent nations of Asia and Africa. However, by the time of the Cultural Revolution, China was involved in acrimonious disputes with many of these same nations, and their relations could have been described as anything but "peacefully coexistent." The Five Principles of Peaceful Coexistence were reemphasized in the post-Mao period, and were considered the basis for relations with all nations, regardless of their social systems or ideology.[21]

Decision Making and Implementation

Information related to leadership and decision making often is kept secret in China. Even knowledgeable observers cannot understand fully the structure of Chinese foreign policy organizations or how they make or implement decisions. What is known about them is subject to conflicting interpretations about the relative power and influence of particular individuals, institutions, and policies.[22]

Since 1949, China's foreign relations have become increasingly more complex, as China has established formal diplomatic relations with more nations, joined the United Nations (UN) and other international and regional political and economic organizations, developed party-to-party ties between the Chinese Communist party (CCP) and foreign political parties, and expanded trade and other economic relations with the rest of the world. These changes have affected foreign relations in significant ways. The economic component of China's international relations has increased dramatically since the late 1970s; more ministries and organizations have become involved in foreign relations than ever before; and the Chinese foreign policy community is more experienced and better informed about the outside world than it was previously.[23]

Despite the growing complexity of Chinese foreign relations, one fundamental aspect of foreign policy has remained relatively constant since 1949: power for the most important decisions has been concentrated in the hands of a few key individuals at the top of the leadership hierarchy. In the past, ultimate foreign policy authority rested with such figures as Mao Zedong and Zhou Enlai. Beginning in the late 1970s, major decisions were understood to have depended on paramount leader Deng Xiaoping. In the 1980s, Deng initiated steps to institutionalize decision making and make it less dependent on personal authority, but the ousters of key leaders like Hu Yaobang and Zhao Ziyang and the foreign policy crisis following the June 1989 Tiananmen incident and other events greatly complicated this transition.[24]

In general terms, however, one can say that since the death of Mao in 1976, China under Deng Xiaoping has undertaken a program of reform and opening to the outside world. The political system as a result is evolving from a totalitarian to an authoritarian model. China's foreign policy decision making has also been in a process of transformation from a "strong-man" model to one more characterized by bureaucratic, sectorial, and regional competition.

As the Long March generation passes from the scene, the new generation of political leaders lack both authority and charisma to dominate foreign policy decision making. Foreign affairs bureaucracies have become increasingly influential. At the same time, in the process of decentralization and opening to the outside world, new actors like the defense industry, the People's Liberation Army (PLA), and provincial authorities, which had previously played little role in foreign policy decision making, have now gained a stronger voice in foreign affairs. Already overseas arms sales by the defense industry and the PLA and pirating of intellectual properties, textile quota evasion, and aggressive marketing of prison-labor products by provincial authorities have become major points of contention between China and the West. This trend, which started in the late 1970s, has essentially not been affected by the crackdown in June 1989 and is likely to continue through the decade with the current economic reform program.

Government and Party Organizations. Under the top leadership lie the foreign affairs bureaucracies of ministerial ranking. These bureaucratic institutions represent the foreign policy elements of the three major systems of Chinese political power: the party, the government, and the military. Officially these institutions make decisions over the details in their implementation of foreign policy decisions made by the central leadership. According to their respective functions, they can be roughly placed into three main categories: (1) policy consultation, coordination, and supervision–the Central Foreign Affairs Leading Small Group (LSG) and the Foreign Affairs Office of the State Council; (2) policy recommendation and implementation–the Ministry of Foreign Affairs (MFA), the Ministry Of Foreign Trade and Economic Cooperation (MOFTEC), the CPC Central (Committee) International Liaison Department (ILD), and the Second Directorate of the PLA General Staff Department (GSD); (3) information and research–Xinhua News Agency, the Third Directorate of the PLA GSD, and academic foreign affairs research institutes. Of the bureaucracies and institutions, only the MFA, MOFTEC and ILD play official policy roles. Others only represent bureaucratic interests in foreign policies, with the PLA one of the newest.

In the 1980s and 1990s, more Chinese organizations became involved in China's foreign relations than at any time previously. The CCP Secretariat and the State Council together carry the major responsibility for foreign policy decisions. High-level party and government organizations such as the CCP's Central Committee and Political Bureau; the CCP and state central military commissions; the National People's Congress; and such leaders as the premier, the president, and the CCP general secretary also are involved in foreign relations to varying degrees by virtue of their concern with major policy issues, both foreign and domestic.[25]

As China's contacts with the outside world have grown in the post-Mao period, party and government leaders at all levels increasingly have become involved in foreign affairs. The president of the People's Republic fulfills a ceremonial role as head of state and also is responsible for officially ratifying or abrogating treaties and agreements with foreign nations. In addition to meeting with foreign visitors, Chinese leaders, including the president, the premier, and officials at lower levels, travel abroad regularly.[26]

Until the late 1980s, the Political Bureau was the primary party organization involved in foreign policy decision making. Since then, the State Council has referred major decisions to the Secretariat for resolution and the Political Bureau for ratification. Under the party Secretariat, the International Liaison Department has primary responsibility for relations between the CCP and foreign political parties. Other CCP Central Committee organizations whose work is related to foreign relations are the United Front Work Department, responsible for relations with overseas Chinese, the Propaganda Department, and the Foreign Propaganda Small Group.[27]

The highest organ of state power, the National People's Congress, traditionally appears to have had only limited influence on foreign policy. Since the early 1980s, however, the National People's Congress has become more active on the international scene by increasing its contacts with foreign legislative bodies. Through its Standing Committee and its Foreign Affairs Committee, the National People's Congress has a voice in foreign relations matters and occasionally prepares reports on foreign policy issues for other party and government bodies.[28]

As the primary executive organization under the National People's Congress, the State Council has a major role in foreign policy, particularly with regard to decisions on routine or specific matters. Greater questions of policy might require party involvement. As in the past, the Ministry of Foreign Affairs is the most important institution involved in conducting day-to-day foreign relations, but many other ministries and organizations under the State Council also have functions related to foreign affairs. These include the Ministry of Foreign Trade and Economic Cooperation, the Ministry of Finance, the Ministry of National Defense, the Bank of China, and the People's Bank of China. In addition, more than half of the other ministries, which oversee such disparate areas as aeronautics, forestry, and public health, have bureaus or departments concerned explicitly with foreign affairs. These offices presumably handle contacts between the ministries and their foreign counterparts.[29]

Ministry of Foreign Affairs. The Ministry of Foreign Affairs has been one of China's most important ministries since 1949. Each area of foreign relations is overseen by a vice minister or assistant minister. The ministry is divided into departments, some geographic and some functional in responsibility. The regionally oriented departments include African affairs, Asian affairs, North American and Oceanian affairs, Latin American affairs, Russian and East European affairs, West Asian and North African affairs, and West European affairs. There also is a Taiwan Affairs Department and a Hong Kong and Macao Affairs Office. The functional departments are responsible for administration, cadres, consular affairs, finance, information, international laws and treaties, international organizations and affairs, personnel, protocol, training and education, and translation. Below the department level are divisions, such as the United States Affairs Division under the North American and Oceanian Affairs Department.[30]

A recurring problem for the ministry and the diplomatic corps has been a shortage of qualified personnel. In the first years after the founding of the People's Republic, there were few prospective diplomats with international experience. Premier Zhou Enlai relied on a group of young people who had served under him in various negotiations with Guomindang, U.S., Soviet, and other officials to form the core of the newly established Ministry of Foreign Affairs. Zhou himself held the foreign ministry portfolio from 1949 to 1958. In the second half of the 1960s, China's foreign affairs sector suffered a major setback during the Cultural Revolution. Higher education was disrupted, foreign-trained scholars and diplomats were attacked, and all of China's ambassadors except the one to Egypt were recalled. The ministry practically ceased functioning. It was an era when foreign exchanges largely were limited to meetings with "friendship" delegations from Maoist communist parties and other radical organizations that visited China under CCP auspices.[31]

Starting in the early 1970s, the foreign affairs establishment was rebuilt. Foreign affairs personnel now are recruited from such specialized training programs as the ministry's Foreign Affairs College, the College of International Relations, the Beijing Foreign Languages Institute, and international studies departments at major universities. Foreign language study is still considered an important requirement, but it increasingly is supplemented by substantive training in foreign relations. Foreign affairs personnel benefit from expanded opportunities for education, travel, and exchange of information with the rest of the world. In addition, specialists from other ministries serve in China's many embassies and consulates; for example, the Ministry of National Defense provides military attaches, commercial officers are drawn from the Ministry of Foreign Trade and Economic Cooperation, and some personnel in charge of cultural affairs come from the Ministry of Culture and the State Education Commission.[32]

Ministry of Foreign Trade and Economic Cooperation. Since the late 1970s, economic and financial issues have become an increasingly important part of China's foreign relations. To streamline foreign economic relations, the Ministry of Foreign Economic Relations and Trade was established in 1982 through the merger of several commissions and ministries. By the late 1980s, this ministry was the second most prominent ministry involved in the routine conduct of foreign relations. Renamed the Ministry of Foreign Trade and Economic Cooperation in 1993, it has an extremely broad mandate that includes foreign trade, foreign investment, foreign aid, and international economic cooperation. Through regular meetings with the Ministry of Foreign Affairs, it participates in efforts to coordinate China's foreign economic policy with other aspects of its foreign policy.[33]

Ministry of National Defense. As in other nations, the military's views on defense capability, deterrence, and perceptions of threat are essential components of China's global strategy. However, little information is available on foreign policy coordination between China's military and foreign policy establishments. The most important military organizations with links to the foreign policy community are the Ministry of National Defense, the State Central Military Commission, and the CCP Central Military Commission. The Ministry of National Defense provides military attaches for Chinese embassies, and its Foreign Affairs Bureau deals with foreign attaches and military visitors. Working-level coordination with the Ministry of Foreign Affairs is maintained when, for example, high-level military leaders travel abroad. In addition, the Ministry of National Defense's strategic research arm, the China Institute for International Strategic Studies, carries out research on military and security issues with foreign policy implications.[34]

The most important link between the military and foreign policy establishments appears to be at the highest level, particularly through the state and party central military commissions. Deng Xiaoping was concurrently chairman of both commissions in the 1980s, as was his successor in these jobs, Jiang Zemin, since 1989. The views of the commissions' members on major foreign policy issues are almost certainly considered in informal discussions or in meetings of other high-level organizations to which they also belong, such as the Political Bureau, the Secretariat, or the State Council. It is significant, though, that compared with earlier periods, relatively few military leaders have served on China's top policymaking bodies since the 1980s.[35]

"People-to-People" Diplomacy. A significant forum for Chinese foreign relations since 1949 has been cultural or "people-to-people" diplomacy. The relative isolation of the People's Republic during its first two decades increased the importance of cultural exchanges and informal ties with people of other countries through mass organizations and friendship societies. In some cases, activities at this level have signaled an important diplomatic breakthrough. The Chinese-U.S. ping-pong exchange in 1971, for instance, helped facilitate the rapprochement between Beijing and Washington at that time. In addition to educational and cultural institutions, many other organizations, including the media, women's, youth, and athletic organizations; and academic and professional societies have been involved in foreign relations. Two institutes responsible for this aspect of Chinese diplomacy are associated with the Ministry of Foreign Affairs and staffed largely by former diplomats: the Chinese People's Association for Friendship with Foreign Countries and the Chinese People's Institute of Foreign Affairs.[36]

The Decision-Making Process. The most crucial foreign policy decisions in the 1980s and early 1990s were made by the highest-level leadership, with Deng Xiaoping as the final arbiter. However, a shift of uncertain importance was under way in the mid-1990s to strengthen the principles of collective and institutional decision making and to reduce party involvement in favor of increased state responsibility. In line with this trend, the State Council makes decisions regarding routine foreign policy matters and refers only major decisions to the party Secretariat or to informal deliberations involving top party leadership. When called upon to make decisions, the Secretariat relies largely on the advice of the State Council and other members of China's foreign affairs community. The importance of the Political Bureau in this process appears to have decreased since the 1980s. Although individual members of the Political Bureau exert influence on foreign policy, the bureau's role as an institution seems to have become to ratify decisions, rather than formulate them. The division between party and government functions in foreign affairs can be summarized as party supremacy in overall policy making and supervision, with the government's State Council and ministries under it responsible for the daily conduct of foreign relations.[37]

These high-level decision-making bodies constitute the apex of an elaborate network of party and government organizations and research institutes concerned with foreign policy. To support the formulation and implementation of policy, especially in a bureaucracy as complex and hierarchical as China's, there exists a network of small advisory and coordination groups. These groups channel research, provide expert advice, and act as a liaison between organizations. Perhaps the most important of these groups is the party Secretariat's Foreign Affairs Small Group (Waishi Xiaozu). This group comprises key party and government officials, including the president, the premier, state councilors, the ministers of foreign affairs and foreign trade and economic cooperation, and various foreign affairs specialists, depending on the agenda of the meeting.[38]

Notes

1. *Beijing Review*, November 1, 1982; *Beijing Review*, April 21, 1986, XVII-XVIII.

2. See, among others, Robert C. North, *The Foreign Relations of China*, Dickenson Publishing Co., Belmont, CA., 1967, pp. 1-9.

3. Jonathan D. Pollack, *Security, Strategy, and the Logic of Chinese Foreign Policy*, Rand Corporation, Santa Monica, 1984, p. 58; Robert C. North, *The Foreign Relations of China*, pp. 1-9; Allen S. Whiting, "Foreign Policy of China," in *Foreign Policy in World Politics*, Roy Macridis, ed., (Englewood Cliffs, NJ: Prentice-Hall, 1985), p. 267.

4. Harry Harding, "Change and Continuity in Chinese Foreign Policy," *Problems of Communism* (Washington, DC), March-April 1983, pp. 1-29.

5. North, *The Foreign Relations of China*, pp. 1-9.

6. Ranbi Vohra, *China's Path to Modernization*, (Englewood Cliffs, NJ: Prentice-Hall, 1987), p. 24; John King Fairbank, *The United States and China*, Harvard U. Press, 1979, pp. 158-161.

7. Harding, "Change and Continuity in Chinese Foreign Policy," *Problems of Communism* (Washington, DC), March-April 1983, pp. 17-18.

8. Ibid., p. 17; Michael Hunt, "Chinese Foreign Relations in Historical Perspective," in Harry Harding (ed.), *China's Foreign Relations in the 1980s*, Yale, 1984, pp. 6-7; John Fairbank, *China Perceived*, Harvard, 1966, p. 56; Xiaoxiong Yi, "China's U.S. policy conundrum in the 1990s," *Asian Survey*, August 1994, pp. 675-91.

9. Fairbank, *The United States and China*, pp. 161-169; Whiting, "Foreign Policy of China," p. 256; Allen S. Whiting, *China Crosses the Yalu*, Macmillian, 1960, pp. 4-5; *Beijing Review*, November 15, 1982, p. 21; *Trends of Future Sino-U.S. Relations: Status and Outlook*, Institute for International Studies of Beijing Academy of Social Sciences, et al., September 1994.

10. Neville Maxwell, book review of *China's Boundary Treaties and Frontier Disputes* by Luke Chang, in *China Quarterly* (London), December 1983, p. 743; Eduardo Lachia, "China Tops List with 10 Border Disputes," *Asian Wall Street Journal* (Hong Kong), April 23, 1983, p. 3; Melvin Gurtov and Byong-Moo Hwang,

China Under Threat: The Politics of Strategy and Diplomacy, (Baltimore: Johns Hopkins University Press, 1980), p. 118; B. W. Cloughley, "Sino-Indian Border: Talks Scheduled but Conflict Possible," *Pacific Defence Reporter* (Kunyung, Victoria, Australia), March 1987, p. 38.

11. Elizabeth Green, "China and Mongolia: Recurring Trends and Prospects for Change," *Asian Survey* (Berkeley), December 1986, pp. 1,343, 1,362.

12. "Hong Kong," *Asia 1985 Yearbook*, (Hong Kong: Far Eastern Economic Review, 1985), p. 146; "Tiny Enclave to Return to Chinese Fold," *Christian Science Monitor* (Boston), March 24, 1987, p. 9; FBIS/China, March 27, 1987, p. W1; John P. Burns, "The Process of Assimilation of Hong Kong (1997) and Implications for Taiwan," *AEI Foreign Policy and Defense Review* (Washington, DC), vol. 6, no. 3, pp. 19-26.

13. Burns, "The Process of Assimilation of Hong Kong (1997) and Implications for Taiwan," p. 24; Thomas B. Gold, "The Status Quo is Not Static: Mainland-Taiwan Relations," *Asian Survey* (Berkeley), March 1987, pp. 300-305; *Chinese Communist World Outlook*, p. 123; Robert Sutter and William Johnson, *Taiwan's Role in World Affairs* (Boulder, CO: Westview, 1994), chapter 1.

14. Mao Zedong, *Report to the Second Plenary Session of the Seventh Central Committee of the CCP*, (Beijing: Foreign Languages Press, 1968), p. 17; Whiting, "Foreign Policy of China," pp. 257-265.

15. Harding, "Change and Continuity in Chinese Foreign Policy," p. 17; Allen S. Whiting, "China and the World," in Allan S. Whiting and Robert F. Dernberger, *China's Future: Foreign Policy and Economic Development in the Post-Mao Era*, (New York: McGraw-Hill, 1977), p. 41.

16. Xinhua, February 3, 1984, in FBIS/China, February 4, 1985, pp. A1-2; Wan Guang, "Trends Toward Global Multipolar Development," *Liaowang Overseas Edition* (Hong Kong), in FBIS/China, March 24, 1987, pp. A2-6; John Garver, *Foreign Relations of the PRC*, (Englewood Cliffs, NJ: Prentice Hall, 1993), part 6.

17. Gurtov and Hwang, pp. 13-14; Fairbank, *The United States and China*, p. 278; Greg O'Leary, "Chinese Foreign Policy—From 'Anti-Imperialism' to 'Anti-Hegemonism'" in *China: The Impact of the Cultural Revolution*, Bill Brugger, ed., (New York: Barnes and Noble, 1978), pp. 243-245. R. I. D. Taylor, "China's Policy Towards the Asia-Pacific," *Asian Affairs* (London) October 1994, pp. 259-269.

18. John Gittings, *The World and China, 1922-1972*, (London: Eyre Methuen, 1974), pp. 158-159; *Chinese Communist World Outlook*, (Washington, DC: U.S. Department of State, Bureau of Intelligence and Research, 1962), p. 11; Whiting, "Foreign Policy of China," p. 262.

19. North, *The Foreign Relations of China*, pp. 128-129; Michael B. Yahuda, *China's Role in World Affairs*, (London: Croom Helm, 1978), pp. 18-19; Harry Harding, "China's Changing Roles in the Contemporary World," in *China's Foreign Relations in the 1980's*, Harry Harding, ed., (New Haven: Yale University Press, 1984), p. 178.

20. Harding, "China's Changing Role in the Contemporary World," pp. 178-179; Mao Zedong, *Report to the Second Plenary Session of the Seventh Central Committee*

of the CCP, (Beijing: Foreign Languages Press, 1968), p. 17; Peng Di, "Are There Changes in China's Foreign Policies?" *Liaowang Overseas Edition* (Hong Kong), in FBIS/China, March 25, 1986, p. A1; Gurtov and Hwang, p. 10; Kim, *China and the World*, p. 8; Whiting, "Assertive Nationalism in Chinese Foreign Policy," *Asian Survey* (Berkeley), August 1983, p. 916.

21. Samuel Kim, *China and the World*, pp. 8, 153, 189, 209; *Chinese Communist World Outlook*, p. 84; Zhao Ziyang in *Beijing Review*, March 25, 1986, XVIII; North, *The Foreign Relations of China*, pp. 141-142.

22. A. Doak Barnett, *The Making of Foreign Policy in China: Structure and Process*, (Boulder, Westview Press, 1985), pp. xi-xiii; Whiting, "Foreign Policy of China," pp. 265-267; Robert S. Ross, book review of Barnett's book listed above, in *Pacific Affairs*, (summer 1986), pp. 296-297; M. B. Yahuda, "The Ministry of Foreign Affairs of the People's Republic of China," in *The Times Survey of Foreign Ministries of the World*, Zara Steiner, ed., (London: Times Books, 1982), p. 154.

23. Michael Okensberg, "China's Confident Nationalism," *Foreign Affairs* (New York), vol. 65, no. 3, p. 519; James R. Townsend and Brantly Womack, *Politics in China*, (Boston: Little, Brown and Co., 1986), pp. 388-389; Lian Yan, "The CPC's Relations with Other Parties," *Beijing Review*, July 7, 1986, p. 22; Barnett, *The Making of Foreign Policy in China*, pp. 3, 93.

24. Barnett, *The Making of Foreign Policy in China*, pp. 7-8, 11, 16-17; North, p. 69; John Gittings, *The World and China, 1922-1972*, (London: Eyre Methuen, 1974), pp. 268-271.

25. Barnett, *The Making of Foreign Policy in China*, p. 32.

26. Oksenberg, "China's Confident Nationalism," p. 502; Barnett, *The Making of Foreign Policy in China*, pp. 27-28; Whiting, "Foreign Policy of China," p. 282.

27. Barnett, *The Making of Foreign Policy in China*, pp. 46-69; Lian Yan, "The CPC's Relations With Other Parties," *Beijing Review*, July 7, 1986, pp. 22-25.

28. Barnett, *The Making of Foreign Policy in China*, pp. 29-30.

29. Oksenberg, "China's Confident Nationalism," p. 502.

30. Barnett, *The Making of Foreign Policy in China*, pp. 75-82.

31. Yahuda, "The Ministry of Foreign Affairs of the PRC," pp. 154-158; Barnett, *The Making of Foreign Policy in China*, pp. 76, 81, 88; Whiting, "Foreign Policy of China," pp. 268-269.

32. Yahuda, "The Ministry of Foreign Affairs of the PRC," pp. 154-158; Barnett, *The Making of Foreign Policy in China*, pp. 76, 81, 86-91.

33. Barnett, *The Making of Foreign Policy in China*, pp. 93-96.

34. Yahuda, "The Ministry of Foreign Affairs of the PRC," pp. 156-157; Barnett, *The Making of Foreign Policy in China*, pp. 96-104; Whiting, "Foreign Policy of China," p. 266.

35. Barnett, *The Making of Foreign Policy in China*, pp. 97-100.

36. North, *The Foreign Relations of China*, p. 103; Barnett, *The Making of Foreign Policy in China*, pp. 105-110; Whiting, "Foreign Policy of China," p. 282.

37. Barnett, *The Making of Foreign Policy in China*, pp. 16, 20, 32-33, 51; Yahuda, "The Ministry of Foreign Affairs of the PRC," p. 159.

38. Barnett, *The Making of Foreign Policy in China*, pp. 42-54, 68-69.

3

China's Emergence as a Global Actor

Under the leadership of Mao Zedong, between 1949 and 1976, China was capable of wide swings in the conduct of foreign policy. During the 1950s, Mao charted a pro-Soviet, anti-United States course; in the 1960s, China shifted to a posture antagonistic to both superpowers; and during the early 1970s, Mao sanctioned a realigning of China toward a rapprochement with the United States in opposition to perceived Soviet expansion. Throughout this period, Chinese leaders under Mao mixed hard and soft tactics in foreign affairs in ways that showed a strong willingness to threaten or use force in order to seek advantage or to respond to perceived encroachment or pressure from outside. China cultivated the image of an aggrieved "have not" power determined to struggle to change the world–at least over a period of time. Beijing supported revolutionary third world political movements and gave arms and training to radical insurgencies directed against established governments.[1]

Foreign analysts were able to discern core goals in Chinese foreign policy throughout this period. Notably, these goals involved support for the security of the Chinese state and its communist leadership; development of China's wealth and power; and a strong desire to stand strong and independent in world affairs. Nevertheless, the frequent shifts in priorities and tactics sometimes caught Chinese officials themselves unaware or unresponsive, leading to leadership confusion and conflict. Also, domestic politics occasionally spilled over into the foreign policy arena, leading to sometimes serious foreign policy debates among leaders. Perhaps the most graphic example of the latter occurred in the mid- to late 1960s, during the most violent phase of the Cultural Revolution. This period saw a collapse of Chinese foreign policy amid a broader collapse of Chinese government and party institutions, reflecting the life-and-death struggle for power then under way among the senior leaders.

The internal chaos of this stage of the Cultural Revolution was matched by the stridency of Maoism in foreign affairs. China was alienated from most of its foreign supporters and stood in direct opposition to both the United States, which was deepening its military involvement in Southeast Asia, and the Soviet Union, which was building its military power along China's northern border as a defensive measure and possible lever to press China. The 1969 border conflict brought China and the Soviet Union to the brink of war. Chinese security was more endangered than at any time since at least the Korean War (1950-1953), and arguably since the establishment of the People's Republic.

Toward Greater Pragmatism, 1969-1989

Adroitly maneuvering to save China in this time of danger, while protecting themselves from leadership adversaries who ultimately perished in the struggle for power, Premier Zhou Enlai and his close associates laid out and followed a more pragmatic, less ideologically driven plan for Chinese foreign policy. Subsequent leaders, notably Deng Xiaoping, established domestic development strategies that served to reinforce the trend toward relative moderation and continuity in Chinese foreign policy.

China's relationship with the superpowers, and especially the Soviet Union, remained at the heart of its foreign policy through much of the late cold war period. In particular, Soviet power repeatedly impeded both China's efforts to expand its influence in Asian and world affairs and its ability to secure China's broader foreign policy goals of security, independence, and development.[2]

Balancing the Superpowers, 1969-1976

During the 1969-1976 period, China was beginning to emerge from the violent domestic conflict and international isolation caused by the Cultural Revolution. The Soviet military buildup and the border clashes between China and the Soviet Union prompted a major reassessment in Chinese foreign policy that focused on countering the Soviet threat to Chinese security. As the United States was pulling back militarily from

Asia, Beijing saw an opportunity to work with the United States, its former adversary, against Soviet "hegemonism" in Asia.

China also used this opening to the United States to support its broader effort to gain greater international recognition. Beijing's entry into the UN in 1971 was a high point in this effort. The China-United States agreement in the Shanghai Communiqué, signed during President Richard M. Nixon's visit to China in 1972, said that both sides opposed the efforts of an unnamed third party (presumably the Soviet Union) to establish "hegemonism" in Asia. Subsequently, Beijing cited this understanding to encourage worldwide efforts to block the expansion of what China called "Soviet hegemonism." China was sharply critical of any moves by the United States or others that it perceived as efforts to accommodate Soviet expansion.

While China was generally supportive of the gradual U.S. withdrawal from Vietnam set under the terms of the Agreement Ending the War and Restoring Peace in Vietnam signed in Paris in January 1973, it was alarmed by the rapid collapse of pro-U.S. regimes in South Vietnam and Cambodia in 1975. Beijing feared that expanding Soviet power and a unified Vietnam would fill the power vacuum left by the United States. Chinese pronouncements encouraged the United States to remain actively involved militarily, economically, and politically in Asia and pointedly warned Asian countries to beware of Soviet efforts to fill the vacuum created by the United States pullback.

The China-United States accommodation that emerged during this period was restricted largely to strategic factors. Because of ongoing leadership struggles, China remained unwilling to break away from Maoist development policies emphasizing Chinese "self-reliance." China also remained very cautious in developing educational, cultural, and technical contacts with the outside world that might be called into question by the ideologically rigid members of the so-called Gang of Four–Maoist radicals who had significant influence over policy at this time.

Domestic Reform and External Outreach, 1977-1980

The period from 1977 to 1980 began following the death of Mao, the purge of the Gang of Four, and the rehabilitation of more pragmatic leaders led by Deng Xiaoping. Deng and his reform-minded colleagues began a major economic and political reform effort designed to end the ideological struggles of the past and to improve the material well-being of the Chinese people. In foreign affairs, they broadened the basis of China's interest in contacts with the West and the rest of the developed world from common anti-Soviet strategic concerns to include greater economic, technical, and other exchanges.[3]

Foreign policy initiatives supported the new quest to achieve economic modernization by helping to promote economic contacts with various countries that could benefit China's modernization and by helping maintain a stable and secure environment in Asian and world affairs that was conducive to Chinese modernization efforts. Chinese leaders put aside past ideological, political, and other constraints in order to seek beneficial economic and technical interchange with a wide range of industrialized and developing nations. They halted or cut back support to third world Maoist insurgents and political groups that would impede smooth economic exchanges abroad; sharply reduced Chinese foreign assistance to the third world; and showed an increased willingness to play down past Maoist pretensions to change the world.

Chinese leaders focused their foreign policy concerns on establishing a "peaceful environment" (that is, a balance of power) around China's periphery in Asia. China could not, on its own, safeguard its interests in this region, which remained more heavily influenced by the Soviet Union and the United States. China continued to see the main danger of instability and adverse development in Asia as coming from the Soviet Union and its allies and associates. Thus, Beijing was particularly concerned by the Soviet-Vietnamese strategic alignment that allowed Vietnam in late 1978 to invade Cambodia, overthrow the Chinese-backed Khmer Rouge regime there, and successfully resist the subsequent Chinese military incursion into Vietnam.

These economic and strategic imperatives explain China's decision to normalize diplomatic relations with the United States in 1978; the Peace and Friendship Treaty signed by China and Japan on August 12, 1978; and China's highly vocal effort at this time to encourage a worldwide "antihegemony front" to contain the expansion of the Soviet Union and its proxies in Asia and elsewhere in the third world. As it was in the 1969-1976 period, Beijing was especially critical of perceived efforts by the United States or others in the West to accommodate or "appease" perceived Soviet or Soviet-backed expansion in the interest of United States-Soviet arms control or other concerns. Beijing also was supportive of a continued strong effort by the United States and its allies to maintain a firm military and diplomatic position against Soviet expansion in Asia and elsewhere.

Reassessment and an Independent Foreign Policy, 1980-1989

Throughout the 1980s, Chinese leaders were generally supportive of the strong U.S.-led international response to the Soviet invasion of Afghanistan in December 1979. The election of Ronald Reagan and the buildup of U.S. military strength in the early 1980s were seen by Beijing as complementing similarly strong efforts against Soviet expansion by U.S. allies in Western Europe and Asia. As a result, China came to view Soviet expansion as held in check for the first time in more than decade–a trend that Beijing judged was likely to continue to pose difficulties for Moscow, which was preoccupied with its leadership succession and deepening economic malaise.

Meanwhile, Chinese leaders began to reassess their close alignment with the United States in light of Reagan's earlier strong statements in favor of support for Taiwan. In response, Beijing opted in 1981 and 1982 for a more "independent" posture in foreign affairs that struck a favorable political chord at home and among developing countries sympathetic to China.

Nevertheless, Leonid Brezhnev and subsequent Soviet leaders were unwillingly to reduce Moscow's military forces around China's periphery or to decrease support for Asian countries, such as Vietnam and India, that served as local counterweights to Chinese influence. Moreover, Chinese leaders also clearly recognized the importance of their newly developed economic ties with the United States. As a result, after two years of political crisis in China-U.S. relations that saw tough negotiations and public disputes with the Reagan administration over U.S. arms sales to Taiwan and other issues, Chinese leaders set limits on China's independent foreign posture. They compromised on heretofore sensitive disputes and consolidated ties with the United States during Reagan's visit to China in 1984. The Reagan administration facilitated this change by increasing the flow of U.S. technology to China and by minimizing public references to differences with Beijing over Taiwan and other issues.

In the mid-1980s, with the rise to power of Mikhail Gorbachev and his reform-minded colleagues in the Soviet Union, China and the Soviet Union moderated past differences and appeared determined to improve political, economic, and other bilateral concerns. Leaders of both sides focused on internal economic-related political reform, and expressed interest in fostering a stable, peaceful international environment conducive to such domestic change. Ideological, territorial, and leadership differences between Beijing and Moscow were deemed less important. However, the two sides remained divided largely over competing security interests in Asia. Gorbachev began to accommodate China's interests in this area by starting to pull back Soviet forces from Afghanistan, Mongolia, and other places around China's periphery. Concurrently, Chinese military planners began to revise substantially China's strategic plans. They downgraded the danger of Soviet attack and allowed for a major demobilization of Chinese ground forces.

The Soviet initiatives also reduced Chinese interest in cooperating closely with the United States and its allies and associates in Asia to check possible Soviet expansion. But China's growing need for close economic and technical ties with these countries compensated to some degree for its decreased interest in closer security ties with them. Chinese leaders also wished to improve relations with the Soviets in order to keep pace with the rapid improvement of Gorbachev's relations with the United States and Western Europe; otherwise, Chinese leaders ran the risk of not being consulted when world powers debated international issues important to China.

During this period, the United States and its allies found the Soviet Union more accommodating than China on matters of interest to the West. At the same time, the change in China's Soviet policy reduced the perceived U.S. need to sustain and develop close strategic cooperation with China against the Soviet Union. Some analysts judged that the United States did not consider economic interchange with China was important enough to compensate for the reduced anti-Soviet strategic cooperation, even though China remained important for Asian security and international arms control. As a result, long-standing bilateral and other irritants in China-United States relations over human rights, treatment of intellectuals, and Tibet appeared to take on more prominence in China-United States relations.[4]

Foreign Relations in the 1990s

Developments Since 1989

The sharp international reaction to China's harsh crackdown on dissent after the June 1989 Tiananmen incident caught Chinese leaders by surprise. They reportedly had expected industrialized nations to restore stable relations with China after a few months. They had not counted on the rapid collapse of communism in Eastern Europe, the subsequent march toward self-determination and democratization throughout the Soviet republics, and ultimately to the end of the Soviet Union in 1991. These unexpected events diverted the industrialized nations from returning to China with advantageous investment, assistance, and economic exchanges, called into question China's strategic importance as a counterweight to the Soviet Union, and posed the most serious challenge to the legitimacy of the Chinese communist regime since the Cultural Revolution.[5]

In response to the dramatic international political events of the late 1980s and early 1990s, Beijing used foreign affairs to demonstrate the legitimacy and prestige of its communist leaders. High-level visits and trade and security agreements were planned to enhance Beijing's image before skeptical audiences at home and abroad. To reestablish internal political stability Chinese leaders gave high priority to the resource needs of the military and public security forces.

Recognizing that communist ideology was not popular enough to support their continued monopoly of power, leaders in Beijing played up more traditional themes of Chinese nationalism to support their rule. Foreign criticisms of the communist system in China were portrayed not as attacks against unjust arbitrary rule but as assaults on the national integrity of China. These attacks were equated with earlier "imperialist" pressures on China in the nineteenth century and the first half of the twentieth century.[6]

Meanwhile, pro-economic reform statements made during Deng Xiaoping's tour of South China in 1992 forced other Chinese senior leaders out of their hesitant approach to economic modernization after June 1989. Deng called for faster growth and increased economic interchange with the outside world. This call coincided with the start of an economic boom on the mainland that continued into the mid-1990s. Double-digit annual growth rates caused inflation, dislocation, and numerous social problems, but they clearly caught the attention of the outside world. Many of China's well-to-do neighbors, such as Hong Kong and Taiwan, already had positioned themselves well in the post-Tiananmen period to take advantage of the mainland's rapid growth. They were followed rapidly by West European and Japanese entrepreneurs. U.S. business interests in the China market grew markedly from 1992 to 1994 and were credited with playing an important role in convincing the Clinton administration to stop linking U.S. most-favored-nation treatment to improvements in China's human rights conditions.[7]

China's post-Mao leaders needed to foster a better economic life for the people of China in order to justify their continued monopoly of power. These leaders could not rely, as Mao did, on enormous personal prestige as successful revolutionaries, or on the attractiveness of communist ideology after a century of chaos. They had little of Mao's prestige, and the attractiveness of communist ideology was largely a thing of the past. China has depended critically on foreign trade, and related foreign investment and assistance, for its economic development. It has depended particularly on its neighbors for aid, investment, and trade benefits, and on the United States and other major consumer markets to absorb its exports. Therefore, to ensure their political survival, China's leaders emphasized their concern with maintaining a "peaceful" international environment that would facilitate the continued trade, investment, and assistance flows so important to Chinese economic well-being.

Thus, the leadership put aside past ideas of self-reliance, and allowed the Chinese economy to become increasingly integrated into the world economy. Beijing made efforts to meet the requirements of the United States and others regarding market access, intellectual property rights, and other economic issues, and wanted to become a member of the General Agreement on Tariffs and Trade (GATT) and a founding member of the World Trade Organization (WTO). Chinese leaders accepted commitments and responsibilities stemming from their participation with such international economic organizations as the World Bank, the Asian Development Bank, and the Asian Pacific Economic Cooperation (APEC) forum.

Chinese leaders remained sensitive on matters of national sovereignty and international security issues. But they adjusted to world pressure when resistance appeared detrimental to broader Chinese concerns. Examples of this adjustment included their cooperation with the international peace settlement in Cambodia in 1991, willingness to join the 1968 Treaty on the Non-Proliferation of Nuclear Weapons and to halt nuclear tests by the end of 1996 under an international agreement, willingness to abide by terms of the Missile Technology Control Regime, and efforts to help the United States reach an agreement with North Korea in October 1994 over the latter's nuclear weapons development program. Beijing also endeavored to meet international expectations on other transnational issues, such as policing drug traffic, curbing international terrorism, and working to avoid further degradation of the global environment.

It is easy to exaggerate the degree of Chinese accommodation to international concerns, however. Beijing's continued hard line against outside criticism of China's political authoritarianism and poor human rights record graphically illustrated the limits of Chinese accommodation. China continued to transfer sensitive military technology or dual-use equipment to Pakistan, Iran, and other potential flash points, despite criticism from Western nations. Furthermore, Chinese political and military leaders were not reluctant to use rhetorical threats or demonstrations of military force to intimidate those it believed were challenging its traditional territorial or nationalistic claims in sensitive areas such as Taiwan, the South China Sea, and Hong Kong.[8]

In short, Beijing approached each issue on a case-by-case basis, each time calculating the costs and benefits of adherence to international norms. By 1991, for example, Beijing saw that maintaining its past support for the Khmer Rouge in Cambodia would defeat its broader interests in achieving a favorable peace settlement in Cambodia and solidifying closer relations with the Association of Southeast Asian Nations (ASEAN) countries, Japan, and the West–all of whom saw continued Chinese aid to the Khmer Rouge as a serious obstacle to peace. Similarly, in 1994, Beijing had to announce its decision to stop nuclear testing by the end of 1996 and join a comprehensive nuclear test ban, or risk major friction in its relations with the United States, Japan, Western Europe, and Russia.

Underlying the case-by-case approach has been a rising sense of nationalism among Chinese leaders. Viewing the world as a highly competitive, state-centered system, Chinese leaders remain deeply suspicious of multilateralism and interdependence. They tend to see the world in more traditional balance-of-power terms, and therefore argue that the world is becoming more multipolar (that is, there are a number of competing nation-states) than multilateral (a system where nation-states sacrifice their independence and freedom of maneuver for the sake of an interdependent international order).[9]

Chinese suspicions of many multilateral efforts center on the role of the United States and the other industrialized nations. These nations are seen as "setting the agenda" of most multilateral regimes to serve their own particular national interests, in the process giving short shrift to the interests and concerns of newly emerging powers like China. For instance, many leaders in China see foreign efforts to encourage or press China to conform to multilateral standards on international security, human rights, and economic policies and practices as motivated by the foreign powers' fear of China's rising power, their unwillingness to share power fairly with China, and their desire to "hold down" China–that is, to keep it weak for as long as possible.

Relations with the United States

Beijing recognizes that the United States exerts predominant strategic influence in East Asia and the Western Pacific, is a leading economic power in the region, surpassed only by Japan, and is one of only two world powers (along with Russia) capable of exerting sufficient power around China's periphery to pose a tangible danger to Chinese security and development. As the world's remaining superpower, the United States also exerts strong influence in international financial and political institutions, such as the World Bank and the United Nations (UN), that are important to Beijing. The United States also has a role in areas of particular sensitivity to Beijing, notably policy regarding Taiwan and international human rights.[10]

China's growing strength since the mid-1980s has increased the importance of the U.S. role in Asia. Few of China's neighbors are willing to challenge or express strongly different views than those held by China on major issues. They privately support a significant U.S. military presence in the region, partly because it serves as an implicit counterweight to China's military power. They and more-distant industrialized nations also privately support firm U.S. efforts to open China's markets, end unfair commercial practices, and protect the integrity of the world trading system. They also appreciate the U.S. efforts to press China to end nuclear testing and proliferation of equipment and technology for weapons of mass destruction.[11]

China, too, sees the United States as the key link in the international balance of power affecting Chinese interests. This judgment goes far toward explaining why Chinese leaders so avidly sought a visit to China by President Bill Clinton from the time he was elected in 1992. It would signal to all at home and abroad that the United States had muffled its opposition to and endorsed cooperation with the Beijing government. Of course, as noted above, some Chinese leaders remain deeply suspicious of U.S. motives. They believe the U.S. government is conspiring to weaken and undermine the Chinese leadership and "hold back" China from a more prominent position in world affairs.[12]

Relations with Asian Neighbors

Japan

China's relations with Japan reflect a delicate balance of economic and security concerns. Japan is China's major source of foreign assistance and advanced technical equipment. Moreover, the Japanese use their economic might and slowly growing military power to support greater economic development and peace in Asia.

Meanwhile, as part of its more relaxed stance regarding Russian policy in Asia, Beijing has muted or reversed past vocal support for greater Japanese defense efforts, the Treaty of Mutual Cooperation and Security signed by Japan and the United States in 1960, and the United States military presence in Japan. It also has muffled public support for Japanese claims to what Tokyo calls the Northern Territories, islands northeast of Hokkaido occupied by Moscow since the end of World War II.

But as the perceived danger of Soviet military expansion has subsided, some official Chinese pronouncements and popular demonstrations have registered sharply critical views of Japan's growing role in Asian affairs. Some have warned bluntly about the danger of revived Japanese militarism; criticized U.S. encouragement of greater Japanese military spending; and sharply attacked alleged Japanese efforts to "infiltrate, control, and exploit" the Chinese and other Asian economies.

Other, more sophisticated Chinese have registered concerns over alleged expanding Japanese efforts to use economic-backed power to gain political and economic influence in parts of Asia considered sensitive by China. Thus, some Chinese officials have expressed concern that Japan would use improved trade and aid relations with Vietnam, Laos, and Cambodia to build strong influence there.[13]

An authoritative assessment by Asian affairs specialist Allen Whiting of the recent Chinese views of the dangers posed by Japan concluded that senior PRC security analysts see Japan as China's most serious long-range military threat.[14] This concern has remained unabated over time despite Japan providing major amounts of foreign aid, loans, investment, technology, and trade. Younger Japan specialists do not share this view but have no visible impact on their elders, as shown by interviews over the past decade. During this period war games consistently targeted Japan's air and naval threat.

Multiple rationales support this perception, the most basic being the classic admonition, "Past experience, if not forgotten, is a guide to the future." Repeated Japanese aggression from 1894 through 1945 provides a basis for public and private statements reflecting the legacy of national humiliation and suffering. Vivid media presentations commemorating the 1937 Rape of Nanking and the 1945 victory over Japan renew anger over the past and raise alarm over the future.

Chinese concern over the threat posed by Japan is argued in varying realpolitik scenarios. Japan must acquire military power to protect its economic power, or alternatively Japan's economic power will prompt it to become a military power. Japan will lose faith in the U.S. security treaty and expand its defense capability, or alternatively Japan will break with the United States over trade issues and go it alone as a military power. By whatever reasoning, Japan's future military threat is seen as certain.

Comparing Japanese and Chinese naval capabilities lends credence to some concern. Japanese destroyers and frigates are superior in quantity and quality. Tokyo's submarine fleet is growing steadily. Air and sea coverage 1,000 nautical miles from Tokyo presents an extensive defense screen. Technological, material, and human resources provide an ominous edge of advantage in a prolonged arms race. Sino-Japanese disputes over ownership of the East China Sea and the associated Senkaku islands with potentially large oil and natural gas reserves make such a race well worth winning. Expressions of concern over Chinese power projection in the South China Sea threatening Japan's interests reinforce suspicion in Beijing that Tokyo will insinuate itself into the Spratly Islands controversy.

According to Whiting's accounts in a December 1993 future security symposium, sixty percent of the Chinese participants reportedly saw Japan as the top threat by 2020. Its military expenditure will be first in the world, believe the Chinese, twenty-five times higher than Beijing's. Papers focused on Japan's ability to produce nuclear weapons, ambitions toward Taiwan, the revival of Japanese militarism, strategy toward China, and "Factors Leading to Anti-China Wars by Japan." In contrast with a present political U.S. threat, that foreseen from Japan places prime responsibility on the PLA for defending the entire span of maritime territory claimed by China. Given assumptions based on historical experience and vital ocean resources at stake, PLA threat assessments of Japan are crucial to the long-term stability of East Asia.

Despite their often deep-seated concerns, however, Chinese leaders for the time being have been loathe to allow such concerns to interfere substantially with China's interest in encouraging greater trade, investment, and assistance from Japan.[15] In particular, Japan in the 1990s has remained preoccupied with serious internal problems, including a protracted economic downturn and the most unsteady political leadership situation in forty years. Under these circumstances,

Tokyo generally continues to seek to accommodate China's growing power through aid and diplomacy, while Beijing sees no near-term danger from Japan.

The Koreas

Beijing has long given pride of place to managing relations with its strategically important neighbor, Korea. Since World War II, China fought a major war there, competed avidly with the United States, the USSR, and Japan for influence on the peninsula, and continues to see developments there as vitally important to Chinese national security.

Beijing has worked since the mid-1980s to reduce tensions associated with the dangerously volatile military confrontation between North Korea and the U.S.-backed Republic of Korea (South Korea). It sees the tense arms race on the peninsula as working against Chinese interests (in the 1980s, the Soviet Union used its ability to provide advanced fighter aircraft and other equipment China would not provide to gain greater influence in Pyongyang). Military confrontation would pit China, an ally of North Korea, against its main economic partners in the United States and Japan, who support South Korea. The continued North-South split also has slowed Chinese efforts to open greater economic exchanges with economically dynamic South Korea. China has made considerable progress in trade relations with South Korea. The annual trade represents many times the value of China's trade with North Korea. But Beijing has hesitated to move faster in exchanges with South Korea for fear of alienating North Korea. The Chinese were especially sensitive that North Korea's leader, Kim Il Sung, who died in 1994, groomed his reportedly unstable son, Kim Jong Il, for an uncertain political succession, and was trying to develop weapons of mass destruction, notably an atomic bomb. China and South Korea announced the establishment of diplomatic relations on August 24, 1992, but Beijing was careful to counsel caution on the part of U.S.-led international efforts to force Pyongyang to abandon its nuclear weapons program.

From a strategic point of view, Chinese officials understand that a nuclear North Korea risks military confrontation on the peninsula, and could prompt South Korea, Japan, and possibly Taiwan to develop nuclear weapons–greatly complicating China's security and diverting attention and resources away from Beijing's top priority, economic modernization. Beijing appears to be in a quandary, however, as to what to do about it.

On the one hand, China is reluctant to put pressure on North Korea. Apart from any remaining sense of "socialist solidarity," Beijing would be highly disturbed by the prospect of a military conflict in a neighboring area. Beijing also feels a need to keep open lines of communication with North Korea as critical to maintaining Chinese influence on the peninsula and helping to preserve its special channels of communication with the North Korean Army and party–elements of power likely to be pivotal in determining the leadership succession in Pyongyang following the death of Kim Il Sung.

On the other hand, Beijing has a strong interest in not alienating important international actors like the United States, Japan, members of the UN Security Council, and South Korea. They provide the markets, infrastructure, development loans, and aid that have been of critical importance in China's economic modernization. If those actors were uniform in pushing a tougher stance toward North Korea, China might feel compelled to go along.

Over the longer term, some Chinese observers worry about the implications of Korean reunification. Some see a reunified Korea as a hedge against emerging Japanese power, but others fear that Japan could come to dominate the peninsula in opposition to China's influence there. They also worry about the economic and security challenges a reunified, possibly nuclear-armed Korea would pose in its own right.[16]

Southeast Asia

As Vietnam withdrew forces from Cambodia in the late 1980s, China worked hard to ensure that a peace agreement would guarantee complete Vietnamese military withdrawal and the establishment of a new government in Phnom Penh that was not dominated by the Vietnamese. The collapse of the Soviet Union increased Vietnam's incentive to accommodate China over Cambodia and other disputes, and China was ready to reciprocate in order to secure its southern boundary and play a prominent role in the Cambodian settlement. Beijing pressed its client, the Khmer Rouge, not to disrupt the Cambodian settlement process, which China saw as helping it secure influence over Vietnam, Cambodia, Laos, and other nations in Southeast Asia.

There remains a risk that some other power or coalition of countries would emerge to challenge and resist Chinese interest in Southeast Asia. Japan is one possibility. Beijing seems satisfied with the situation that has emerged where a number of regional and other powers are active in the region in ways that have not fundamentally challenged Chinese interests. One area of possible exception involves the conflicting territorial claims of China and Southeast Asian nations to islands in the South China Sea. There, assertive Chinese military actions appear to belie Chinese diplomats' expressions designed to reassure Southeast Asian nations of Chinese intentions. China has also worked with U.S. oil companies to assert its claims to resources under the sea.[17]

South Asia

Elsewhere in Asia, China is an important foreign policy player but distance and geographic barriers keep it from exerting as strong an influence as in Northeast and Southeast Asia.[18] India's regional ambition and defense buildup support its ability to face China along the disputed border. But the two sides downplay tensions, and relations have improved, especially since Prime Minister Rajiv Gandhi visited Beijing in December 1988–the first high-level state visit since the 1962 border war.

India had depended heavily on the Soviet Union for advanced military equipment, but by the early 1990s it needed to find other suppliers. It also sought to reach out to China, Japan, the United States, and Western Europe. Although China was prepared to reciprocate Indian gestures of good will, it continued to supply Pakistan, India's main strategic rival on the subcontinent, with an array of aircraft, tanks, and other military equipment.

Taiwan and Hong Kong

Beijing is following a carrot-and-stick policy toward Taiwan, with the long-term goal of establishing a situation that will cause Taiwan's leaders to begin negotiations with Beijing on the reunification of Taiwan with the mainland on terms acceptable to the PRC.[19] Beijing's carrots focus on the attractiveness of the mainland to Taiwan's investors and traders. Taiwan's economic stake in the mainland is growing by leaps and bounds. Trade in 1994 was worth $20 billion; cumulative investment was worth an estimated $20 billion in 1994. Though reluctant to get into any formal negotiations with Beijing over reunification, Taiwan has been prompted by burgeoning cross-Strait exchanges to allow an active, albeit unofficial, dialogue between Taiwan and the mainland to deal with practical issues in cross-Strait relations. Beijing supports the dialogue and would like to expand its scope to issues relating to reunification.

Recent developments in cross-Strait relations include PRC leader Jiang Zemin's January 30, 1995, pronouncement of "eight points" regarding mainland-Taiwan relations. Although the substance of Jiang's proposals was subject to varying interpretations, the tone of his message was moderate. Taipei has responded in kind. The Nationalist party-ruled government has also taken several steps in recent months to ease commercial restrictions on contacts with the mainland. This is part of a broader government effort to develop Taiwan into a "regional operations center."

Beijing's "sticks" focus on: a) threats to resort to military force if Taiwan declares independence or otherwise further compromises the PRC claim to Taiwan (these threats are backed by repeated military exercises in the Taiwan Strait area); and b) strong efforts to block Taiwan's recently increased efforts to gain greater formal recognition in world bodies and in international affairs in general.

Beijing and Taipei continue to compete strongly for official international recognition. At present, Beijing holds the upper hand, as most large or otherwise important countries have recognized Beijing and, at the latter's insistence, broken official ties with Taipei. Taiwan has official relations with fewer than thirty countries, and most are small. Taipei has also lost out to PRC pressure in most official international organizations. Compromises have been reached allowing Taipei to continue participating in the Asian Development Bank and to join the forum on Asia Pacific Economic Cooperation (APEC), along with the PRC and Hong Kong, in November 1991. Taipei has also focused recently on gaining entry to the UN, UN affiliates, the GATT/WTO, and other official international organizations. Beijing either opposes such representation for Taiwan or sets conditions compatible with its interests.

The Chinese nationalist leadership in Taiwan has endeavored to offset this adverse international trend by engaging in what it calls "pragmatic diplomacy." Under recently sanctioned policy guidelines of "one country-two governments" or "one country-two areas," Taipei officials attempt to win official recognition from countries already having official ties with Beijing. Thus far, Taipei has won over a handful of small countries in this way. The expense involved–Taipei usually accompanies its diplomatic initiatives with offers of assistance–has provoked controversy in Taiwan. Since the PRC still insists that it is the only legitimate government of China, it breaks relations with countries that establish official ties with Taipei.

Another channel focuses on Chinese nationalist officials' efforts to build ties, short of formal official relations, with a wide range of important developed and other countries. This so-called "substantive" diplomacy has seen dozens of countries upgrade their informal offices or other interactive mechanisms to manage effectively their growing economic interchange with Taiwan. By 1993, Taiwan claimed to have unofficial relations with 150 countries, to have established ninety offices in sixty countries that did not maintain diplomatic relations with Taiwan, and to be the site of thirty-seven offices of foreign governments that did not maintain diplomatic relations with Taiwan.

Meanwhile, Taiwan leaders headed by President Lee Teng-hui have attempted to use informal visits–so-called "vacation diplomacy"–to build Taiwan's relations with top leaders in Asia and North America. Beijing has strongly pressured the United States and other governments against accepting such Taiwan visits. This led to a crisis in U.S.-PRC-Taiwan relations following Lee's visit to Cornell University in June 1995.

Beijing has hardened its policies toward Hong Kong in recent years–a reflection of Chinese leaders' uneasiness that their nationalist aspirations toward the territory may be thwarted to varying degrees by indigenous forces aided and abetted by outside supporters. It has been reinforced by domestic politics in Beijing that require leaders to appear firm on such sensitive issues of national sovereignty or risk being pushed aside by others appealing to the strong nationalist sentiments among the Chinese communist leadership. The need for firmness on these issues is thought to be particularly acute during a period of leadership transition with the fading of senior leader Deng Xiaoping.

With the signing of the Sino-British agreement of 1984, Beijing knew that Hong Kong would revert to Chinese control in 1997. Chinese expectations of a gradual and smooth transition, dealing with pliant British colonial administrators, were upset by the 1989 Tiananmen demonstrations. On the one hand, many in Hong Kong saw the PRC crackdown as foreshowing PRC rule in Hong Kong and pressured Britain to do more to guarantee Hong Kong's autonomy after 1997. The government of Prime Minister John Major and his governor in Hong Kong, Chris Patten, followed this path with a series of policy initiatives that greatly irritated Beijing. On the other hand, Beijing's sensitivities over Hong Kong were heightened by the Tiananmen events. Chinese leaders came to view critics in Hong Kong as a major source of support for dissent in the PRC. They were determined to exert greater control and influence over developments in Hong Kong in order to curb such political opposition. Beijing also suspected that British authorities were being profligate in dealing with Hong Kong government budget reserves in the period up to 1997.

Although Britain and China continue to cooperate on a number of transition issues, China has responded to Patten's political reforms by asserting it will nullify all existing representative institutions in Hong Kong in 1997 and establish new ones in line with PRC goals. With this in mind, Beijing has established a shadow government of Hong Kong figures willing to work closely with Beijing. Meanwhile, projects continue to go forward, notably those dealing with a new airport. But Beijing has blocked others seen as not in China's interest.

Relations with Other Countries

Russia and the Newly Independent States

The military threat posed to China by the Soviet Union was downgraded substantially by PRC leaders in the 1980s and is now not of major immediate importance.[20] Indeed, at no time in the past has the PRC been so free from great power military pressure and threat. Russia, the newly emerging central Asian countries, and the new Mongolia do not pose a substantial national security threat to China over the near term. Beijing can relax its military guard against them.

Instability in these areas could pose a danger to China's desire to maintain firm control of minority-populated areas along the inland frontier of China. The collapse of communism in the USSR has also put pressure on PRC leaders to justify their continued efforts to legitimate the Chinese Communist party as one of the few remaining ruling communist parties in the world.

China continues to develop a mutually advantageous economic relationship with Russia. Trade has grown and significantly includes over $1 billion in Russian military sales to China in recent years. The sales have included jet fighters and advanced submarines. The two sides have reached general agreement about their disputed borders, but a few key areas remain unresolved.

In a 1993 security symposium in China only ten percent of Chinese participants foresaw Russia as China's greatest threat by 2020, arguing that territorial disputes and minority nationalities straddling the border would cause conflict. Veteran generals, on the other hand, saw Russia as an eventual weight to balance off against U.S. and Japanese threats. Reciprocally analysts see China as necessary for Russia to balance off against the United States and Europe as well as Japan.

Sino-Russian summit meetings in 1992, 1994, and 1995 marked the progressive resolution of border differences, sharply increased trade, and significant transfers of Russian weapons and military technology to China. Agreement on withdrawal of forces by 100 kilometers on both sides, due by 2000, followed large unilateral reductions in regional deployments. Some see troublesome possibilities–these are dissenting murmurs in a chorus of praise for prospective Sino-Russian relations.

Borderland Threats

Beijing threat perceptions in Xinjiang are twofold: pan-Islamic and pan-Turkic subversion.[21] These perceptions are grounded in historic revolts against Chinese rule as recently as 1946. The double threat reemerged with the collapse of the Soviet Union spawning independent republics along the Xinjiang border. Riots and demonstrations of varying cause are uniformly denounced in the local press as "splittism" or "counterrevolutionary," allegedly stimulated by "foreign sources." The actual origin, size, and nature of these outbreaks are uncertain but perceptions in Urumqi and Beijing attribute worst-case implications for security.

Russia is no longer the threat behind local dissidence as in the 1930s and 1940s. Instead the presence of independent Kazakhstan, Kirghiztan, and Tajikistan across the border is seen in Beijing as a mixed blessing. Flourishing cross-border trade opens up possibilities for Xinjiang's economy otherwise largely isolated from the booming coastal provinces. On the other hand trade and travel open a political window to self-rule as against Chinese domination. Ethno-religious ties cannot be closely controlled as they were during the Soviet period.

The actual security threat is peripheral in every sense of the word. No true unity exists among the seven million Uighurs, one million Kazakhs, and another 300,000 non-Han living among some six million Chinese with a strong PLA concentration. Yet "national separatism still remains the principal threat to Xinjiang's stability" according to a 1993 official report. Logistical support for the PLA depends mainly on a single railroad vulnerable to sudden sandstorms and floods. Xinjiang, spanning 1.6 million square kilometers, strategically borders eight countries. Economic importance lies in the Tarim Basin with one-seventh of China's total oil reserves and one-fourth of total gas reserves. In this perspective security threats in Xinjiang take on greater significance than justified by reality.

Tibet poses a different security threat because of the international as well as indigenous prestige of the Dalai Lama, seen in Beijing as backed by Washington in a drive for Tibetan independence. The still-disputed border with India over which the two countries fought in 1962 adds a strategic dimension to the problem. As in Xinjiang, official reports claim "the situation in Tibet is basically stable, but the antisplittism struggle there remains intense." A vital strategic road linking the two regions traverses territory claimed by India.

Middle East

Since the 1980s, Beijing has used arms sales and transfers of sensitive technology to gain economic profits and garner influence throughout the Persian Gulf region. China has sold several billion dollars of arms to Iran, Iraq, and Saudi Arabia. Its influence suffered a setback after the 1990-1991 Persian Gulf War when it supported both sides, but Beijing worked hard to reestablish strong ties with Iran and others in the region during the ensuing period. Nevertheless, few world conflicts had lent themselves as readily to Chinese weapons sales, and Chinese transfers declined sharply after the Persian Gulf War.[22]

Participation in International Organizations

The end of the cold war has seen a rise in importance of international organizations. China has adjusted its policies to take these new realities into account, placing greater emphasis on international organizations, especially the UN. By virtue of its permanent seat on the Security Council, China will continue to play a major role in world decisions. Other powers that might be inclined to pressure China need to take account of China's UN role in assessing their policies.

International trade practices also affect how China conducts its foreign relations. The industrialized nations and the financial institutions they lead have required countries such as China to adhere more closely to free-market economic development strategies. This undermines China's desire to follow certain neo-mercantilist strategies in order to build foreign exchange reserves to purchase needed commodities, including high technology. While Chinese leaders often resist outside pressures for more reform and ease of access to the Chinese economy, they also strive to maintain access for foreign markets in order to gain foreign exchange and purchase high technology.

The post-cold war international efforts to curb the sale of weapons systems and technology associated with weapons of mass destruction concern segments of the People's Liberation Army (PLA) and others in the Chinese leadership. They rely on these sales for bureaucratic and personal advantages and to gain foreign exchange needed to purchase needed technology and supplies abroad. The sales also build better political relations and other ties China's military could use to gain access to information, technology, and other material that industrialized nations try to keep away from China.[23]

Beijing appears generally cooperative in working with enhanced international efforts to curb the flow of drugs, to pressure those who harbor terrorists, and to deal with worldwide environmental issues. Significantly, such cooperation involves infringement on traditional Chinese concepts of national sovereignty, but Beijing has gone along with international efforts in these areas with little complaint and often with considerable enthusiasm.

Human rights issues are often a bone of contention between China and other powers, especially the Western nations. Beijing takes particular offense at heightened world efforts to press it to bring its human rights practices into closer alignment with the broad standards for participation, accountability, and democracy followed by many other nations. It sees such pressure as an affront to China's national sovereignty, designed to undermine the legitimacy and power of the Chinese communist regime. Beijing has been particularly concerned when human rights issues are used in conjunction with calls for greater freedom or self-determination in places like Tibet and Taiwan. Such outside advocacy is seen to amount to little more than disguised efforts to overthrow China's government and split the nation apart.

Assessment

Several key themes emerge from an analysis of China's international behavior. Chinese leaders see security around its periphery as less likely to be disrupted by a major international power than at any time since 1949. But the reduced big-power military threat does not preclude possible conflicts between China and its neighbors over territory or other issues. Nor does the reduced threat automatically translate into growing Chinese influence in Asia or sanguine Chinese leadership attitudes regarding the evolving balance of influence in Asia. Regional economic and military powers–such as Japan, Indonesia, and India–are among international leaders asserting their influence in the post-cold war era.

Still, regional security trends are generally compatible with China's primary focus on internal economic modernization and political stability. So long as the regional power balance remains stable and broadly favorable to Chinese interests, Beijing is likely to emphasize pragmatic development of economic contacts in its foreign affairs. At least some leaders in Beijing, however, appear prepared to embark on a more assertive Chinese stance in the region, presumably after China achieves solid progress in its economic modernization program.

Ideological and leadership disputes have less importance for Chinese foreign policy than in the past. Although leaders might be divided between conservative-minded and reform-minded officials, the differences within the leadership over foreign affairs in the mid-1990s appear markedly less than at any time during the Maoist period.

Beijing's foreign policy has come to stress economic ties to other countries–especially the Western-aligned, industrialized nations–more than in the past. Particularly as a result of the new openness to foreign economic contacts and the putting aside of Maoist policies of economic self-reliance, Beijing has come to see its well-being as more closely linked to continued good relations with important industrialized nations, notably Japan and the United States. These nations provide the assistance, technology, investment, and markets China needs to modernize effectively.

China's overall pragmatic adjustments to world affairs do not depend on just one or two leaders. Although Deng Xiaoping assumed senior foreign policymaking duties from Mao Zedong and Zhou Enlai, the policies generally follow an outline agreed upon among senior Chinese leaders, who in turn are advised and influenced by a wide range of experts and interest groups in China. Many of these groups have a strong interest in dealing pragmatically with world affairs–particularly by seeking strong economic, technological, and administrative interconnections between Chinese enterprises and interest groups and their counterparts outside China. Beijing's leaders are loath to pursue policies that could jeopardize China's economic progress in an increasingly interdependent world. Nevertheless, a substantial segment of the Chinese leadership remains suspicious of U.S. pressure and very sensitive regarding issues of national sovereignty.

Notes

1. Among the many useful reviews of Chinese foreign policy and behavior see A. Doak Barnett, *China and the Major Powers in East Asia*, (Washington, DC: Brookings, 1977); Harry Harding, ed., *China's Foreign Relations in the 1980s*, (New Haven: Yale University Press, 1984); Harry Harding, *A Fragile Relationship: The United States and China Since 1972*, (Washington, DC: Brookings, 1993); Samuel Kim, ed., *China and the World*, (Boulder, CO: Westview Press, 1993); Robert Sutter, *Chinese Foreign Policy-Developments After Mao*, (New York: Praeger, 1985); Yufan Hao and Guocang Huan, eds., *The Chinese View of the World*, (New York: Pantheon, 1989); Allen Whiting, ed., *China's Foreign Relations*, (Philadelphia: ANNALS, January 1992); and John W. Garver, *Foreign Relations of the People's Republic of China* (Englewood Cliffs, NJ: Prentice Hall, 1993).

2. This analysis draws heavily from Robert Sutter, *Chinese Foreign Policy in Asia and the Sino-Soviet Summit: Background, Prospects and Implications for U.S. Policy*, CRS Report 89-298F, Congressional Research Service, Washington, DC, May 15, 1989, pp. 7-11.

3. The political reforms fell notably short of political pluralism or democracy as there remained strong measures to prevent dissent from emerging as a serious challenge to the regime.

4. See Harding, *A Fragile Relationship*, op. cit.

5. Among useful analyses of this period are Lloyd Vasey, "China's Growing Military Power and Implications for East Asia," *Pacific Forum*, CSIS, August 1993; Ming Zhang, "China and Its Major Power Relations," *The Journal of Contemporary China*, (fall 1994); Thomas McNaugher, "A Strong China: Is the U.S. Ready?," *Brookings Review*, (fall 1994); Ralph Cossa, "China and Northeast Asia: What Lies Ahead?, *Pacific Forum*, CSIS, February 1994; Chong-Pin Lin, "China Military Modernization: Perceptions, Progress and Prospects," *Security Studies*, (summer 1994); Robert McNamara, et al, "Sino-American Military Relations: Mutual Responsibilities in the Post-Cold War Era," National Committee on U.S.-China Relations, November 1994.

6. Discussed among others at an international forum on U.S.-Chinese Relations, Woodrow Wilson Center for Scholars, Washington, DC, November 7, 1994.

7. See among others Robert Sutter and Kerry Dumbaugh, *U.S.-China Relations*, CRS Issue Brief 94002, Congressional Research Service, Washington, DC (updated regularly).

8. For background, see *China As A Security Concern in Asia*, CRS Report 95-465, December 22, 1994, p. 28.

9. See among others *Trends of Future Sino-U.S. Relations and Policy Proposals*, Institute for International Studies of Beijing Academy of Social Sciences, et al., September 1994, and *Sino-U.S. Relations: Status and Outlook–Views from Beijing*, CRS

memorandum, August 15, 1994.

10. See, among others, *Trends of Future Sino-U.S. Relations*, cited in note 9.

11. See, among others, sources cited in note 5.

12. See, among others, *Sino-U.S. Relations: Status and Outlook–Views from Beijing*, CRS memorandum, August 15, 1994.

13. See *China in World Affairs–Background, Prospects and Implications for the United States*, CRS Report 92-747S, October 1, 1992, pp. 17-18.

14. Whiting has published several important pieces on China-Japan relations, notably *China Eyes Japan*, (Berkeley: University of California Press, 1989). This assessment draws from a draft paper he prepared for a *China Quarterly*-Council on Advanced Policy Studies conference in Hong Kong, July 1995.

15. See among others, Allen Whiting, ed., *"China Foreign Relations,"* the *Annals*, January 1992.

16. See among others U.S. Congressional Research Service Report No. 92-747S, *China in World Affairs*, by Robert Sutter, October 1, 1992, pp. 17-18.

17. For background, see CRS Report 92-118 F, *Indochina and Southeast Asia Under Change*, by Robert Sutter and Jeffrey Young, January 31, 1992, p. 19.

18. For background, see CRS Report 92-747S, *China in World Affairs*, by Robert Sutter, October 1, 1992, p. 20.

19. See among others, CRS Issue Brief 94006, *Taiwan–Recent Changes and U.S. Policy Choices* and CRS Issue Brief 94051, *Hong Kong's Political Transition*.

20. For background, see CRS Report 92-747S, *China in World Affairs*, October 1, 1992, p. 15; and the draft paper by Allen Whiting referred to in note 14.

21. This is based on the analysis in Allen Whiting's conference paper of July 1995.

22. See, among others, CRS Issue Brief 92056, *Chinese Missile and Nuclear Proliferation*, by Robert Shuey and Shirley Kan; Washington, DC (updated regularly).

23. See, for background, CRS Report 92-747S, *China in World Affairs*, op. cit., pp. 21-22.

4

Determinants of China's Future in World Affairs

China's role in world affairs during the next decade will be determined by how a range of possible political, economic, social, military, and foreign policy trends combine to shape China's future.

The decline in Deng Xiaoping's health focused new attention on Beijing's central leadership and the role it plays in China's future. It is important to note, however, that China today is not the China of Mao Zedong when central leaders could dictate policy changes in defiance of economic, social, and international realities. China's future will be determined by a mix of leadership judgments interacting with the economic, political, social, military, and foreign policy trends reviewed below.[1]

Leadership Dynamics

Political problems, especially perceived differences among the leadership elites in Beijing, have traditionally been given pride of place in Western analyses of contemporary China. Such attention was justified in view of the magnitude and consequences of the political shifts that took place during Mao's reign and Deng's struggles to move the economy away from central planning in the late 1970s and 1980s. Today, differences among leadership elites in Beijing are of less importance.

During the Maoist period (1949-1976), Chinese leadership differences often were wide ranging and had broad implications for China's internal and foreign policies. The differences sometimes resulted in "life and death" struggles between contending factions whose policy preferences ranged along a spectrum, including pragmatic collaboration with the United States and the West on one side, and strident hostility to most of the outside world on the other. The stakes of such leadership differences were high. Those who came out on the losing side faced disgrace, financial ruin, hard labor, torture, and sometimes death. By contrast, policy, personnel, and other differences among Chinese leaders today are much less severe and have much less serious implications for themselves and for drastic policy changes.

Following the death of Mao (1976) and the rise of more pragmatic Chinese leaders bent on economic modernization and reform in the late 1970s, debate among Chinese leadership elites has focused on the dynamics of nation building. Some groups favored the central government's retention of considerable control over the economic development process. This strategy would result in slower economic growth in the interest of avoiding socially disruptive developments. Others favored sharp reduction in state control in order to spur market-driven economic growth. They argued that more rapid economic growth over the long run would help Chinese authorities deal more effectively with social and other dislocations stemming from economic and other changes.

Over time, the range of this debate has narrowed. Indeed, the results of the communist party's fall 1992 14th Congress and subsequent party and government meetings have reflected a high degree of leadership consensus on how to carry out reform. This new consensus supported a more market-driven approach to economic reform. It also reflected caution over political change seen in leadership decisions since the crackdown on political dissent in 1989. Several factors contributed to this unusual degree of consensus behind the mix of economic reforms and authoritarian politics:

- The demise of the USSR and the recasting of international competition and security in terms of economic strength lent impetus to accelerated economic performance and reform.
- The deaths of key conservative elders (e.g., Chen Yun, Wang Zhen, Li Xiannian, and Hu Qiaomu) removed obstacles to the economic reform agenda.

Greater leadership unity has also been seen in the sensitive areas of ideological doctrine and personnel assignments. The major doctrinal debates that had characterized differences over Chinese development strategies for so long now appeared to be a thing of the past. After Deng Xiaoping's trip through southern China in early 1992, the Politburo endorsed his conclusion that leftism (orthodox Marxist and Maoist ideas) is a greater danger to China than rightism (Western and liberal values). A few months later the 14th Party Congress endorsed the concept of a "socialist market economy." This formulation, which was selected over more conservative alternatives such as a "socialist planned market economy," for the first time formally assigned market forces a much higher priority than the central plan as the principal regulatory mechanism for the economy.

Other developments regarding personnel changes argued for more uniform support of economic reform:

- Several prominent conservative leaders have been removed from office (Song Ping, Wang Renzhi, and Gao Di).
- A vigorous proponent of economic reform, Zhu Rongji was elevated to the standing committee of the Politburo in 1992, and serves concurrently as the executive vice premier of the State Council.
- Two other officials believed sympathetic to reform–Qiao Shi and Li Ruihuan–have taken over the chairmanships of the country's two central legislative bodies.

All of the above did not imply that Chinese leaders would remain unified in the period ahead. The personnel decisions made at the 1992 Party Congress and later were preceded by intense political struggle among competing factions and resulted in the choice of compromise candidates in several cases. Obviously Beijing's leaders are well aware that the still uncertain succession question means that policies and positions will be dealt with not just on their merits, but on how they will affect the careers of Chinese political leaders. Those who favor more conservative doctrine and policy also still have access to official media to air their views.

In 1995, signs of fluidity in elite-level politics continued as the maneuvering around the succession to Deng Xiaoping intensified. There were at least two competing groupings in the central party leadership. The more conservative group (widely believed to include Jiang Zemin, Li Peng, and Zou Jiahua) favored a slower rate of economic growth, a more cautious approach to economic reform, a less extensive opening of the Chinese economy to the rest of the world, and the maintenance of an authoritarian political system. The reformers (probably including Zhu Rongji, Qiao Shi, Wan Li, Tian Jiyun, and Li Ruihuan) advocated bolder economic reform, fuller integration with the international economy, and often faster economic growth. Notably, some of the reformers appeared to support a reassessment of the Tiananmen crisis, the political rehabilitation of former Prime Minister Zhao Ziyang, and a greater role for legislative assemblies in the political process.[2]

[For brief biographies of six important leaders in current Beijing politics, see Appendix.]

These two leadership groups, in turn, reflected an even broader range of opinion outside the national leadership. Although no longer prominently represented on the Politburo, conservatives were still active and criticized the loosening of administrative and ideological controls over society, the embrace of some capitalist economic policies, and the adoption of what they regard as an overly accommodative posture towards the United States. These conservatives were said to have the support of some prominent veteran officials.

Conversely, although there is no sign that national leaders are prepared to advocate sweeping political reform, there are clearly those in China–especially younger officials and most intellectuals in the major cities–who will press for more rapid progress towards political liberalization.

At present, there is a notable turn away from the three year market reform boom evidenced since Deng Xiaoping's tour of south China in 1992. As the leadership transition has moved forward, a conservative emphasis on central control, economic balance, and social stability has prevailed. President Jiang Zemin and Premier Li Peng have taken the lead, seeking to further entrench their political positions and either remove or mollify potential challengers.

It seems likely that the conservatives will not only face opposition from advocates of continued active reform, but will confront economic, social, and other systemic problems that will make renewed economic and probably political change necessary. In particular, Beijing cannot afford the public largess necessary to continue present economic policies, which subsidize the urban population and appease the localities. It needs to continue moving toward privatization of state enterprises and market reform. Also, party corruption–an increasingly serious problem, probably cannot be remedied without greater rule of law–a change requiring political reform.

It is possible that the leadership succession will be carried out smoothly. Although the new leaders have more narrow bases of political power than did Deng and leaders of his generation, they may be able to manage internal differences amicably. Viewed retrospectively since the

Maoist period, it seems clear that the steadily narrowing range of debate in Beijing over policy, doctrine, and personnel means that there is less controversy in these areas. It also seems evident that prospects for a major disruptive change coming from disputes in these areas are less than in the past.

Prudence and past experience nonetheless argue against certainty in looking at China's leadership transition. Although there are more institutional mechanisms in Chinese leadership politics, personalities and particularistic connections remain central in determining power in China. Outside observers with little knowledge of these personal and particularistic factors are hard put to offer a definitive prediction of leadership dynamics in Beijing. Based on current knowledge, there appears to be ample opportunity for continued serious divisions within the leadership over both power and policy. This could be reflected in periodic reshufflings of personnel, as one faction gains temporary advantage over the other. It might also be reflected in chronic immobility, in which a divided leadership is unable to make timely and coherent decisions.

Beijing's Power Structure and Decision-Making Process: Implications of the Leadership Transition

The post-Deng Xiaoping leaders will exert power, and make and carry out decisions, through the array of power mechanisms and decision-making processes available to them. Depending on personal preferences and circumstances, senior leaders in China have tended to use different kinds of mechanisms to exert their influences, and to come to and carry out decisions. The post-Deng Xiaoping leaders are unlikely to be exceptions to this rule.

There is little specific, concrete information as to how senior Chinese leaders reach decisions on significant issues and insure that those decisions are carried out to their satisfaction. In general terms, the Chinese power structure may be divided into three main pillars:

- The state or government;
- The party; and
- The military.

The day-to-day decision making has been delegated by the senior leaders to the important institutions and ministries within each of the pillars. Daily running of the government is the responsibility of the State Council and its working organs. It can be assumed that the ministries operating under the authority of the State Council have substantial independence in running each ministry's daily affairs but that highly important decisions are made primarily by the State Council and/or the party.

The main institution in the party apparatus is the Standing Committee of the Politburo, which makes all important decisions concerning the party. Day-to-day running of the party apparatus is the responsibility of the party Secretariat. Most of the important decisions on matters of policy and personnel are adopted under the authority of the party. It is assumed that the seven-member Standing Committee is the most powerful institution in the PRC.

The main military institution is the Central Military Commission, which has connections to both the party and the state, but is most strongly linked to the former. The commission's chairman (Jiang Zemin) and main vice-chairman (Liu Huaqing) are both party Standing Committee members. The military is further divided into a myriad of offices and departments, several different branches, and seven military regions.

There is a significant overlap of senior leaders' authority (especially between the state and party), which prevents the development of any separation of powers within the PRC political system. Thus it is difficult to say which pillar actually makes the ultimate decisions on issues of great import for any given issue area. There exists no explicit institutionalized decision-making structure. Reforms in the 1980s toward a more formalized decision-making structure were undermined by, and in part blamed for, the catastrophic events of June 1989. It is perhaps safest to assume that all vital decisions relating to the party, state, or military are made by a small group of Standing Committee members in consultation with party elders and influential members of interests groups and ministries most directly affected by decisions.

Evolution of Decision Making. In the Maoist era, decision making was often a highly personalized affair. Major policy shifts were either authorized or formulated by Mao. Bureaucratic and regional interests were kept in check through campaigns and purges. Mao had the ability to remove rivals if he desired and during his rule the center generally could command the obedience of the provinces.

Deng Xiaoping acceded to power in part by promising an end to the Maoist politics that threatened political careers and stifled dissent within leadership confines. For Deng, this reduced his ability to manipulate other leaders. Coupled with his lack of unquestioned authority (relative to Mao), this has meant that Deng has had to build consensus on reform measures and serve as a broker among reformist, conservative, and other factions. His success in these functions has helped to reduce the threat political instability poses to economic modernization. The bargaining has increased the ability of the provinces to lobby for their interests and resist some central directives.

The next generation of leadership, while vigorous, better educated, and more skilled in economic matters, does not possess a leader with the great authority and vital horizontal political links of Deng. They will likely have to broker political interests even more than Deng did, and will be less able to impose bold ideas on fellow leaders.

With no dominant leader likely to emerge in the immediate future, greater emphasis may be put on alliance- and coalition-building. The party may continue to place a premium on leadership stability and unity, and leaders may prefer to see that the leadership succession question is decided amongst themselves in a more predictable and controllable process.

Important Institutions and Levers of Power. Recently prominent institutions of power include the party Politburo's Standing Committee of seven top leaders; the party's Central Military Commission; the People's Liberation Army (PLA), the People's Armed Police, the Public Security Bureau, and related organs of defense and internal security; the State Council and associated government ministries; and the national legislature, the National People's Congress, led by its Standing Committee.

The PLA's influence will likely be felt in any leadership succession. The PLA has traditionally influenced civilian affairs and has been called in to end social unrest. Part of Deng's reform program included reducing the military's role in civilian affairs. This may have worked too well to suit Deng in 1989, as many military leaders were reportedly wary of following party orders to crack down on the Tiananmen demonstrators. The military representation in the party's Central Committee has increased since Tiananmen, as has the size of defense budgets. The appointment in recent years of two elderly officers to lead the military may reflect Deng Xiaoping's concerns over securing the unwavering loyalty of the PLA for China's future civilian leaders.

Economic modernization is the linchpin of party legitimacy. Thus institutions that play a vital role in influencing economic modernization are important sources of power. These institutions include: The Ministry of Foreign Trade and Economic Cooperation (MOFTEC), the

State Economics and Trade Office, the Central Banks, and institutions that deal with science and technology.

The influence of regional leaders on decision making has increased substantially as decentralization of power has proceeded over the past fifteen years. The support of regional leaders could be crucial to the leadership succession and in carrying out decisions of the new central leaders.

Party elders–contemporaries of Deng Xiaoping–are now few in number but have exerted important influence throughout the reform era. Precisely how they influence policy is not known, although it likely has more to do with widespread personal connections and prestige than with formal levers of power.

Power Bases of the Current Elite

Jiang Zemin now currently holds all of the top posts in the state, party, and military organs. This is unusual in PRC politics, and may mean little politically. The only other PRC leader to hold all these posts concurrently was Hua Guofeng, who was pushed aside by Deng Xiaoping at the start of the reform period in the late 1970s. If the party leadership is wary of engaging in a leadership struggle and is more amenable to a sort of collective leadership, Jiang may stand to gain as he already holds the nominally most powerful posts. Jiang's weakest ties are with the military, but he has been working steadfastly to improve them (see Appendix for biographic sketch).

Li Peng is currently the premier of the PRC's State Council and the chief conservative on the Politburo's Standing Committee; his major patron among the party elders was Chen Yun. Li is also believed to be the major implementor of China's post-Tiananmen foreign policy. Li has few military ties.

Qiao Shi has had extensive experience in the party's security and intelligence apparatus. He reportedly has control of the dossiers of the current leadership, which is an important source of power within the regime. Qiao is now chairman of China's primary legislative organ, the NPC, and he is reportedly trying to transform that legislature from a rubber stamp body to a genuine power source. Qiao has few overt military ties.

Zhu Rongji is currently the leader most responsible for the economy. He is most closely identified with economic reform. Zhu was the head of the People's Bank and is overseeing trade and state enterprise reform, as well as energy and natural resources development and the Chinese stock market. Zhu's duties require him to travel extensively around China and insure that provincial leaders follow central directives. This could help him expand ties with regional leaders, or cause them to dislike him if he is seen as forcing provinces to abide by unpopular central directives. Zhu's influence over the economy could be an important source of power, but if the economy sputters substantially he could suffer politically. Zhu has few military ties.

Yang Shangkun currently holds no positions but is considered a still healthy party elder. Yang has the strongest military ties of any potential successor to Deng.

Zhao Ziyang does not have many military ties. In fact many military leaders might oppose his return to power given his opposition to the military intervention ending the Tiananmen demonstrations. Zhao does enjoy strong regional support, especially in the economically important south. Zhao is also closely identified with the liberal causes of economic and political reform.

Local Politics

Economic reforms have been accompanied by a large-scale devolution of authority from the central party and government organs to provincial and other local authorities who are taking the lead in promoting flexible schemes to foster economic growth. There is a danger that local authorities will become so influential as to undermine and eventually challenge central authority.

Provincial authorities have been given greater control over personnel appointments in their jurisdictions; greater authority to approve imports, exports, and foreign investment projects; greater access to tax revenues and to the profits of state enterprises; and greater power over domestic investment decisions. Provincial leaders, always able to lobby the center on matters of policy and resource allocation, are increasingly able to evade or even defy decisions with which they disagree.

The power of the provincial leaders also may be reflected in their growing role in the central elite. No fewer than six provincial and municipal leaders (from Tibet, Shanghai, Beijing, Shandong, Guangdong, and Tianjin) were added to the Politburo at the 1992 14th Party Congress–the largest increase in such officials since the Cultural Revolution. Similarly, the proportion of central committee members taken from the local regions rose from twenty-five percent at the 13th Congress to over sixty percent at the 14th Congress.

The decentralization of political power in China recently has been a disorderly process. It poses serious difficulties for Beijing's leaders, who are trying to cool down the currently overheated Chinese economy. Yet it is easy to exaggerate the implications for China's future. In particular, prospects for the political fragmentation of China–often cited in Western press reporting and some China experts' analyses about China–appear fairly remote. The central government still controls the allocation of economic resources that are critical to most of the country's provinces. The party's central personnel apparatus appoints the top officials at the provincial level, and central leaders still control the PLA and the Public Security apparatus. Alongside these political factors for unity must be placed the emergence of an economic system that is more highly integrated nationally than ever before, and the popular nationalistic ideal of China as a nation-state.

Economic Modernization: The Linchpin of Political Legitimacy

Economic modernization remains a fundamental determinant of the future of China.[3] Post-Mao leaders have recognized that their hold on power rests heavily on their ability to achieve concrete economic success and to make life materially better for the vast majority of the Chinese people. They are aware that they have little of Mao's prestige as a successful revolutionary and nationalist leader, and that the hold of communist ideology on the minds of the Chinese people is a thing of the past. Performance is seen as what counts, and economic performance is the linchpin of the continued political legitimacy of the communist leaders in China.

Bad statistical reporting notwithstanding, Maoist China had quite respectable (over eight percent annually) rates of economic growth, on average. It achieved much in bringing China from its largely agrarian roots and produced an impressive array of industrial and technological establishments. In the course of these efforts, however, tens of millions lost their lives. Waste and inefficiency reached a point in the late 1970s that a consensus was reached among post-Mao leaders on the need to move away from state-controlled development, harness some free-market vitality, and to open China more to the outside world. What followed was basically a pragmatic, trial-and-error approach that is now building

China into a more modern and efficient market-centered economic power.

Efforts focused first on rejuvenating the stagnant rural economy, resulting in several years of rapid growth, which, by the mid-1980s, had doubled the income of the average farmer. Dominated by large state-controlled enterprises, the urban economy posed a more difficult management problem. Nonetheless, progress in the direction of greater decentralization and reliance on market forces has been evident since the 1980s. Chinese officials now claim that roughly eighty percent of commodities in China are distributed through market channels at prices largely set by market forces.

Reliance on decentralized decision making–a feature of economic reform efforts–has given local authorities a greater say in economic matters. Prior to the reform, economic policies were largely inflexible and dictated from Beijing or from provincial capitals. Reforms have given local officials greater leeway to adapt policies and implementation to fit their conditions. Since the early 1980s, China's economy has grown at an average of nearly nine percent a year in real terms. Living standards for much of the Chinese population have improved steadily over the past decade and a half, and consumer goods and food supplies are abundant throughout much of the country.

Beijing's trial-and-error approach to economic reforms has not been without significant drawbacks. For instance:

- In many cases, the regime has delayed the hardest reform steps–such as closing money-losing state factories or trimming surplus workers from state enterprise payrolls–out of fear of social unrest.
- Reforms have widened the gap between rich and poor regions of the country.
- Local decision-making authority has been accompanied by rising levels of corruption.
- Despite substantial reform over the past decade and a half, the regime still has problems tuning China's economy to achieve stable long-term growth. Economic cycles in China tend to be severe. To curb economic overheating, Beijing must step in with blunt measures–such as cutting off new lending–when inflation and other unwanted side effects emerge.

In the late 1970s and 1980s, there was strong debate from often widely varied perspectives in the Chinese leadership on how to handle China's economic development and reform. Today, the leadership appears more united on these issues.

In 1992, Beijing registered a booming 12.8 percent growth rate. The boom continued in 1993 at a rate of 13.4 percent. With such rapid growth came dislocations and renewed inflation. Beijing decided in mid-1993 to strengthen measures to cool the economy under the direction of Vice Premier Zhu Rongji. The cooling plan proved to be not as sweeping and draconian as past government efforts to curb inflation during previous "boom-bust" cycles associated with Chinese reform. Beijing still wants to see economic growth at a more sustainable, less disruptive level of around nine percent a year. Its main problem comes from local officials bent on pursuing entrepreneurial endeavors with sources of capital outside central control.

At a communist party plenum on November 11-14, 1993, it was decided to push forward with greater growth and reform and moderate the earlier measures to dampen growth and inflation. Results in 1994 showed continued economic overheating along with some indications that efforts to rein in rapid economic growth were beginning to work.

- An eleven percent growth rate for 1994.
- Continued inflation rates over twenty percent.
- Continued very active foreign investment.
- Continued widening in gap of per capita income between better-off urban residents and poorer rural dwellers.

On balance, the economic fundamentals in the Chinese economy remain strong. China has the natural resources, the human capital, and access to foreign technology and capital to sustain growth rates of the past decade into the next century. It is also at the geographic center of the world's most dynamic economic region. But China continues to face major economic impediments, including inadequate transportation and electric power systems, large population growth, an emerging business law system, and inadequate fiscal and monetary control mechanisms.

Regime-Society Relations

A focal point of analytical concern in the West recently has been the nature of regime-society relations in China.[4] If there is going to be a big challenge to China's new leaders and a big change in direction in Chinese policy and practice, many analysts believe, it will be ignited by friction as the regime's injunctions and conflicting trends in the society rub together. Adding fuel to this fire is widespread discontent with growing official corruption.

There has been mounting evidence of discontent in both rural and urban areas. Many city-dwelling intellectuals, workers, and others were thought to have been seriously alienated from government authority following the repression of the Tiananmen demonstrations of 1989. This may have moderated over the years but not disappeared.

Urban dwellers also contain the largest groups in the society whose benefits are being fundamentally challenged by the economic reform policies. They are unused to economic insecurity and some are thought to be willing to restrict reform in order to preserve their benefits (e.g., guaranteed jobs, low-cost housing, health-care). Others, of course, welcome the enormous increase in personal freedom that comes from the breakdown of the so-called work unit system that has dominated the life of workers and others associated with state-controlled enterprises and other places of employment. In particular, the individual worker is no longer dependent on the unit and its sometimes capricious and overbearing leaders for the essentials of life (salary, housing, schooling for children, rations if applicable). On balance, it seems fair to conclude that most urban workers in state-controlled enterprises–while they might welcome new freedom–are unused to and fearful of the possible negative consequences for them that could result from "jumping into the sea" of market-oriented enterprise in Chinese cities.

In the countryside, the terms of trade and government procurement practices for agricultural goods have taken a turn relatively disadvantageous for farmers after the high growth in peasant income fostered by government policies in the late 1970s and early 1980s. Prices of consumer goods and agricultural inputs have risen, far outpacing government procurement prices for agricultural commodities. Local officials responsible for purchasing grain and other mandated crops have sometimes used their allocations of cash to speculate in real estate or local enterprises. They have provided peasants with "IOUs" for their crops–a practice that has set off a number of peasant demonstrations and riots. Local officials have often established a sometimes dizzying array of taxes, fees, and levies from the peasants in order to help support local services and to provide capital for entrepreneurial endeavors supported by local officials. The cumulative effect of all these practices has been large-scale popular discontent and many reports of strikes, demonstrations, and sometimes violent riots against local officials and the broader administrative system that supports them.

In the past, the center could endeavor to deal with such problems through party channels, using the so-called "rectification" campaigns to weed out corrupt or abusive local officials in order to insure continued effective government. Current conditions in China make such an approach less likely to succeed. Reformers in Beijing are following policies that tacitly endorse the widespread entrepreneurship shown by local officials. The scope of corruption and misuse of funds has reportedly become so widespread that there may not be enough untainted cadre or local officials uninvolved in these practices to replace or sanction the errant local cadre.

Behind this state of affairs rests a widespread cynical view of power and politics in China. In the past, the vision of Marxism-Leninism had created an important incentive to motivate party-government cadre to insure their loyalty to central discipline. Today that ideology is widely viewed as bankrupt, and has often been replaced by a more particularistic, self-serving mentality where cadre work hard to benefit mainly themselves, their families, and their localities.

Democratic societies have established usually effective institutions to deal with local-central conflicts of interest and friction between the society and the state. China has few of these mechanisms. The policy consensus in Beijing seems to preclude any significant political change to establish them in the near future. The result is likely to be continued friction between the society on the one hand and the organs and officials of government, especially central government, on the other.

The Military

The PLA remains the ultimate instrument of central control over society and possibly resisting localities. At the same time, the PLA remains important as a possible arbiter should central, civilian policymakers reach an impasse on sensitive decision points involving domestic or foreign policies.[5]

The army today is leaner, led by more professionally competent officers, and less inclined to identify with local interests than in the past. The PLA has gone through a series of important changes and reforms under Deng Xiaoping's leadership. These have involved:

- Rotation of local military commanders;

- The establishment of more regular retirement of senior-level leaders;
- Reduction in the number of military regions;
- Increased centralization of the chain of command; and
- Big cuts in force levels, along with incremental efforts to modernize PLA training, equipment, and personnel procedures.

At the 14th Party Congress in 1992, PLA leaders thought to have strong political ambitions were demoted in ways designed to firm up the principle of civil control of the military and reduce the chances of the emergence of a rival base of power. The consensus on the policies of economic reform and political authoritarianism reached at the Congress and later leadership meetings also suggested that the PLA leadership was prepared to adhere to and support current policies.

Analysts remain unwilling to rule out an extraordinary intervention by the PLA into the political process. For one thing, it seems likely that the death of Deng Xiaoping will remove the leader with the most civilian *and* military prestige and create a power vacuum that will be difficult to fill. Few of the apparent contenders for power have extensive PLA experience. For the most part, party-government leaders and PLA leaders are following different career paths that make communications between the two more difficult. Thus, to achieve their interests, PLA leaders may feel compelled to resort to–albeit reluctantly–unauthorized actions. Second, politically ambitious PLA leaders who were demoted at the last Congress are still in the leadership or still retain considerable political influence; they may try to revive their political fortunes.

Against this backdrop, it is quite possible that a combination of factors such as policy indecision in Beijing and instability or disturbances in the provinces could provide sufficient justification for at least some PLA leaders to intervene in politics. Such intervention would be harder to stop in the absence of senior leaders like Deng Xiaoping. How this intervention would take place is difficult to foresee. Some suggest that the size and difficulty of administering China would force the military to work through existing party-government mechanisms. The military would rule in the name of party-government authority. A serious danger posed by any such military intervention would be seen if competing military leaders were vying for power. In such cases, a split in the PLA would presumably reflect a split in the leadership as a whole and add greatly to the administrative difficulties of ruling the country.

Foreign Policy Concerns

Chinese foreign policy changed markedly during the Maoist period (1949-1976). It moved from reliance on the USSR and strident opposition to the United States to a posture of strong opposition to both the United States and the USSR and finally to an approach that relied strategically on reconciliation with the United States to deal with the danger posed by the Soviet threat. After Mao died, Chinese leaders emphasized domestic policies of development that required markedly increased economic contacts abroad and gave added impetus to Beijing's desire to sustain good relations with the West and to avoid disruptions around the periphery of China that would complicate the Chinese drive toward modernization.[6]

Major changes have taken place in the international balance of power since the late 1980s (e.g., the collapse of the Soviet Union) and in China (e.g., the Tiananmen incident), but Chinese foreign policy continues to adhere to the general outlines established in the years after Mao's death. So long as China remains preoccupied with internal developments and international actors avoid initiatives seen as posing fundamental challenges to the Chinese leadership, Beijing seems likely to continue to follow the relatively narrow range of policies that it has adhered to in the past fifteen years.

As noted in the previous chapter, several trends have characterized the Chinese approach to foreign affairs in the post-Mao period, notably:

- Chinese leaders now face a security environment around China's periphery that is less likely to be disrupted by a major international power than at any time in the past.
- Regional security trends have been generally compatible with China's primary concern with internal economic modernization and political stability.
- Ideological and leadership disputes have had less importance for Chinese foreign policy than in the past.
- Chinese foreign policy has become more economically dependent on other countries, especially the Western-aligned, developed countries, than in the past. They have provided the assistance, technology, investment, and markets China needs to modernize effectively.
- China's overall pragmatic adjustments to world affairs have not been dependent on just one or two leaders in China. Although Deng Xiaoping picked up senior foreign policymaking duties

from Mao Zedong and Zhou Enlai, the policies followed represented, in broad terms, a consensus among senior Chinese leaders who have been advised and influenced by a wide range of experts and interest groups in China.

There remains the distinct possibility that outside forces (e.g., the United States and Taiwan) may adopt policies that challenge fundamental Chinese interests and prompt a strongly assertive Chinese response. For example, Beijing has threatened repeatedly that it would resort to force to halt movement in Taiwan to declare the island an independent country. Some analysts also judge that Beijing may revert to a tough anti-U.S. posture if the United States escalates sanctions and other pressures on China's communist regime. Hostilities in Korea that threaten vital Chinese security interests also would possibly prompt a forceful Chinese response.

Notes

1. Analysis in this section benefitted greatly from analyses contained in the *Cambridge History of China*, vol. 14, parts I and II; in the volumes on China released periodically by the U.S. Congressional Joint Economic Committee; and for the most recent period, from discussion by Harry Harding, David M. Lampton, David Shambaugh, and Albert Keidel, among others, at the Third Japan-U.S. Symposium on China, sponsored by the Japan Institute of International Affairs, Tokyo, July 15-16, 1993; H. Lyman Miller, "The Fourteenth Party Congress," *Washington Journal of Modern China*, (spring 1993); David Bachman, *Fourteenth Congress of the China Communist Party*, Asia Society, November 1992; Chong-pin Lin, "The Coming Chinese Earthquake," *The International Economy*, May/June 1992; Anne Thurston, "The Dragon Stirs," *Wilson Quarterly*, (spring 1993); David Shambaugh, "Losing Control: The Erosion of State Authority in China," *Current History*, September 1993; Gerald Segal, "China After Deng," *Jane's Intelligence Review*, November 1994; Arthur Waldron, "China's Coming Constitutional Changes," *ORBIS*, (winter 1995); and Harry Harding, "On the Four Great Relationships: The Prospects for China," *Survival*, (summer 1994).

2. Of course, in a period of leadership transition, Chinese leaders may choose not to follow their policy preference, but adhere to a different line for tactical political reasons. In the recent past, for example, party Chairman Jiang Zemin moved from cautious support for reform, to more rigorous support following Deng Xiaoping's tour of southern China in 1992, to the more cautious support we see today.

3. Analysis in this section is based heavily on CIA, *China's Economy in 1992 and 1993: Grappling With the Risks of Rapid Growth*, July 30, 1993, and *China's Economy in 1993 and 1994: The Search for a Soft Landing*, July 22, 1994. It also benefitted from the periodic assessments of the Chinese economy published in several volumes by the U.S. Congress, Joint Economic Committee, (e.g., "China Under the Four Modernizations," 1982; "China's Economy Looks Toward the Year 2000," 1986; and "China's Economic Dilemmas in the 1990s," 1991). Other notable views are seen in writings of Dwight Perkins and Nicholas Lardy in the *Cambridge History of China*, vol. 14, parts I, and II and Harry Harding, "China's Second Revolution," (Washington, DC: Brookings Institution, 1987).

4. See sources in note 1, especially works by Anne Thurston, David Shambaugh, and Chong-pin Lin.

5. Analysis in this section is taken in particular from discussion at the Institute for International Security Studies and China Association of Policy Studies conference on the PLA, June 1993; Michael Swaine, "The Military and Political Succession in China," Rand Corporation, 1992; discussion at the Third Japan-U.S. Conference on China, noted above; and discussion at the U.S. Defense Department Net Assessment Office, Conference on China's Future, August 1994. For background, see Shirley Kan, *China's Military: Roles and Implications for U.S. Policy Toward China*, CRS Report 91-731F, October 3, 1991. An example of the military playing a strong role in political evolution in transitional states was seen notably during the events in the Russian Republic in September 1993.

6. For background, see among others, Robert Sutter, *China in World Affairs*, CRS Report 95-265S, January 31, 1995, p. 19. While the content of Chinese policy changed, some goals remained broadly consistent: the security of the Chinese state and communist leadership; development of China's wealth and power; and Chinese strength and independence in world affairs.

5

The U.S. Factor

The outlook for Chinese foreign policy over the next ten years remains uncertain. Optimists in the West tend to extrapolate from the pragmatic trends seen in Chinese foreign policy behavior since the death of Mao and the rise of pragmatic nation-building policies of Deng Xiaoping. They argue that the logic of post-Mao foreign policy will continue to drive Chinese leaders in directions of greater cooperation, accommodation, and interdependence with the outside world, and especially China's neighbors and the advanced developed countries led by the United States. According to this view, as China becomes economically more advanced, it will undergo social and eventually political transformation that will result in a more pluralistic political decision-making process in Beijing that will, in turn, act to check assertive or aggressive Chinese foreign actions or tendencies. Moreover, as Beijing becomes more economically interdependent on those around China and the advanced developing countries, it will presumably be less inclined to take aggressive or disruptive actions against them.[1]

Pessimists in the United States and elsewhere in the West are more inclined to focus on the strong nationalistic ambitions and intentions of the Chinese leaders. They are often struck by the strong nationalistic views of at least a segment of PRC leaders in the past few years who voice deep suspicion of U.S. pressures directed against China. These Chinese leaders see these U.S. pressures and other U.S. policies, such as support for Taiwan, as fundamental challenges to China that must be confronted and resisted.

In the past, Chinese nationalistic ambitions ran up against, and were held in check by U.S.-backed military containment or Soviet-backed military containment. Later, Beijing's need for advantageous foreign economic interchange to support economic development at home, and thereby legitimate continued communist rule in China, caused it to curb assertive, nationalistic behavior abroad. But the pessimists believe that Beijing has now or will soon reach a point of economic development where it will no longer need to cater so much to outside concerns. For example, the government in Beijing may have reinforced its political legitimacy by its record of material progress in recent years. Also, China's economy has become such a magnet for foreign attention that the Sino-foreign tables could be reversed–that is, foreign countries now will feel an increasing need to accommodate China or risk being closed out of the booming China market, rather than China feeling a need to accommodate foreign interests.[2] China is now widely acknowledged as a world-class economic power and possibly a nascent superpower. None of this is unrecognized by China's leadership.

Whether China will follow the path of the optimists or pessimists, or some other future course, will depend heavily on two sets of factors.

1. Internal–political stability and the course of economic and political performance; and
2. External–the interaction of Chinese relations with key states around its periphery and Chinese adjustment to international trends in the so-called "new world order."

Internal Variables

Developments inside China that could cause a shift from pragmatism to a more assertive and disruptive emphasis on nationalism in Chinese foreign policy are:

- a major economic failure or change in political leadership. These could prompt Beijing's leaders to put aside their current approach to nation-building and adopt a more assertive foreign policy; this could be accompanied by harsher reactions to internal dissent and to Western influence in China; and
- the achievement of such a high level of economic success and social-political stability that Chinese leaders would feel confident that China was strong enough to pursue its interests in the region and elsewhere with less regard for the reaction or concerns of other countries.

Some have argued that it might be good for Asian and world stability if China continued to make progress toward economic modernization, but failed to achieve full success.[3] Under these circumstances, Beijing's leaders would likely continue to see their interests as best served by pursuing a moderate, conventional nation-building program. They would likely remain preoccupied with the difficulties of internal modernization and would not achieve a level of success that would allow for a more forceful policy in Asian and world affairs for some time to come.

An examination of variables governing China's development and reform efforts suggests that Beijing appears to face such future prospects. Beijing's leaders are unlikely to achieve fully their current development objectives for some time because of significant economic constraints, the complications from efforts to implement proposed reforms, and leadership and political instability. Major short-term economic constraints include an inadequate transportation system, insufficient supplies of electric power, an expanding government spending deficit, money-losing state enterprises, and a shortage of trained personnel. Long-term impediments include growing population pressure, the difficulty of obtaining enough capital to develop available energy resources and general industry, and the slowdown of agricultural growth after the rapid advances in the recent past.[4]

Reflecting these and other important constraints, the Chinese leadership at present continues to delay some changes in prices and economic restructuring because it fears they would have serious consequences for Chinese internal stability. Such changes can trigger inflation and cause hoarding. Closing inefficient factories forces workers to change jobs and perhaps remain unemployed for a time. Decentralized economic decision making means that local managers can use their increased power for personal benefit as well as for the common good. The result of these kinds of impediments has been a zig-zag pattern of forward movement and slowdown in economic reforms.

The problems of political stability focus on leadership succession–as principal leader Deng Xiaoping slowly fades–and the difficulty Beijing has in trying to control students, workers, and others demanding greater accountability, less corruption, or other steps that would curb central authority. The repeated political difficulties over the results of the economic reforms and political measures continue to demonstrate the volatility of politics in China.

Of course, the widely publicized difficulties of the reform efforts sometimes obscure their major accomplishments and the political support that lies behind them. Reflecting the rapid economic growth in China over the past seventeen years, the constituency favoring economic reform includes representatives of coastal provinces, enterprise managers, prospering farmers, many intellectuals, and technically competent party officials. The major alternatives to current policies (e.g., Maoist self-reliance and Soviet-style central planning) have been tried in the past and have been found wanting. Some of the followers of purged party leader Zhao Ziyang provided an alternative favoring greater political as well as economic reform, but thus far no leader has emerged with a program with viable support or constituency able to lead China in a direction markedly different than the current communist party-led development effort. Thus, on balance, it appears likely that Beijing will remain focused on economic reform while stressing the need for political stability, even in the event of strong leadership and political disputes and economic complications in the next few years. Nevertheless, analysts are sometimes concerned about what they see as Chinese assertiveness in the post-cold war order in Asia.

As analysts assess internal variables affecting China's future, the following questions appear relevant:

- *Political leadership*: How long will the recent broad consensus on economic reform and political authoritarianism last? Will a struggle for power following the death of Deng Xiaoping lead to an impasse in policymaking on domestic or foreign policy questions? What mechanisms will emerge to deal with expected continuing differences among central leaders and between them and provincial and local government leaders?

- *Economy*: How well will government authorities manage recent efforts to cool down the economy and control unwanted side effects (inflation)? Over the longer term, will it be possible to establish enough market control mechanisms in order to avoid the sharp and wasteful "boom-bust" economic cycles of recent years? Are there sufficient incentives for central and local authorities to work together on economic policies that will foster more efficient growth, curb lagging non-market enterprises, deal effectively with transportation, power, and other bottlenecks, and give all major sectors of the Chinese economy a meaningful stake in economic reform?

- *Society*: Will cleavages among significant groups in society (e.g., successful entrepreneurs versus low-paid employees in government-run enterprises) grow as a result of continued economic reform? Will relatively disadvantaged groups adopt extralegal means to register their grievances or will political and other mechanisms be established allowing these groups to have more of a say in government policy? How will authorities deal effectively with the widespread corruption among officials at central and local levels?

- *Military*: Will PLA and civilian leaders continue to cooperate closely in the post-Deng Xiaoping leadership? Will the PLA continue recent trends toward a more professional and streamlined force, or will PLA leaders feel impelled to get involved more deeply in post-Deng leadership politics? Does the PLA's heavy involvement in market-oriented enterprises sap its ability to serve as a coercive force against social discontent or resisting local authorities, or its ability to serve its primary goal of national defense?

External Relations

The foreign powers around China's periphery and those who have an important role to play regarding Chinese interests in international organizations, trade, and global issues could influence the course of Chinese foreign policy in several ways. Some may adopt policies on issues sensitive to Beijing that would prompt Chinese leaders to subordinate pragmatic interests for the sake of protecting Chinese territorial or other national claims. Most notable in this regard are outside challenges to China's claims to disputed territories. In the case of Taiwan, for example, if the leaders in Taipei were to formally declare independence from the mainland, Beijing might be hard put not to follow through on its repeated pledge to use force to stop such a development. In the case of disputed claims to islets in the South China Sea, Chinese naval forces could be expected to respond promptly to any effort by Vietnam or others to expand their territorial holdings by force.

On global economic issues, there is uncertainty as to how far the Chinese government will go in compromising with or retaliating against the United States and others unless China is allowed expeditiously to enter the WTO.[5] What is clear, however, is that a major shift toward protectionism among the developed countries would clearly undermine the basis of China's export-led growth. It could lead to a major shift in China's foreign policy, away from continued cooperation with the developed countries. By the same token, if foreign powers were to appear to "gang up" against China and impose sanctions because of PRC arms exports, human rights, or other policies, this too might prompt a serious Chinese reevaluation of the costs and benefits of cooperation with the international status quo.

In contrast to those who argue against heavy or provocative external pressure on China are those who argue against the dangers of appeasement or weakness in the face of China's growing strength. Even those who want foreign countries to "engage" closely with China often add that this must be done from a firm position. As a recent Trilateral Commission Study concluded, "a cooperative approach may not elicit a constructive Chinese response. . .the strength and prosperity of the Trilateral Countries–not their weakness–generate Chinese respect. Such classic considerations as balance of power, realism and a keen sense of Trilateral interests must also govern Western and Japanese thinking about China."[6]

As analysts assess external variables affecting China's future, the following questions appear relevant:

Are foreign powers–notably the United States–increasing or reducing political, economic, or other pressures on China's political system? Does an interdependent economic strategy continue to hold sufficient benefits for China as to outweigh the costs China pays in terms of diminished sovereignty and accommodating international pressures and irritants? Will developments around China's periphery and elsewhere in world affairs continue to be basically compatible with China's development strategy, or will events (e.g., Taiwan's declaration of independence; major international confrontation with North Korea; Japanese decision to develop nuclear weapons; rise in U.S. trade protectionism) prompt a sharp, more assertive Chinese response? Has greater Chinese economic and military power prompted PRC leaders to be more assertive in backing nationalistic, territorial, or other demands?

U.S. Policy Approaches

Beijing acknowledges that the United States still exerts predominant strategic influence in Asia, is a leading economic power in the region, and is capable of posing a real danger to Chinese security and development.

There is general agreement in the United States that Washington should use its influence in order to have Beijing conform to international norms and over time to foster changes in China's political, economic, and security systems compatible with American interests. At the same time, there is little agreement in Washington on how the United States should achieve these objectives. In general, there are three approaches influencing current U.S. China policy and little indication as to which approach will ultimately succeed.[7]

On one side is an approach favored by some in the Clinton administration, the Congress, and elsewhere who argue in favor of a moderate, less confrontational and "engaged" posture toward China. Some in this camp are concerned with perceived fundamental weaknesses in China and urge a moderate U.S. policy approach out of fear that to do otherwise could promote divisions in and a possible breakup of China with potentially disastrous consequences for U.S. interests in Asian stability and prosperity. Others are more impressed with China's growing economic and national strength and the opportunities this provides for the United States. They promote close U.S. engagement with China as the most appropriate way to guide the newly emerging power into channels of international activity compatible with American interests.

Sometimes underlying this moderate approach is a belief that trends in China are moving inexorably in the "right" direction. That is, China is becoming increasingly interdependent economically with its neighbors and the developed countries of the West, and is seen as increasingly unlikely to take disruptive action that would upset these advantageous international economic relationships. In addition, greater wealth in China is seen as pushing Chinese society in directions that seem certain to develop a materially better-off, more educated, and cosmopolitan populace that will over time press its government for greater representation, political pluralism, and eventually democracy. Therefore, U.S. policy should seek to work ever more closely with China in order to encourage these positive long-term trends.

A second, tougher approach is that of some U.S. advocates inside and out of the U.S. government who have doubts about the interdependence argument. These U.S. policymakers and opinion leaders stress that Beijing's officials still view the world as a state-centered competitive environment where interdependence counts for little and compromises sovereign strength. China's leaders are seen as determined to use whatever means at their disposal to increase China's wealth and power. At present, Beijing is seen biding its time and conforming to many international norms as it builds economic strength. Once it succeeds with economic modernization, the argument goes, Beijing will be disinclined to curb its narrow nationalistic or other ambitions out of a need for international interdependence or other concerns for world community. When strong enough, China, like other large powers in the past, will possess great capabilities and attract many friends and allies.

Under these circumstances, this approach encourages U.S. leaders to be more firm than moderate in dealing with China. Rather than trying to persuade Beijing of the advantages of international cooperation, the United States is advised to keep military forces as a counterweight to rising Chinese power in Asia; to remain firm in dealing with economic, arms proliferation, and other disputes with China; and to work closely with traditional U.S. allies and friends along China's periphery in order to deal with any suspected assertiveness or disruption from Beijing.

A third approach is favored by some U.S. officials and others who believe that the political system in China needs to be changed first before the United States has any real hope of reaching a constructive relationship with China. Beijing's communist leaders are seen as inherently incapable of long-term positive ties with the United States. U.S. policy should focus on mechanisms to change China from within while maintaining a vigilant posture to deal with disruptive Chinese foreign policy actions in Asian and world affairs. The development of an authoritarian superpower more economically competent than the USSR is not to be aided.

Uncertainty in the U.S. Approach to China

Caught up in the drama of the recent changes inside China, Western specialists and other observers have understandably focused on internal variables and factors as the most important determinants of China's future. Indeed, most foreign powers, led by Japan, Russia, India, the ASEAN states, and others around China's periphery have appeared willing in recent years to accommodate and work with China, and to avoid actions and pressures that could prompt a sharp adjustment or shift in Chinese policy or a change in China's future policy orientation.

Not so the United States. U.S. policy now intrudes on such a wide range of issues sensitive to Beijing and to the future of China's policy as to represent perhaps the most critical current variable in determining China's future direction.

- The United States clearly has it within its power through trade sanctions or protectionist trade measures to seriously complicate PRC economic development plans.

- The United States has the option at this time to instigate or exacerbate regional security tensions over China's rising power in ways that could seriously complicate China's desire for an accommodating security environment in the region.
- The United States also plays a key role in such sensitive territorial questions for the PRC leadership as Taiwan, Tibet, Hong Kong, and the South China Sea. Any PRC leadership that does not handle these issues appropriately is widely seen as vulnerable to challenges from others in the communist hierarchy. Beijing's leaders' view of the challenges posed by such territorial problems also is seen as going far toward determining PRC willingness or reluctance to associate closely with outside powers and develop an interdependent approach to world affairs.
- Sharp tensions in U.S.-China relations would presumably force key countries in the region like Japan, South Korea, Russia, and Australia, and key international actors like the international financial institutions that provide several billion dollars of aid to the PRC annually, to feel the need to choose between Washington and Beijing on important issues–choices with unpredictable and potentially serious implications for China's ability to sustain a cooperative foreign environment.

By the same token, the United States also appears to have a potentially large influence on encouraging China to engage with the world in a positive and constructive way. With its superior military strength and intelligence capabilities, the United States could take the lead in reassuring Asian states over China's growing military power and at the same time reassuring China of the regional response to China's rise. As the world's largest economy, the United States can play a very important role in determining the most constructive ways to engage the Chinese economy in the WTO and other multilateral economic organizations. U.S. policy on issues like Taiwan, Tibet, Hong Kong, the South China Sea, and other territorial questions sensitive to Beijing could be formulated in ways that encourage constructive PRC responses to accepted international norms. Similar arguments can be made regarding U.S. policy toward trade, arms proliferation, human rights, environment, and other questions now at the center of U.S. interaction with China.

In a word, a case can be made for the argument that for the time being, the United States has it within its power to move the direction of

PRC policy in one way or the other. Whether U.S. policymakers realize their influence and what they propose to do with it remains to be seen.

An effective U.S. policy toward China, whether tough or accommodating, does not seem likely in the near future. There remains too much uncertainty and unpredictability in the conduct of U.S. foreign policy in the post-cold war environment to allow for such an organized American approach. There are many reasons for this knotted situation in U.S. foreign policy.

Numerous issues and variables affecting U.S. policy make it difficult to chart its general direction. The task is made all the more difficult because the previous framework for U.S. policy, based on the primacy of security issues and opposition to Soviet expansion, is now obsolete. Imperatives of economic competitiveness, democracy, human rights, and other values have achieved greater prominence in U.S. policymaking. The ability of the executive branch of government to use the argument of U.S. strategic competition with the Soviet Union as a means to keep foreign policymaking power in its hands is also at an end. American policymaking will likely reflect more sharply the pluralistic nature of U.S. society and the various pressure groups and other representative institutions there for some time to come.

History has shown that this fluidity and competition among priorities is more often than not the norm in American foreign policy. Presidents Wilson and Roosevelt both set forth comprehensive concepts of a well-integrated U.S. foreign policy, but neither framework lasted long. The requirements of the cold war were much more effective in establishing rigor and order in U.S. foreign policy priorities, but that era is now over. In retrospect, it appears as the aberration rather than the norm in the course of U.S. foreign policy.

In general terms, there appear to be three distinct tendencies or schools of thought concerned with U.S. foreign policy after the cold war.[8] Although contemporary U.S. foreign policy advocates cover a wide range of opinion and issues, one can discern these three approaches. By understanding what these schools stand for and observing the actions of U.S. policy in specific areas regarding China, one can get a better sense as to how difficult it will continue to be to predict the future direction of U.S. policy toward China.

On one side are Americans who are concerned with what they see as a relative decline in U.S. power, which in turn complicates U.S. efforts to protect important interests abroad. They call for the United States to work harder to preserve important interests abroad, but with fewer U.S. resources and less U.S. influence available to do the job. These leaders' review of recent developments causes them to expect further changes in world affairs, sometimes in unexpected ways. They see relatively limited or declining U.S. power and influence to deal with those changes.

They stress in particular several "realities" governing the current U.S. approach to Asia and the Pacific and world affairs in general:

- U.S. attention to China, Asia and the Pacific, and elsewhere abroad has been diverted by the need to focus on pressing U.S. domestic problems.
- U.S. government decision making will remain difficult because of the possibility that the executive branch will remain in control of one U.S. political party, and the Congress in control of another party.
- The U.S. government and the U.S. private sector have only limited financial resources to devote to domestic and foreign policy concerns.
- The priorities in U.S. policy toward China will remain unclear. Security, economic, and cultural-political issues will vary in receiving top priority in U.S. policy.
- There remains no obvious international framework to deal with foreign issues. U.S. policy must use a mix of international, regional, and bilateral efforts to achieve policy goals.

Under these circumstances, these advocates see a strong need for the United States to work prudently and closely with traditional U.S. allies and associates. Their cautious approach argues, for example, that it seems foolish and inconsistent with U.S. goals not to preserve the long-standing U.S. stake in good relations with Japan and with friends and allies along the periphery of Asia and in Oceania. Their security policies and political-cultural orientations are generally seen as in accord with U.S. interests. Although opinion surveys sometimes claim that the American public and some U.S. leaders see Japan as an economic competitive "threat" to U.S. well-being, these observers stress a different line of argument. They highlight the fact that few polls of U.S. public opinion or U.S. leaders support the view that it is now in America's interest to focus U.S. energies on the need to confront the Japanese economic threat, in a way that confrontation with the Soviet Union came to dominate U.S. policy during the cold war.

In the view of these advocates, caution is in order in anticipating future U.S. relations with other major regional actors–the former Soviet

Union, China, and India. All three are preoccupied with internal political-development crises. Few appear to be seeking to foment tensions or major instability in the region. All seek better ties and closer economic relations with the West and with the advancing economies of the region. U.S. policy would appear well advised, they say, to work closely with these governments wherever there is possible common ground on security, economic, or political issues.

In considering U.S. assets available to influence trends in the region, these advocates call on U.S. leaders to go slow in reducing the U.S. military presence in the region. The economic savings of such a cutback would be small; the political costs could be high inasmuch as most countries in Asia have been encouraging the United States to remain actively involved in the region to offset the growing power of Japan or the potential ambitions of China or others.

A second major school of thought on U.S. foreign policy emerged in the 1990s. These proponents have argued for major cutbacks in U.S. international involvement and a renewed focus on solving U.S. domestic problems concerning crime, drugs, lagging economic competitiveness and educational standards, homelessness, poverty, decaying cities and transportation infrastructure, and other issues. Variations of this view are seen in the writings of William Hyland, Patrick Buchanan, and other well-known commentators, and in the political rhetoric of Ross Perot.

Often called an "American First" or "Neoisolationist" school, these advocates argue for sweeping cuts in U.S. military, diplomatic, and foreign assistance spending abroad. They are skeptical of the utility of the international financial institutions, the United Nations, and the international efforts to promote free trade through the GATT, WTO, and other means. They argue that the United States has become overextended in world affairs; has been taken advantage of in the current world security-economic system; and must begin to retreat from international commitments in order to gather together the resources needed to deal with American domestic problems. As to specific recommendations, these proponents tend to favor a complete U.S. pullback from foreign bases; drastic cuts in foreign assistance and foreign technical/information programs; and termination of various international economic talks that help to perpetuate a world trading system, which they see as basically contrary to American economic interests. Many in this school favor stronger government intervention in the domestic U.S. economy and related areas of promoting technology, education, and social welfare. Some favor trade measures that are seen as protectionist by U.S. trading partners.

Meanwhile, on the other side of the debate lies a third, somewhat less well articulated school of thought. This school of thought generally judges that U.S. policy needs to more strongly and actively promote U.S. views of the world political, military, and economic order; to press those countries that do not conform to the U.S. view of an appropriate world order; and to lead strongly in world affairs, attempting to avoid compromises and accommodations with others that would reduce the impact and strength of U.S. leadership.

This school of thought has always been present in American politics. But it appears far stronger today than at any other time since at least the 1960s for several reasons:

- *Impact of Reagan policies*–After a prolonged period of introspection and doubt following the Vietnam War, the oil shocks, and the Iran hostage crisis, U.S. opinion became much more optimistic about the United States and its future after two terms of Ronald Reagan.
- *Victory in the cold war*–This represented a great accomplishment for the U.S.-backed system of collective security and for U.S. political and economic values.
- *Persian Gulf War*–U.S. military doctrine, equipment, and performance were strong; U.S. ability to lead in a world crisis also appeared strong.
- *Economic developments*–Although the United States is seen facing still serious difficulties, advocates point to analysts who are now more optimistic about U.S. ability to prosper in the increasingly competitive world economic environment.
- *Values-Culture*–The United States is seen as better positioned than any other country to exert leadership in all major areas of cultural influences; i.e., ideas and values, political concepts, life-style, and popular culture.

The perception of a power vacuum in the world, in which the United States more freely exerts its influence, drives further consideration of this school of thought. Thus, proponents of this viewpoint are not deterred by the seeming decline in economic resources available to U.S. policymakers. In particular, the former Soviet Union, China, and India are likely to remain internally preoccupied for some time. Meanwhile, Japan and Germany are acknowledged to be economically powerful; but politically they have shown themselves to be uncertain as to how to use their new power and culturally they appear to be not nearly as influential as the United States.

In recent years, advocates of this third tendency have been most vocal in pressing their concern for strong U.S. policy in support of U.S. political values of democracy and human rights. In this regard they have sometimes argued for a more active U.S. foreign policy, leading some recipient countries to view U.S. policy as illegitimate interference in a country's internal affairs. They have also reinforced the strength and determination of the U.S. case in opposition to economic or trading policies seen in the United States as grossly inequitable or predatory; and they have reinforced strongly the U.S. policy against the proliferation of weapons of mass destruction. Other areas where they have exerted more influence involve international sanctions against countries that harbor terrorists, promote the drug trade, or grossly harm the world environment. They have also pushed the U.S. government to be more assertive in promoting humanitarian relief and in recognizing politically the legitimacy of people's right to self-determination.

In sum, it is not hard to see the evidence of clashes among these three, often competing tendencies in U.S. policy toward China. Most obvious in recent years have been those of the third group who have strongly pursued human rights, arms proliferation, trade practices, and other issues with China. They have pressed Beijing hard to meet U.S. sanctioned international norms, threatening sometimes very serious economic or other actions if China did not conform. By contrast, the more cautious and accommodating first group sees the strong advocates of U.S. values and concerns as being unrealistic about U.S. power and unwilling to make needed compromises with the Chinese government and others in order to protect U.S. interests in relations with China.

Notes

1. Discussed, among others, in Ming Zhang, "China and the Major Power Relations," *The Journal of Contemporary China*, (fall 1994).

2. Discussed, among others, in Chong-Pin Lin, "Chinese Military Modernization: Perceptions, Progress and Prospects," *Security Studies*, (summer 1994).

3. Reviewed in *China in Transition*, CRS Report 93-1061S, December 20, 1993, p. 23. Of course, among other arguments are those that stress that an economically successful China would be very closely integrated with and dependent on the world economy, and would not be disruptive in world politics.

4. See among others CRS Issue Brief 93114, replayed on pp. 3-17 in Senate Document 104-3, cited in chapter 1, note 1.

5. Discussed, among others, in CRS Issue Brief 94002, replayed on pp. 196-210 in Senate Document 104-3, cited in chapter 1, note 1.

6. Yoichi Funabashi, et al., *Emerging China In A World of Interdependence*, Trilateral Commission, May 1994.

7. Reviewed in CRS Report 95-265-S, *China in World Affairs,* replayed on pp. 175-195 in Senate Document 104-3 cited in chapter 1, note 1.

8. For background, see Robert Sutter, *East Asia and the Pacific: Challenges for U.S. Policy,* (Boulder, CO: Westview Press, 1992), pp. 155-158.

6

The U.S.-China Relationship

A review of the twists and turns in recent U.S. policy toward China not only says something about the lack of consensus and effectiveness in U.S. policy. It also graphically illustrates how deeply involved the United States has become in such a wide range of issue areas of importance to China and its political leadership. It is hard to imagine another element in the equation of factors that will determine China's future role in world affairs that is more important and more uncertain than the United States.

Recent Policy Evolution

During his campaign for president in 1992, Bill Clinton staked out a position on China that was markedly different from that pursued by the Bush administration.[1] He stated his belief that the United States should use its economic leverage to promote democracy in China. He supported congressional action to link China's MFN status with its human rights policies, and supported a number of other congressional initiatives.

Decision on MFN: 1993

The annual MFN decision in 1993 was the administration's first major test on U.S.-China relations. Under U.S. law, China's eligibility for MFN status is subject to an annual renewal, which the president must request by June 3, and which automatically goes into effect if Congress does not enact a joint resolution of disapproval within sixty days. On May 28, 1993, President Clinton issued a Report to Congress and an executive order, which effectively continued China's unconditional MFN status for another year (through July 1994), but placed conditions on China's MFN status in succeeding years.

Under the president's executive order, the secretary of state may not recommend an extension of China's MFN treatment in 1994 unless he determines (1) that China has abided by its 1992 agreement with the United States to halt exports of prison labor products to the United States, and (2) that an extension will substantially promote the freedom-of-emigration objectives in the Jackson-Vanik Amendment to the 1974 Trade Act. In addition, in making his recommendation the secretary must determine whether China has made overall significant progress in human rights, including:

- adhering to the Universal Declaration of Human Rights;
- releasing and acceptably accounting for political prisoners;
- ensuring humane treatment of prisoners;
- protecting Tibet's religious and cultural heritage; and
- permitting international radio and television broadcasts into China.

The executive order further stated that the administration would pursue other legislative and executive actions to ensure that China complied with trade agreements and adhered to the Non-Proliferation Treaty (NPT), Missile Technology Control Regime (MTCR), and other nonproliferation commitments.

On the whole, the immediate reaction to the president's MFN decision was positive. House and Senate sponsors of legislation conditioning the granting of MFN, both democrats, expressed their support for the president's executive order over their own bills. In effect this suspended, for the remainder of the year, what had become a rancorous annual congressional debate on MFN conditionality; neither bill was acted upon in 1993. Many thought that Chinese officials also seemed relieved over the May 28 decision; although the Chinese Foreign Ministry lodged a "strong protest"–the first such protest since February 1990–its statements concerning the decision were relatively restrained. Chinese officials were aware that the two MFN bills pending before Congress would have greatly reduced the administration's flexibility in determining China's future MFN status.

Policy Initiatives, 1993-1994

The breathing spell that the May 1993 MFN decision bought for U.S.-China relations lasted less than three months. By late summer, several of the long-standing irritants in the relationship were newly raw. As a series of confrontations developed over human rights and weapons proliferation, neither the United States nor China appeared to be pursuing consistent policies. The relationship, far from being stabilized, eroded further with a rapidity that startled administration observers. During August and September 1993, China issued strong protests against a number of U.S. actions, accompanied by unusually harsh rhetoric criticizing American intentions and objectives. Concerned about the state of U.S.-China relations, U.S. officials began a reassessment of U.S. policy, a process that culminated in September 1993 with the president's signing of an action memorandum.

U.S. policy toward China entered a new phase in September 1993. According to press reports, President Clinton signed a classified "action memorandum" in mid-month that defined the new policy direction. Administration officials termed the new approach a policy of "comprehensive engagement." In conjunction with the new policy, a procession of high-level U.S. officials visited Beijing. Together, they represented all three of the contentious issues that had driven U.S.-China relations in recent years–human rights, trade, and nonproliferation.

President Clinton met with China's President Jiang Zemin at the November 1993 APEC conference in Seattle; the administration on March 30, 1994, announced new, liberalized licensing procedures for the export of high-technology items to China and other proscribed countries that had once been controlled by the now-defunct Coordinating Committee on Multilateral Export Controls (COCOM); and, most significantly, the president, on May 26, 1994, announced his decision to extend China's MFN status for another year despite Beijing's failure to meet the human rights criteria in his 1993 executive order.

Resumption of Military Contacts

The visit of Assistant Secretary of Defense Charles Freeman (November 1993) effectively ended the ban on high-level military contacts that had been in place since June 5, 1989. Although the United States had developed close military ties and cooperation with China during the 1980s–even selling China some military equipment and weapons systems–military contacts had been suspended since the 1989 Tiananmen Square crackdown.

The decision to resume military contacts reportedly reflected U.S. administration officials' concerns about a number of disturbing trends in China. In particular was the observation by U.S. officials that the People's Liberation Army (PLA), formerly a chief proponent of closer U.S. ties, had begun to reassess its views of China's security threats. U.S. experts believed the PLA was developing deep suspicions of American intentions toward China, and was becoming more inclined to challenge U.S. political and military interests. According to U.S. press reports, a classified U.S. Intelligence Estimate on China warned that China's military leaders were beginning to see the United States, and not the former Soviet Union, as China's principal enemy. The Clinton administration apparently hoped that the Freeman visit and future military dialogues would help defuse this trend.

Status of Missile-Related Sanctions

On January 7, 1994, the administration announced that China and the United States would begin nonproliferation talks in Washington on January 26, 1994, to address reports of Chinese export of M-11 missile technology and equipment to Pakistan and resulting U.S. sanctions imposed on August 24, 1993. In addition, the U.S. Commerce Department was authorized to approve export licenses for three U.S. communications satellites, which were to be sent to China for launch, on the grounds that the satellites were not covered by the August 24, 1993, sanctions; it had been anticipated that the licenses would be a casualty of the U.S. sanctions. On October 4, 1994, the United States and China signed an agreement allowing the export of high technology satellites to China that were frozen as a sanction against Beijing's secret transfer of missile components and technology to Pakistan. China agreed that once the sanctions are ended, it will abide by rules of the international Missile Technology Control Regime (MTCR).

Asia Pacific Economic Cooperation Forum (APEC) Meeting, November 1993

The 1993 Ministerial and Leaders' Meeting of APEC, which the

United States hosted in Seattle in November 1993, provided another opportunity for the administration to engage with Chinese leaders. Prior to the APEC meeting, on November 17, 270 members of the U.S. House of Representatives signed a letter to President Clinton expressing their concern for China's lack of progress in meeting conditions on human rights, trade, and the prevention of weapons proliferation. When President Clinton met with China's President Jiang Zemin in a private ninety-minute meeting during the APEC summit, he urged the Chinese leader to demonstrate "early concrete progress" on these conditions. He also specifically asked China to permit International Red Cross inspections of Chinese prisons; begin a dialogue with the Dalai Lama, Tibet's spiritual leader; and allow U.S. Customs officials to inspect Chinese prisons under the terms of a U.S.-China agreement of August 1992 covering exports of prison-made goods. Mr. Jiang responded with a conventional Chinese deflection–that U.S.-China dialogue should be conducted on the basis of mutual respect, without "interference in one another's affairs"; and that the United States would have to lift its remaining sanctions before meaningful negotiations could take place.

Also during the APEC leaders' meeting, Secretary of State Christopher, meeting with Chinese Foreign Minister Qian Qichen, told his counterpart that the United States was dropping its long-standing opposition to China's purchase of an $8 million Cray supercomputer. U.S. officials defended the decision by saying that it was a good will gesture toward China, and that monitoring of the supercomputer's use will assure it is not used by the military. China has said that the computer will be used for weather forecasting.

Secretary of State Warren Christopher's Visit to Beijing, March 1994

On March 11, 1994, Secretary of State Christopher took to Beijing the message that China needed to make rapid further progress on human rights in order to satisfy the conditions of the 1993 executive order. Reinforcing this point, the secretary's trip was preceded by the visit of John Shattuck, U.S. assistant secretary of state for human rights affairs, who made a point of meeting with a prominent Chinese dissident. Chinese leaders appeared strongly opposed to, even defiant of, the U.S. position. In particular, Chinese security forces detained prominent Chinese activists and some Western journalists prior to Secretary Christopher's visit. In the aftermath of the secretary's visit, U.S. officials publicly expressed satisfaction that the visit resulted in progress on the two mandatory provisions of the 1993 executive order: clearing blocked Chinese passports to facilitate emigration; and a second memorandum of understanding (MOU) on preventing exports of products made by prison labor. But privately, many observers expressed concern that China's widely publicized stance during the Christopher visit would not make the president's impending decision on MFN any easier.

President Clinton's 1994 Decision to Renew China's MFN Status

In a press conference on May 26, 1994, President Clinton announced that he had decided the United States should renew China's MFN trading status despite Beijing's failure to meet the human rights conditions in his 1993 executive order. Furthermore, he stated that he was moving to "de-link" human rights from China's MFN status, saying that the United States had "reached the end of the usefulness of that policy." Acknowledging that China continued to commit very serious human rights abuses, the president also announced that he was extending the Tiananmen sanctions imposed against China; banning the import of munitions from China, principally guns and ammunition; and inaugurating a new program to support those working for human rights improvements in China. This program is to include: increased broadcasts for Radio Free Asia and the Voice of America; increased support for nongovernmental organizations (NGOs) working on human rights in China; and working with American businesses to develop voluntary principles for business activity in China.

The New Arms Embargo on Imports. The arms embargo announced by the president on May 26 went into effect at 12:01 a.m. on May 28, 1994. The embargo places a complete prohibition on the imports from China of articles on the Munitions Import List of the Bureau of Alcohol, Tobacco, and Firearms (BATF), including articles for which current valid import permits are held or articles that may be en route. According to the U.S. Customs Service, such imports were projected to total approximately $200 million in 1994. Current information was that the only articles on the Munitions Import List that China exports to the United States are ammunition, firearms, firearms parts and accessories (for example, rifle scopes), and gas masks. Under several sets of U.S. government regulations (the Department of State's International Traffic in Arms Regulations–22 CFR 126.1(a), and the Treasury Department's Regulations on the Importation of Arms, Ammunition, and Implements

War–27 CFR 47.52(a)), U.S. policy is to prohibit imports of defense icles from countries subject to a U.S. arms *export* embargo. According the U.S. Customs Service, China has been exempted from this policy ce 1989. The president's May 26 decision brings U.S. policy toward ina into conformity with U.S. regulations.

Congressional Reaction. On August 9, 1994, the House of presentatives considered three measures relating to China's MFN tus, and enacted one that essentially codified the president's initiatives. e first measure was H.J. Res. 373, which would have disapproved sident Clinton's recommendation that MFN be extended to China for ther year. This resolution would have had to have been approved by h houses by August 31 before it could go into effect. Its August 9 eat in the House, by a vote of 75-356, effectively killed the measure 1994.

The House also considered two alternative proposals addressing the e of MFN for China. Under the rule, both measures were being red as substitutes to the United States-China Act of 1994 (H.R. 4590, oduced by Representatives Pelosi, Bonior, and Gephardt). One stitute, also by Pelosi, was identical to the bill itself. It would have uired the secretary of state to encourage American businesses to adopt the voluntary code of conduct mentioned above. In addition, the substitute provided for two alternative provisions, which essentially would have limited the measure's punitive effects to goods produced by Chinese government entities, while protecting MFN status for goods produced by China's private-sector entrepreneurs or joint ventures with foreign partners:

- it declared that even if Congress passed a joint resolution of disapproval, MFN status would be denied only to those imported products that are produced, manufactured, or exported by Chinese state-owned enterprises; and
- it declared that if Congress did not pass a joint resolution of disapproval, MFN status would not be extended to imports of goods made or exported by the Chinese military or a defense industrial trading company, or to goods in most major products categories made or re-exported by Chinese state-owned enterprises.

The second substitute, offered by Representative Hamilton, in effect codified the president's May 26 decision recommending MFN be extended to China, except for the president's initiative to prohibit imports of Chinese arms and ammunition. The House adopted the Hamilton substitute by a vote of 280-152, and rejected the Pelosi substitute by a vote of 158-270.

Subsequent Actions

The Clinton administration moved to solidify aspects of U.S.-China relations, but developments also reflected a number of issues in contention:

- Commerce Secretary Brown led a large business delegation to China in August 1994, signing $5 billion in contracts. China also agreed to resume the off-again, on-again human rights dialogue with the United States.
- The Clinton administration proposed only minor adjustments in U.S. relations with Taiwan as a result of a lengthy Taiwan policy review announced on September 7.
- Foreign Minister Qian signed agreements on October 4, 1994, allowing the United States to lift sanctions imposed as a result of China's sale of missile components to Pakistan; and pledging to work to end the production of fissile material for nuclear weapons.
- Defense Secretary Perry held four days of talks with senior military and government leaders in Beijing.
- President Clinton discussed North Korea, arms proliferation, trade, human rights, and other issues with China's president at the APEC leaders' meeting in Indonesia on November 14, 1994. The Chinese president was enthusiastic about the U.S.-North Korean nuclear accord.
- Beijing threatened to end commercial agreements with the United States unless it got into GATT by year's end, and it canceled Secretary Pena's visit to China on account of his visit to Taiwan in early December.
- U.S. Trade Representative Kantor on December 31, 1994, threatened trade sanctions worth over $1 billion unless Beijing met U.S. intellectual property rights (IPR) conditions by February 4. The United States began such formal trade sanctions on February 4, and China immediately announced

retaliatory steps. The trade conflict was averted by an agreement reached on February 26, 1995.

- Assistant Secretary of State for Human Rights John Shattuck held two days of fruitless talks in Beijing in mid-January 1995. In February 1995, Beijing complained about the annual U.S. State Department report on China's human rights conditions and strongly protested U.S. support for a UN resolution critical of Chinese human rights.
- Energy Secretary O'Leary oversaw the signing of agreements in China with a reported value of several billion dollars.
- The United States and China reached agreement on March 12, 1995, regarding market access disputes and China's WTO membership.

Congressional Initiatives. While passing almost unanimously separate House and Senate resolutions urging President Clinton to look past Beijing's objections and allow Taiwan's president to make a private visit to the United States, Congress considered in May legislation in the House and Senate that was strongly critical of China. Specifically, the State Department authorization bill (H.R. 1564) and the foreign aid authorization bill (H.R. 1563) had numerous such provisions. The provisions were incorporated into a larger foreign policy bill (H.R. 1561) in mid-May. The legislation:

- criticized China's stance in the territorial dispute in the South China Sea and asserted that any attempt by a "nondemocratic power" to push its claims on others would be seen as a matter of "grave concern" to the United States;
- contained provisions amending the Taiwan Relations Act to supersede U.S. obligations undertaken in a 1982 U.S.-PRC communiqué on arms to Taiwan, and to press the Clinton administration to grant visas to Taiwanese officials visiting in a private capacity;
- strongly criticized China's "gulag" and overall human rights record, urging the president not to visit China under these circumstances, and requiring the administration to submit reports and take other actions to promote greater human rights in China;
- reaffirmed the congressional view that Tibet is "an occupied country," that the State Department should establish a "special

envoy" for Tibet, and that regular State Department reports be issued regarding the status of U.S. relations with Tibet;

- restricted U.S. spending for family planning activities in China, unless it is certified that China no longer conducts forced abortions; and
- set a series of conditions regarding U.S. policy on the September 1995 International Conference on Women to be held in Beijing.

In mid-May, the Senate Foreign Relations Committee began markup on legislation (S.908) on foreign policy authorization that also took strong issue with China's practices and behavior. Among other provisions, it:

- supported a visit of Taiwan's president to the United States;
- set conditions on U.S. participation in the 1995 International Women's Conference in Beijing;
- amended the Taiwan Relations Act to have it supersede the U.S.-PRC communiqué of 1982 restricting U.S. arms sales to Taiwan;
- established reporting requirements and called for the appointment of a U.S. special envoy for Tibet;
- criticized PRC forced labor practices and exports of forced labor products; and
- changed the name of the Taiwan office in the United States.

Taiwan's President's Visit, MFN Renewal. President Clinton bowed to congressional pressure in deciding on May 22, 1995, to allow Taiwan's president to make a private visit to the United States. Beijing protested strongly and canceled some high-level visits. The president on June 2, 1995, announced that he would renew MFN treatment for China for another year.

By mid-June, Beijing had cut off or suspended several important channels to the United States as a result of Taiwan's president's visit. At that time, Chinese officials and media were virtually uniform in depicting the U.S. actions as the latest and most important U.S. government conspiracy to use relations with Taiwan and other means to "contain" China.

Beijing attributed U.S. motives to a basic American fear of China's rising power and influence in the world, and a determination on the part of the United States to check the "Chinese threat."

At the time, Beijing indicated that only "concrete" action by the U.S. government–at minimum a pledge by the Clinton administration that it would not give a visa to other senior Taiwanese leaders–would allow U.S.-China relations to go forward. To underline the point, Beijing called home its ambassador, refused U.S. offers to send Under Secretary of State Tarnoff to China for talks, and rebuffed reported U.S. queries about a possible U.S.-Chinese summit. Beijing also escalated political and military pressure on Taiwan and on Lee Teng-hui in particular. These pressures included the most provocative military exercises in the Taiwan area and the most hostile rhetoric against a Taiwan leader seen in over twenty years.[2]

The tough PRC approach continued until the August 1 meeting between Secretary of State Christopher and Chinese Foreign Minister Qian Qichen in Brunei.[3] Chinese officials saw no particular accommodation by Christopher of Chinese demands on Taiwan, as the secretary confirmed to the world media that the United States was not prepared to promise not to allow senior Taiwanese visitors to travel in a private capacity to the United States. Nonetheless, Chinese officials and commentary soon adjusted their view of the United States to allow for some forward movement in U.S.-PRC relations. Significant steps included:

- Private acknowledgment by several Chinese officials in the United States that the U.S. government is indeed not conspiring to contain China, even though these same officials judge that senior leaders in Beijing continue to believe the conspiracy theory;[4]
- Strong efforts by the PRC Embassy in Washington and other PRC officials to build better ties with Congress. Senior Chinese leaders in Beijing went on record strongly endorsing interaction with Congress, with Foreign Minister Qian stating on August 18 that "China is willing to increase contacts and exchanges with the U.S. Congress and welcomes more U.S. congressmen to visit China;"[5]
- China's agreement to the previously rebuffed visit by Under Secretary Tarnoff and to move ahead similarly with plans for a U.S.-China summit; and
- China's publicly acknowledged willingness–for the first time–to consider the appointment of former Senator James Sasser as ambassador to China.[6] Beijing's refusal to consider the

appointment had stalled the nomination for many months. China reportedly decided to return its ambassador to Washington following his withdrawal in June.

Meanwhile, China improved the overall atmosphere in U.S.-China relations by releasing detained human rights activist Harry Wu after his conviction in August–a step that eased the way for First Lady Hillary Clinton to attend the International Women's Conference in Beijing in September.

China's more moderate approach to the United States stood in marked contrast to Beijing's continued harsh pressure against Lee Teng-hui. In effect, Chinese officials and media now acknowledged that Lee's visit reflected more the strong desire of Lee and others in Taiwan to assume a greater role in international affairs than it did a U.S. conspiracy to use the "Taiwan card" to check the growth of Chinese power and influence.

A sharply worded New China News Agency commentary of August 22 provided the most authoritative justification to date of Beijing's shift toward more moderation toward the United States.[7] At one level, the commentary was harshly critical of "hegemonists" in the U.S. media and elsewhere who had brought Sino-U.S. relations to their "lowest ebb" in sixteen years. (U.S. media reaction to the Chinese commentary focused on the harsh anti-U.S. rhetoric in the piece.)[8] In fact, however, the Chinese commentary carefully differentiated between the so-called U.S. "hegemonists" in the media (*Time* magazine, the *New York Times*, and the *Washington Post* specifically were mentioned), and "quite a few sensible people" in the United States who oppose the containment strategy advocated by the hegemonists. The commentary clearly implied that the Clinton administration was among the "sensible people" and that the hegemonists in the media and elsewhere were becoming increasingly "unpopular" in the United States. The commentary did not link Congress with one side or the other in the American debate.

Chinese officials privately offered a somewhat different rationale for China's shift and also provided a somewhat more optimistic outlook for U.S.-China relations. One official recently returned from many weeks of consultations in Beijing advised that at the recent PRC leadership meetings at the seaside resort of Beidahe, senior Chinese leaders reportedly reconfirmed their view that the U.S. government may be conspiring to contain China. But these officials also recognized China's need for a workable relationship with the United States. Thus, while suspicious of U.S. intentions, and determined to resist any perceived U.S. efforts to "contain" China, Chinese leaders recognized a need for China to work pragmatically with the United States in areas of importance to China. The official added that Chinese leaders recognize that at present "China needs the United States more than the United States needs China."[9]

Another official specializing in Sino-American relations assessed the current situation this way in August 1995. Since the United States refused to provide Beijing with the concrete action it sought on Taiwan, there would remain a certain coolness and distance in the U.S.-PRC relationship for some time to come. Nonetheless, Beijing will move forward in areas of Sino-American relations where it saw important advantage for China.[10] The official was cautiously optimistic about the outlook for the visit of Under Secretary of State Tarnoff and for the proposed summit meeting between President Clinton and President Jiang Zemin, even though he acknowledged that no substantial "breakthrough" in bilateral relations appeared likely.

Jiang Zemin's Political Profile and China's Policy Toward the Clinton-Jiang Summit Meetings, October-November 1995

Subsequent reports by Chinese officials and official media in fall 1995, along with observations by some prominent U.S. officials and experts with close contacts with China, pointed to Chinese President Jiang Zemin's rising power and influence in the Chinese leadership, especially following a series of important Chinese leadership meetings in August-September 1995.[11] Some Chinese officials' private descriptions of the Chinese policy deliberations at those meetings asserted that Jiang strongly defended a moderate PRC stance toward the United States and was successful in achieving a consensus behind such a stance despite the deeply felt skepticism and criticism from other Chinese leaders urging a harder line toward the United States.

The officials consulted implied that Jiang's support for a moderate U.S. policy would be made easier if the Clinton administration were able to ease U.S.-China relations on issues important to China such as Taiwan, lifting existing U.S. sanctions on China, ending U.S. efforts to criticize China on human rights issues at the UN Human Rights Commission and easing China's entry into the World Trade Organization. They were not optimistic that the administration would be willing or able to offer any such gesture to Jiang in the foreseeable future.

Recent Signs of Jiang's Rising Power

In addition to recent scholarly articles and private assessments of senior U.S. experts[12] that Jiang indeed has consolidated his leading role in the post-Deng Xiaoping era, several pieces of evidence seem to reinforce this view of Jiang's prominence.

- Senator Dianne Feinstein told the Senate Foreign Relations Committee on October 11 that it was her belief that Jiang now consolidated his power and that the United States should use the opportunity to revive relations with Beijing. The senator recently returned from China where she met with Jiang for four hours. As a result of her past relations with Jiang (San Francisco and Shanghai were "sister" cities when Senator Feinstein and President Jiang were respective mayors) Senator Feinstein has spent more time with Jiang than any other senior U.S. official.
- At the recent party plenary meeting in Beijing, Jiang was seen to have improved his influence with the senior military leadership by securing the appointment of two senior leaders associated with him to the policymaking Military Affairs Commission, and the appointment of another senior military leader associated with him to be the new chief of the army's General Staff.[13]
- Also at the party meeting, Jiang gave a speech on tasks for China's future that communist officials in Hong Kong equated with a landmark Mao Zedong speech charting the course for China's future in the mid-1950s. The officials made it clear that Jiang's efforts were intended to be equated in importance with the Mao directive.[14]
- In an interview with *U.S. News and World Report* disclosed on October 16, Jiang appeared to moderate substantially Beijing's tough line toward Taiwan and President Lee Teng-hui in effect since Lee's visit to the United States in June. In particular, Chinese official commentary had accused Lee of being a double-crosser with whom the Chinese government could not deal and urged that he be replaced.[15] Jiang said in his interview, by contrast, that Lee Teng-hui was invited to visit Beijing for

talks and that Jiang was willing to travel to Taiwan for talks with Lee if invited.

- Chinese officials privately recounted Jiang's role in the recent policy deliberations in Beijing over policy toward the United States. According to the officials, Jiang, the Foreign Ministry, and other purported supporters of a moderate Chinese approach toward the United States were put on the defensive by the Clinton administration's reversal of policy in granting a visa to Lee Teng-hui. At that time, many Chinese officials claimed to have seen a change in U.S. policy toward China and to have become convinced that the United States was determined to use Taiwan and other issues to hold back and "contain" the emergence of China's power and influence in world affairs. At the leadership meetings in August and September, Jiang was said to have argued strongly against such a hard line and to have succeeded in winning leadership endorsement of a view of U.S. policy as not one of "containment" but one of "engagement with an element of containment which is rising." On this basis, Jiang and the Chinese leaders reportedly were prepared to resume a working relationship with the United States despite U.S. refusal to grant concessions on Taiwan and other issues sought by Beijing at the time.

Implications and Outlook for U.S. Policy

Chinese officials and some U.S. observers who believe that Jiang Zemin is a rapidly rising power in Chinese politics and is playing a central role in determining policy toward the United States have suggested that a more forthcoming and flexible U.S. policy toward China would allow for more forward movement by Jiang and the Chinese leadership on issues important to the United States. They averred that Jiang was "frustrated" by the perceived absence of any such flexibility or gesture from the Clinton administration in the weeks leading to the October 24 summit meeting, even though in their view Jiang was signaling an interest in better relations. As an example of such a "signal" to the United States, some observers point to Jiang's admission in the interview with *U.S. News and World Report* that China needed to do a better job in "lobbying" the U.S. Congress and pointedly invited senators and representatives to visit China.

Chinese officials cited have suggested that the main outcome of the Clinton-Jiang meetings may be the meetings themselves rather than any particular issue of substantive improvement. Although Chinese officials say they could be surprised by some U.S. policy initiative at the summit or at the Clinton-Jiang meeting slated for Japan in November, they tended to be pessimistic about prospects for substantial improvements in U.S.-Chinese relations over the next year. They believed that attitudes toward China in the United States remain decidedly mixed, while U.S. election year politics were seen as likely to make the Clinton administration reluctant to take positive initiatives toward the current Chinese government. By the same token, the Chinese leadership was seen as unwilling to make unilateral gestures to Washington. Nevertheless, Chinese officials made clear that Beijing's policy is to seek to avoid deterioration in relations if possible, as the United States is seen as by far the most important foreign determinant in China's future development.

Specific Issues

Taiwan and U.S.-PRC Relations

The fallout of Taiwan's President Lee Teng-hui's June 1995 visit to the United States included a carefully calibrated PRC effort to cut off or suspend contacts and communications with the United States and Taiwan over a range of important policy questions.[16] Beijing also conducted military missile tests near Taiwan and appeared to highlight its detention of Chinese-American human rights activist Harry Wu to show its unhappiness with U.S. policy. In this atmosphere, prospects for a resumption of U.S.-PRC and Taiwan-PRC contacts were unclear, especially since domestic politics in Beijing, Taipei, and Washington appeared to work against meaningful efforts by the three parties to deal with serious challenges facing their triangular relationship. Options for U.S. policy range from a hard-line response to Beijing's pressure and accommodation of Taiwan's demands, to a stance designed to reinvigorate a meaningful dialogue with Beijing while avoiding steps in relations with Taiwan that would antagonize the mainland government.

Beijing's response to the June 1995 visit of President Lee Teng-hui to the United States has raised a number of concerns for the United States about the future stability of the triangular U.S.-PRC-Taiwan relationship. For many years, U.S. policy has sought to strike a working balance between growing ties with the People's Republic of China (PRC) while sustaining support for Taiwan. Despite generally eased tensions in the Taiwan Strait and extensive Taiwan trade with and investment in mainland China, the two sides remain politically far apart and compete for international influence, especially in the United States.

U.S. policy in this triangular U.S.-PRC-Taiwan relationship has been complicated because:

- many in Congress favor formal efforts to go beyond administration policy to strengthen U.S.-Taiwan relations in ways sure to antagonize the PRC;
- Taiwan is moving away from past advocacy of "one China" to positions favoring an official status for Taipei that would complicate the U.S. "one China" policy and challenge Beijing's claim to sovereignty over the island; and
- Beijing shows little sign of deviating from its claim to Taiwan.

Beijing's Response to Lee's Visit

Toward the United States, Beijing withdrew its ambassador in protest, withdrew a visiting PRC air force chief, and postponed the visit of the Chinese defense minister, the visit of the U.S. Arms Control Agency director to China, and a senior State Department official visit to Beijing planned for July. Beijing also suspended ongoing U.S.-PRC talks on missile technology control and cooperation on nuclear energy. All this was accompanied by a steady drumbeat of harsh protests and invective from Chinese officials and official media.

Taiwan's leaders also have been strongly criticized by PRC media. Concrete action against Taiwan has included the postponement of high-level talks between the leaders of the two ostensibly unofficial organizations that regulate PRC-Taiwan contacts across the Taiwan Strait, and PRC missile tests/military exercises conducted near Taiwan.

Analysts remain unclear as to how far Beijing will go in pushing its critical reaction to President Lee's visit. The August 1, 1995, meeting between the U.S. and Chinese foreign ministers eased tensions to some degree, as did the Bill Clinton-Jiang Zemin meeting in October 1995. Many specialists worry that there is little likelihood of a rapid improvement in the triangular relationship soon. In particular, domestic politics in each country are seen to get in the way of effective and

constructive efforts by any of the three parties to deal with the challenges
facing the triangular relationship today.

Challenges in the Triangular Relationship

In general, the challenges can be characterized as:

- *China's growing economic and related political and military power
  in the East Asian region and throughout the world.* Several years
  of remarkable economic growth have been followed by
  predictions of continued development well into the next century.
  This gives PRC leaders a growing sense of confidence in their
  ability to survive the embarrassment of Tiananmen and the
  traumas of the collapse of international communism to become
  an increasingly influential player on the world stage. It also
  allows for a substantial increase in China's military capabilities
  and reluctance on the part of senior Chinese leaders to defer to
  the pressures of the United States, Taiwan, or others;
- *Taiwan's assertiveness.* Fed by steady and impressive economic
  growth and rapidly changing social conditions, Taiwan has moved
  rapidly in recent years to democratize its political system. The
  result, long sought by the United States, has been a blossoming
  of political pluralism and debate. This has included often
  contentious discussion of such long-repressed issues as the
  identity of the people on Taiwan and the idea that the
  government and people on the island should have a more
  autonomous and independent posture in world affairs. Such
  trends have led to efforts to increase Taiwan's stature in
  international bodies despite the objections of the PRC; and to
  efforts inside Taiwan to move away from past rigorous adherence
  to a one China policy to a more flexible policy seen by Beijing
  as a fundamental challenge to China's traditional stance
  regarding national sovereignty and reunification; and
- *U.S. uncertainty.* The end of the cold war, a change in
  generation of U.S. leaders, the more pluralistic nature of U.S.
  foreign policy decision making in recent years, and other factors
  have led to some confusion about the American role in Asian
  and world affairs. Domestic factors and unanticipated foreign
  developments appear to intervene at various times to push U.S.

decision makers in changing directions without a clear and settled sense of priorities or objectives.

Domestic Determinants

As the three parties attempt to deal with the rising tensions and reduced contacts and communications in their triangular relationship, they are likely to be more hampered than helped by the domestic politics in each country.

- *China is in the midst of a leadership succession struggle.* It is often assumed that under such circumstances, PRC leaders are unlikely to adopt flexible or accommodating policies on issues of national sovereignty, like Taiwan. Indeed, a more politically expedient stance is seen to be one that is suspicious or even hostile to outsiders who challenge Beijing's nationalistic goals. As noted above, it has been widely reported that the prevailing view among senior leaders and supporting officials and intellectuals in China is that the U.S. government is fundamentally hostile to China, and that Taiwan's leaders are moving slowly but surely toward a more autonomous and independent posture antagonistic to PRC objectives of reunification and sovereignty. The Lee Teng-hui visit is seen as a capstone of these sinister U.S. and Taiwanese efforts, confirming PRC suspicions. As a result, Beijing is seen to be reacting with frustration, hostility, and strong measures in order to defend itself from the perceived U.S. efforts and to halt Taiwan's drive toward autonomy.
- *At least up until now, Taiwan has not been dissuaded by Beijing's actions.* Pressed by a widespread domestic demand in Taiwan that those in authority do more to gain Taiwan greater stature in world politics, politicians of the ruling Nationalist party and the opposition party have been very active in seeking opportunities to enhance Taiwan's international role. They have particularly focused their efforts on the United States, especially on the U.S. Congress. Visits by senior leaders from Taiwan to Congress in the first half of 1995 were among the most frequent of any foreign country. In many cases, these Taiwanese leaders are seeking general support for Taiwan's rising role in world affairs, and particular support from them in the competitive

arena of Taiwan domestic politics. The atmosphere in Taiwan remains politically charged as politicians position themselves for the elections of a new legislature at the end of 1995 and for the election of the president in early 1996. Thus, pressure from Taiwan on the United States for additional signs of support seems likely to grow as the year goes on.

- *U.S. domestic politics are also quite active as the republican-controlled Congress vies with the democratic president for leadership on important policy issues, including foreign policy.* On the issue of President Lee's visit, President Clinton became isolated from almost all members of his own party as well as the dominant republicans in Congress, adding to the political pressure to reach a decision on this issue that would smooth the domestic U.S. political controversy before it became a broader issue in the upcoming congressional and presidential election campaigns. It remains to be seen whether members of Congress will press the president for other signs of support for Taiwan (e.g., Taiwan membership in international organizations) in the months ahead.

Tibet

Unhappy with Chinese policies and with what they see as weak Clinton administration policy, advocates in the Congress, media, and elsewhere have pressed the United States to take a tougher stance against the current situation in Tibet. The issue figures prominently in recent foreign policy legislation (HR1561, S.908).

Economic development, fueled by central government subsidies, is changing traditional Tibetan ways of life. While the Chinese government has made efforts in recent years to restore the physical structures and other aspects of Tibetan Buddhism and Tibetan culture damaged or destroyed during the Cultural Revolution, repressive social and political controls continue to limit the individual freedoms of Tibetans.

Because the Chinese government strictly controls access to and information about Tibet, it is difficult to state precisely the scope of human rights abuse there. It is known, however, that Chinese government authorities continue to commit widespread human rights abuses in Tibet, including instances of torture, arbitrary arrest, and detention without public trial, long detention of Tibetan nationalists for peacefully expressing their political views, and rigid controls on freedom of speech and the press, particularly for Tibetans. There are credible reports that authorities in some instances tortured and killed detainees in Tibet.

The authorities permit most traditional religious practices except those seen as a vehicle for political dissent, which they ruthlessly suppress. They continue to detain and prosecute monks and nuns who have expressed dissenting political views in public. Legal safeguards for Tibetans detained or imprisoned are inadequate in design and implementation, and lack of independent outside access to prisoners or prisons makes it difficult to assess the extent and severity of abuses and the number of Tibetan prisoners.

In Tibet, where Buddhism and Tibetan nationalism are closely intertwined, relations between Buddhists and secular authorities continue to be tense. The government does not tolerate religious manifestations and advocating Tibetan independence, and it has prohibited a large traditional festival, which has in the past been used to encourage separatist sentiment. The government condemns the Dalai Lama's political activities and his leadership of a "government in exile," but it recognizes him as a major religious figure.

The Chinese government continues to take steps to ameliorate damage caused in the 1960s and the 1970s to Tibet's historic religious buildings and other aspects of its cultural and religious heritage. The government has expended substantial sums to reconstruct the most important sacred sites of Tibetan Buddhism. A five-year project to restore the Potala Palace (the most important Tibetan Buddhist center) in Lhasa was concluded in August 1994 at a cost of $6.4 million. While the government denies it, the practice of religion in Tibet continues to be hampered by the limits the government imposes on the number of resident monks in several of Tibet's main temples. There are 34,000 Buddhist monks and nuns in Tibet, according to official figures, a small number compared to traditional norms.

Economic Development and Protection of Cultural Heritage. Like China's fifty-four other minority ethnic groups, Tibetans receive preferential treatment in marriage policy, family planning, university admission, and employment. Chinese government development policies have helped raise the living standards of Tibetans, but also have disrupted traditional living patterns. The government has sought to preserve the Tibetan language, but in doing so has encountered the dilemma of how to preserve the language without limiting educational opportunities. In Tibet, primary schools at the village level teach in Tibetan. Many pupils end their formal education after graduating from these schools, which usually only have two or three grades. Those who go on to regional primary schools and beyond, particularly after junior high school, receive much of their education in Chinese, although some areas provide instruction in Tibetan through junior high school. Efforts to expand Tibetan language instruction are hampered by lack of materials and competent teachers at higher levels.

In July 1994, the Chinese Communist party (CCP) and the State Council conducted a large-scale work conference on Tibet. The third of its kind since 1980, this work conference was attended by delegations from the CCP and central government organizations, as well as provincial representatives and delegates from certain urban areas. The conference focused on setting economic development goals, pledging to increase economic activity in Tibet by ten percent a year. The plan included a total of $270 million in investment projects, continuing the government policy of providing substantial budget subsidies to develop Tibet's backward economy. China's leaders also made clear that Tibet would continue to receive central government financial assistance and would retain "special flexibility" in implementing reform policies mandated elsewhere in China. In a speech covered extensively in the Chinese press, President Jiang Zemin reiterated Beijing's willingness to "welcome back" the Dalai Lama to Tibet, so long as "he abandons advocacy of Tibetan independence and ceases activities to split the motherland." Although the work conference approved plans to boost economic development in Tibet, it produced no change in the Chinese government's policy toward Tibet.

The Dalai Lama continues to express concern that development projects and other central government policies encourage a massive influx of Han Chinese into Tibet, which has the effect of overwhelming Tibet's traditional culture and diluting Tibetan demographic dominance in Tibet. Freer movement of people throughout China in recent years and the prospect of economic opportunity in Tibet have led to a substantial increase in the non-Tibetan population (including China's Muslim Hui minority as well as Han Chinese) in Lhasa and other urban areas. Most of these migrants profess to be temporary residents, but small businesses run by ethnic Han and Hui peoples (mostly restaurants and retail shops) are becoming more numerous in or near some Tibetan towns and cities. Roughly one-third of the population of Lhasa is Han Chinese. Chinese officials assert that ninety-five percent of Tibet's official registered population is Tibetan, with Han and other ethnic groups making up the remainder. Increased economic development will likely mean the transfer to, or temporary duty in, Tibet of a greater number of non-Tibetan technical personnel, and may also increase the number of immigrants from China's large floating population seeking to take advantage of new economic opportunities.

Human Rights Abuses in China

China's human rights abuses have been the most visible and constant point of contention in U.S.-China relations since the 1989 Tiananmen Square crackdown, and continue to be so in 1995. Early on, President Clinton had supported linking China's MFN status with its human rights performance, and in a 1993 executive order spelled out the human rights conditions China would have to meet. But by May 26, 1994, the president had decided to "de-link" human rights from China's MFN status, saying that the United States had "reached the end of the usefulness of that policy." The administration's policy change has reactivated congressional interest in pursuing human rights-related legislation on China.

China's human rights record since the president's "de-linkage" decision has presented a mixed picture, with both setbacks and minor improvements providing plenty of ammunition for policy debate. The U.S. State Department's report on human rights practices for 1994 states that the human rights situation in China was marked by "diversity" during the year–that while well-documented abuses continued, China also took new and specific steps to improve its human rights record. Among these were the release of several prominent political and religious prisoners, and the adoption of a new law permitting citizens to recover damages from the Chinese government in cases where their rights have been violated. The most recent Human Rights Watch/Asia report notes that human rights violations in China are continuing, but is silent on whether the situation is improving or growing worse. The 1995 Amnesty International Report states that crackdowns in China have intensified over the past year, and that several new repressive laws have been enacted.

One incident that particularly highlights growing Sino-American tensions over human rights is China's detention on June 19, 1995, of Harry Wu, an American citizen traveling in China under a legitimate Chinese visa. Wu has been charged with espionage, a charge subject to the death penalty in China. Congress, reacting strongly to Mr. Wu's detention, made his case a prominent feature of a number of bills.

A second recent issue regarding human rights involves the Fourth International Conference on Women, held in Beijing in September 1995. Chinese officials attempted to place restrictions on the attendees of the conference–such as prohibiting the attendance of women's delegations from Tibet and Taiwan–and in other respects tried to limit the conference's exposure and visibility. A number of measures before the 104th Congress addressed this issue, usually by trying to place restrictions on the availability of U.S. State Department funds for international conferences unless the United States takes a strong stand on this issue with Beijing.

Apart from these two issues, other human rights issues bedeviling U.S.-China relations have been around for several years. These include: inhumane treatment of prisoners; holding of political prisoners; use of prison labor for producing goods for export; restrictions on freedom of speech, assembly, and the press; restrictions on religious groups; and abuses of ethnic minorities, particularly in Tibet. Although threats to withdraw MFN because of China's human rights abuses have not materialized this year, rhetoric on human rights remains heated in Congress.

Missile Sales and Weapons Proliferation Policies

In 1995, Central Intelligence Agency assessments of Chinese missile component sales to Iran and Pakistan raised the prospect of new U.S. sanctions against China in accordance with U.S. law. This, as well as U.S. concern over prospective Chinese provision of nuclear reactors and nuclear technology to Iran, comes at a time of deteriorating U.S.-China relations due to mounting congressional criticism of the Chinese government's human rights abuses and repression in Tibet, and to Beijing's angry reaction to the visit of Taiwan's president to the United States.

In June 1995, press reports described CIA assessments that:

(1) China had delivered to Iran missile-guidance systems and computerized machine tools that would enable Iran to improve the accuracy of its North Korean-supplied SCUD missiles and construct additional missiles; and

(2) China had delivered to Pakistan component parts of M-11 ballistic missiles. John Holum, director of the Arms Control and Disarmament Agency, seemed to confirm the press reports by stating

that "There are substantial indications of continued missile-related transactions to both countries. We need clarification from the Chinese."

If the Chinese sales to Iran are confirmed, the Clinton administration must impose sanctions on China under the Arms Export Control Act and the Export Administration Act. The United States already has restricted twice (1991 and 1993) the export of satellites to China because of China's sale of M-11 components and technology to Pakistan. The Bush and Clinton administrations subsequently lifted the sanctions after receiving assurances from the Chinese government. The assurances, however, were vague. Secretary of State Baker said in November 1991 that China agreed to observe the guidelines of the Missile Technology Control Regime (MTCR), which the Bush administration "understands" as applying to M-9 and M-11 missiles. In October 1994, Secretary of State Christopher and the Chinese foreign minister issued a joint statement in which China agreed not to export "ground-to-ground missiles" capable of delivering a 500 kilogram warhead 300 kilometers or more. The statement did not mention missile technology.

The 1995 CIA assessments reportedly produced a split within the Clinton administration over the appropriate response. Officials responsible for non-proliferation policy were said to favor the imposition of U.S. penalties on China, citing especially China's assistance to Iran. Officials in charge of relations with China were said to warn of the impact of sanctions on the already worsening U.S.-China relationship, and they reportedly argued that more evidence of Chinese assistance to Pakistan and Iran is required.

Since 1992, the Chinese government has linked its policy on missile sales to Pakistan with the U.S. decision in 1992 to sell F-16 fighters to Taiwan; China views the sale of F-16s as a violation of the 1982 U.S.-PRC communiqué on Taiwan. In June 1995, the Chinese government suspended a planned visit to Beijing by ACDA Director Holum in retaliation for the Taiwan president's visit to the United States. Chinese officials also contend that restrictions under the MTCR (of which China is not a member) also should apply to military strike aircraft. The Bush and Clinton administrations also have been concerned over reported PRC sales of missiles, missile components, and missile fuel to Syria, Saudi Arabia, and Iraq.

Administration officials also have raised inquiries into China's supply of nuclear technology to countries like Pakistan, Algeria, and Iran. China signed the Nuclear Non-Proliferation Treaty (NPT) in March 1992. Prior to that, China "probably provided some nuclear weapons related assistance to Islamabad," according to CIA Director James Woolsey. This reportedly has included nuclear bomb designs, technical assistance for reactors, and nuclear fuel production plants. Since April 1995, the Clinton administration has raised with China proposed Chinese sales of two 300 megawatt nuclear reactors and related technology to Iran. Such assistance is legal under the NPT, but administration officials believe it could assist an Iranian nuclear weapons program.

Hong Kong's Transition to Chinese Rule

Hong Kong has long been a point of U.S. economic, political, and other interests in Asia. Recent developments there have mixed implications for those interests. On the one hand, Hong Kong's economy, increasingly tied to the vibrantly expanding Chinese mainland economy, continues to grow around six percent annually in recent years. Over the last decade, Hong Kong has risen from the fifteenth largest to the eighth largest trader in the world, and its per capita GDP has climbed from $6,000 to $20,000. With a population of six million (half a percent of China's) Hong Kong's economy presently equals one-fifth of mainland China's GDP.

Under the terms of the Sino-British Joint Declaration of 1984, Hong Kong will become a special administrative region (SAR) of China on July 1, 1997. The joint declaration contains assurances that Hong Kong's lifestyle and capitalist economy will remain until the year 2047, and it further states that Hong Kong's freely elected government will retain a level of autonomy over local laws and financial and monetary matters.

In addition, in 1990, the Standing Committee of China's National People's Congress approved the Basic Law for Hong Kong (a so-called mini-constitution), which defined the legal rights of Hong Kong residents; the region's relationship to Beijing; and the political structure and formation of the post-1997 Hong Kong government.

On October 7, 1992, Hong Kong's new governor, Christopher Patten, unveiled proposals to expand the voting franchise in Hong Kong and broaden the scope of democratic institutions. Patten's proposals reflected a growing desire on the part of the colonial government and the people of Hong Kong that, in the aftermath of the 1989 Tiananmen crackdown, Hong Kong should erect safeguards against capricious Chinese government action after 1997. The proposals were seen by the British authorities as consistent with the 1984 Sino-British Joint Declaration, but Beijing disagreed.

For Beijing, Patten's proposals raised a security issue, because it viewed the establishment of more democratic institutions as a threat to its ability to resume unimpeded sovereignty over Hong Kong in 1997. Subsequent Chinese rhetoric denounced the proposals as a violation of the 1984 Sino-British Joint Declaration. In 1993, attempts by both sides to reach a negotiated settlement on the reform package broke down after seventeen frustrating rounds. On December 2, 1993, Governor Patten announced that he would submit part of his reform package to the Legislative Council (Legco) without China's endorsement. Legco finally passed the reform measures in June 1994. District board elections were held the following September. In response, Beijing announced its intention to dismantle all of Hong Kong's democratic institutions after it resumes sovereignty in 1997.

The controversy over Patten's political reforms has represented only the most notable of a series of PRC-Hong Kong political issues that have littered the pathway to Chinese rule. Other issues include perceived threats to the continued rule of law, civil liberties, civil service integrity, and freedom of the press long enjoyed in Hong Kong. The British and Chinese authorities have also been engaged in protracted and sometimes contentious talks over such sensitive economic and other issues regarding major infrastructure projects (e.g., the new Hong Kong airport) and the use of government-owned lands in the territory.

U.S. Interests in Hong Kong. The United States has several areas of interest in these developments.

Economic. Hong Kong is the largest base of American economic operations in Asia. Over 30,000 Americans live and work there; 1,000 U.S. firms have corporate offices in Hong Kong, most of which are used as financial and marketing bases in support of substantial manufacturing facilities in mainland China and as headquarters for business activities throughout Asia. By 1995, U.S. investments in Hong Kong totaled $10.5 billion. According to the U.S. Consul General in Hong Kong, U.S. exports to the territory in 1994 amounted to $11 billion, while U.S. imports were about $9 billion. Hong Kong is the major transshipment point for Chinese products exported to the United States, which were valued at over $20 billion in 1993.

Human rights/democracy. Since the violent 1989 Tiananmen suppression in Beijing, U.S. leaders, especially in the Congress, have paid sometimes close attention to the human rights situation in Hong Kong. They have been generally supportive of Governor Patten's efforts to increase modestly the level of democracy in the territory prior to its reversion to China.

Taiwan. U.S. leaders sometimes view Beijing's handling of the Hong Kong transition as an indicator of the way Beijing would likely handle reunification with Taiwan. Chinese authorities have stated that their "one country-two systems" policy approach to Hong Kong also applies to Taiwan.

MFN, other aspects of China policy. Considerations over Hong Kong have been an important element in the ongoing U.S. debate over China policy since the Tiananmen incident, especially the debate over whether or not the United States should approve MFN tariff treatment for Chinese exports to the United States. On the one hand, critics of China argued in the past that MFN and other favorable treatment for China should be withheld unless Beijing met certain conditions, including a more accommodating Chinese stance on democracy and human rights in Hong Kong. An important counterargument held that cutting off MFN would, among other effects, have a disastrous economic and perhaps negative political impact on Hong Kong, especially as the bulk of Chinese exports to the United States pass through the colony.

U.S. Trade With China

Growth in Trade

U.S.-China trade has risen rapidly since 1980, when MFN status was mutually granted. Total trade (exports plus imports) between the two nations rose from $4.8 billion in 1980 to $48.1 billion in 1994. China is now the sixth largest U.S. trading partner. Over the past few years, the U.S. trade deficit with China has grown sharply, due largely to a surge in U.S. imports of Chinese goods relative to U.S. exports to China (see table 6.1). As a result, the U.S. trade deficit with China has been rising at a faster rate than that of any other major U.S. trading partner. In 1984, the United States had a $61 million trade deficit with China. In just ten years, the U.S. trade deficit with China surged to $29.5 billion, making China the second largest deficit trading partner of the United States behind Japan (see figure 6.1). Available U.S. trade data for 1995 indicate that the U.S. trade deficit in 1995 could rise to about $37 billion.

U.S. Exports to China

U.S. exports to China in 1994 totaled $9.3 billion, accounting for 1.8

TABLE 6.1 U.S. Merchandise Trade with China: 1984-1995[a]

Year	U.S. Exports	U.S. Imports	U.S. Trade Balance
1984	3,004	3,065	-61
1985	3,852	3,862	-10
1986	3,105	4,771	-1,666
1987	3,488	6,293	-2,805
1988	5,033	8,512	-3,479
1989	5,807	11,989	-6,181
1990	4,807	15,224	-10,417
1991	6,278	18,976	-12,698
1992	7,418	25,727	-18,309
1993	8,767	31,535	-22,768
1994	9,287	38,781	-29,494
1995	11,648	48,561	-36,913

[a] In millions of U.S. dollars.
Source: U.S. Department of Commerce. Data for 1995 estimated by CRS based on U.S.-China trade data for January-May 1995.

FIGURE 6.1 U.S. Merchandise Trade with China: 1984-1994[a]

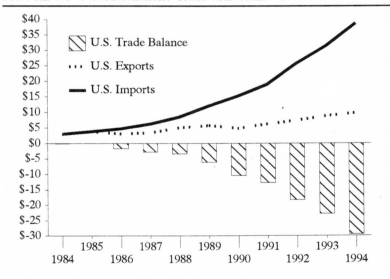

[a] In billions of U.S. dollars.
Source: U.S. Department of Commerce.

percent of total U.S. exports to the world, and making China the fourteenth largest market for U.S. exports. At present, China is a relatively small market for U.S. exports. For example, U.S. exports to China are smaller than those to such Asian countries as Hong Kong, Singapore, South Korea, and Taiwan. However, China is becoming one of the fastest growing markets for U.S. exports. U.S. exports to China between 1990 and 1994 grew by 93.2 percent. U.S. exports to China in 1995 are projected to rise by about twenty-five percent over the previous year.

The top five U.S. exports to China in 1994 were: (1) transport equipment (mainly aircraft and parts), (2) fertilizers, (3) textile fibers, (4) specialized machinery, and (5) telecommunications and sound equipment. Together, these five commodities accounted for over half of total U.S. exports to China (see table 6.2). Aircraft and parts were by far the largest U.S. export to China in 1994, accounting for 20.9 percent of total U.S. exports.

U.S. Imports From China

China is a relatively large source of many U.S. imports. In 1994, imports from China accounted for 5.8 percent of total U.S. imports, making China the fourth largest supplier of U.S. imports. The level of U.S. imports from China nearly doubled between 1991 and 1994; U.S. imports from China are projected to rise by over twenty-five percent in 1995.

The top five U.S. imports from China in 1994 were: (1) miscellaneous manufactured articles (such as toys and games); (2) clothing and apparel; (3) footwear; (4) telecommunications equipment, sound recording, and reproducing equipment (such as telephone answering machines, radios, tape recorders and players, televisions and VCRs); and (5) electrical machinery (see table 6.3). Together, imports of these five commodities accounted for over two-thirds of total U.S. imports from China. U.S. imports from China in 1994 rose by $7.2 billion (or 23 percent) over the previous year. Imports of miscellaneous manufactured articles, clothing, and footwear accounted for a substantial share of this increase.

The surge in U.S. imports of Chinese products over the past few years can be largely explained by two factors. First, China's production of low-cost, labor-intensive products (such as consumer goods) has increased sharply in recent years (due to China's comparative advantage in such

TABLE 6.2 Top Five U.S. Exports to China: 1990 and 1994[a]

SITC Commodity	1990	1994	1990/1994 % Change
Total all commodities	$4,807	$9,287	93.2
Transport equipment[b]	755	1,938	156.3
Fertilizers[c]	544	944	73.5
Textile fibers and wastes	385	761	97.7
Machinery[d]	323	676	109.3
Telecommunications	81	572	606.0

[a] In millions of U.S. dollars. Ranked according to the top five U.S. exports to China in 1994, based on the Standard International Trade Classification (SITC) system, two-digit level.

[b] Not elsewhere specified, excluding road vehicles (mainly aircraft and parts).

[c] Except crude of group 272.

[d] Specialized for particular industries.

[e] Includes sound recording and reproduction apparatus and equipment.

Source: U.S. Department of Commerce. Data obtained by CRS using Tradenet.

TABLE 6.3 Top Five U.S. Imports From China: 1990 and 1994[a]

SITC Commodity	1990	1994	1990/1994 % Change
Total all commodities	15,224	38,781	107.1
Manufactured articles[b]	3,243	8,690	168.0
Apparel and clothing	3,469	6,311	81.9
Footwear	1,477	5,259	256.1
Telecommunications[c]	1,163	3,779	224.9
Electrical machinery[d]	657	2,275	246.3

[a] In millions of U.S. dollars. Ranked according to the top U.S. five imports from China in 1994, based on the Standard International Trade Classification (SITC) system, two-digit level.

[b] Miscellaneous, not elsewhere specified.

[c] Includes sound recording and reproduction apparatus and equipment.

[d] Not elsewhere specified.

Source: U.S. Department of Commerce. Data obtained by CRS using Tradenet.

sectors); U.S. demand for such products has steadily increased as well.

Second, Hong Kong and Taiwan have shifted production of a wide variety of labor-intensive products (such as shoes, toys, and electronic products) into China to take advantage of China's relatively low-cost labor supply. As a result, many of the products that used to be produced in Taiwan and Hong Kong (a large share of which were exported to the United States) are now being produced by Hong Kong and Taiwanese firms in China, then exported.

U.S.-China Trade Issues

Many trade analysts have attributed the growing U.S.-China trade deficit to a variety of Chinese restrictive trade practices, such as high tariffs, quotas, import license requirements, and discriminatory import regulations. Other trade issues of concern to the United States have included China's violation of U.S. intellectual property rights (IPRs), transshipments of textiles to the United States in violation of U.S. textile quotas, and China's alleged use of forced labor for products exported to the United States. Over the past few years, the United States and China have reached agreement on many of these issues:

- On April 26, 1991, the United States trade representative (USTR) designated China under Section 301 for failing to provide adequate protection for U.S. intellectual property rights. A memorandum of understanding (MOU) was reached on January 16, 1992. However, on June 30, 1994, the USTR again designated China under Section 301 for failing to enforce its IPR laws and for restricting market access of intellectual property-related products. On February 4, 1995, the USTR announced that sanctions would be imposed against China by February 26, 1995, unless a new agreement was reached. A preliminary agreement was subsequently reached on February 26, 1995, that pledges China to significantly improve its IPR enforcement regime and market access for U.S. products.

- On October 10, 1991, the USTR initiated a Section 301 investigation of four major Chinese trade barriers, including import prohibitions and quotas, restrictive import license requirements, restrictive standards and certification requirements for imports, and lack of transparency of Chinese trade laws. On October 10, 1992, the United States and China reached an MOU agreement on market access. China agreed to reduce several major trade barriers over the next five years. China suspended its implementation of the MOU agreement in January 1995 after it was unable to obtain membership into the World Trade Organization (WTO) by the end of 1994. However, in March 1995, China agreed to resume its implementation of the MOU, after the United States assured China that it supported China's accession to the WTO and would be flexible on China's accession terms.

- On August 7, 1992, the United States and China signed a MOU to ensure that products made by forced labor in China are not exported to the United States. On March 14, 1994, China agreed to take additional steps to provide access to suspected forced labor camps to U.S. inspectors.

- On January 17, 1994, the United States and China reached an agreement on U.S. import quotas of Chinese textile and apparel products that would allow but limit the growth in China's quota levels and establish mechanisms to deal with Chinese transshipments.

China's increasing trade surplus with the United States and alleged unfair trade practices have become a focal point in the annual congressional debate over China's MFN status. Over the past few years, several members of Congress have attempted to pass legislation terminating or conditioning China's MFN status. On June 2, 1995, President Clinton announced his decision to renew China's MFN status for an additional year. On July 20, 1995, the House tabled legislation (H.J. Res. 96) that would have terminated China's MFN status and instead passed H.R. 2058, which urges the president to press China on human rights, trade, and arms exports, and to report its efforts to the Congress every six months.

While the United States and China have reached agreement on several trade areas, it is likely that tensions will persist in the near future. The trade issues likely to cause the most conflict include:

- *The U.S.-China trade imbalance.* The U.S. trade deficit with China continues to grow sharply and could increase to $37 billion in 1995.
- *Market access.* The United States continues to press China to improve market access for U.S. goods and services by seeking to get China to implement fully the October 1992 MOU on market access. The USTR has noted on several occasions that China has not fully implemented the agreement. For example, China continues to maintain restrictive phytosanitary inspection requirements on agricultural imports. In addition, China has failed to remove all tariff and non-tariff barriers on specific products that were designated under the MOU. Finally, problems remain over the transparency of China's trade laws and regulations. The USTR has warned on several occasions that sanctions could be imposed against China if the agreement is not fully carried out.

- *The World Trade Organization (WTO).* The United States is holding talks with China over its accession to the WTO. The United States has insisted that China make major reforms to its trade regime before it is allowed to become a member of the WTO, including making its trade regime more transparent, significantly reducing government support of domestic firms, and affording national treatment to foreign firms. Chinese officials have argued that China should be allowed to enter the WTO as a developing country, and thus afforded a transitionary period to implement trade reforms after it becomes a WTO member. Chinese officials have been reluctant to reduce several trade barriers out of fear that such measures could be disruptive to certain Chinese industries. China views the United States as the largest impediment to its becoming a member of the WTO.

- *IPR enforcement.* Disputes will likely arise in the future over China's implementation of the February 1995 IPR agreement as well as the pace and degree of market-opening measures. The Chinese government has pledged to conduct extensive raids over the next several months against firms producing pirated materials and to strengthen its IPR enforcement regime. In addition, China pledged to establish a coordinated IPR enforcement approach at all levels of government to stop piracy. However, in the past, the central government has often reported difficulty getting provincial and local officials to enforce laws and regulations issued by the central authorities.

- *Political issues.* U.S.-China economic relations could be affected by U.S. policy towards China on human rights, weapons proliferation, and Taiwan. China might respond to U.S. policies by limiting trade or restricting U.S. investment.

China As A Security Threat in Asia: Alternative Views

Americans disagree as to whether or not China poses a serious security concern for U.S. interests in peace and security in Asia and the Pacific. Many point to rising Chinese defense capabilities and assertive rhetoric to warn of Chinese military-backed expansion. Others judge that the main danger comes from China's weakness. They argue that the possibility of an emerging breakdown in government authority in China could prompt regional disorder and refugee flows seriously undermining Asian stability. Still others see the Chinese "threat" as grossly exaggerated. They stress that Beijing's leaders are in control of the country and see their interests best served by accommodation to their richer and generally better armed neighbors.

A CRS assessment[17] of factors arguing in favor and against viewing China as a military threat concludes:

- China's current military capabilities generally show little sign of China posing a direct threat to the United States for a decade or longer.
- The main perceived danger over the next few years focuses on areas in the Asia-Pacific region where China and other countries important to the United States contest territorial claims. Examples include the South China Sea, Taiwan, and others.
- Perceived Chinese expansionist designs to control these contested areas are currently held in check by limitations in China's military capabilities; insufficient justification in terms of important Chinese security, economic, or political interests; and the likely negative foreign reaction to assertive Chinese action. Each of these factors is subject to change.

U.S. policymakers have a range of unilateral, bilateral, and multilateral options for dealing with China's military power. They involve both positive steps (e.g., resumed high-level U.S.-Chinese military exchanges designed to reassure both sides of the others' intentions) and negative measures (e.g., establishing regional security arrangements designed to curb China's military power).

China: Environment, Energy, and Natural Resources

Economic development, population growth, and increasing purchasing power and consumption combined impose a tremendous burden on China's environment and natural resources. Moreover, because China is so large, its environmental policies and problems have significance for the success or failure of international efforts to protect the global environment (such as those concerning climate change, stratospheric ozone, endangered species, deforestation, and biodiversity). Severe environmental problems are evident in China across nearly the entire spectrum of pollution and natural resource degradation. China is undertaking efforts to control these problems through legislation, but is facing continuing difficulties in enforcement, both due to lack of financial resources and to the immensity of the problems facing the country.

Pollution. China's current high levels of air pollution, as well as its potential for rapidly increasing such pollution as a result of economic development, is perhaps that country's environmental issue of greatest international concern. China's reliance on and inefficient use of coal as its primary energy source have created severe air pollution and health problems in its cities and acid rain damage throughout much of the country and beyond its borders; they have also made China the world's third largest emitter of carbon dioxide. China's energy use increased more than 200 percent between 1970 and 1990, and economic growth goals suggest that energy consumption will continue to grow rapidly. (To appreciate the potential for increased energy consumption, consider that in 1990, the average household energy consumption in China was just 0.03 percent of the energy consumed in an average U.S. home.)

Carbon dioxide emissions, thought to be a key contributor to suspected climate change, are expected to increase substantially unless China places less reliance on coal. A major alternative energy source is hydroelectric power, which provides roughly twenty percent of China's energy. The proposed Three Gorges dam project is expected to increase hydroelectric capacity by fifty percent, but, as discussed below, has significant environmental implications as well. Although China has considerable natural gas reserves, little has been done to develop the infrastructure needed to exploit this relatively cleaner resource.

China's development also poses a challenge to international efforts to control and phaseout stratospheric ozone-depleting substances. China is a party to the Montreal Protocol; however, its consumption of chlorofluorocarbons (CFCs) for refrigeration has increased ninety-nine percent in recent years, and it plans to continue manufacturing millions of refrigerators each year using CFCs as refrigerant. Development and transfer of alternative refrigeration technologies to China may be critical to the success of international stratospheric ozone protection efforts.

Natural Resources. Deterioration of natural resources is a serious problem throughout China. Problems include land degradation—especially erosion and desertification (the spread of desert-like conditions); loss of wildlife habitat and biological diversity; loss of forest resources; and coastal pollution with resulting damage to fisheries and marine resources. Pressure on water resources is causing groundwater resources to dwindle and rivers to become increasingly polluted.

Land Degradation. Cropland makes up only some ten percent of China's total land area, and arid or semi-arid conditions prevail over half of the rest of the country. Weather conditions are extremely variable, and extensive cycles of flooding affect some of the more productive areas. The rate of desertification in China is estimated by some authorities to be about 210,000 hectares (518,700 acres) per year, and economic losses from sandstorms are considerable. The governments of provinces are intensifying recent efforts to plant windbreak forests, and report some 10 million hectares now planted to protect farmland with greenbelts. Other sources of land degradation include salinization from improper drainage of irrigation projects, and water-logging of rice paddies. Soil erosion is a serious problem affecting an estimated 161 million hectares in 1991, up from 129 million hectares in 1985; soil erosion causes reduction in crop yield as well as contributing to siltation and flooding of rivers. Extensive efforts, including reforestation of deforested areas and construction of terraces, are under way.

Forest Management. Only about 13.6 percent of China's land area is tree-covered, and most forests are concentrated in the Northeast and Southwest. This figure represents extensive losses over the past several centuries, as well as current pressure on forests for fuelwood and other uses for timber. Extensive reforestation programs are frequently reported in the press from many different provinces, often to provide shelterbelts against wind erosion and desertification; but it appears that demand for wood still exceeds supply.

Three Gorges Dam. One of the most controversial of China's natural resources issues involves the Three Gorges hydroelectric dam project on the Chang Jiang (Yangtze) River that was approved in 1992 despite widespread objections from environmental groups internationally as well as from some scientific and environmental experts in China. The Three Gorges project, expected to take fifteen to eighteen years to build, would be the world's largest hydroelectric dam, with projected annual power generation of 84 billion kilowatt hours, equivalent to some 40 to 50 million tons of coal per year. In addition to its power production potential, the dam will provide flood control to alleviate the danger of severe flooding in the lower Yangtze River.

Critics of the project have focused on the social impact, since the reservoir behind the dam will involve the relocation of some 1.1 million people from two cities, eleven counties, 140 towns, and 1,351 villages, as well as submersion of 23,800 hectares of cultivated land. Although the government has promised to construct new villages and reclaim wasteland for crops, critics note that such resettlement schemes have a poor record of success in alleviating the intense social and economic problems associated with mass relocations. Ecological concerns include destruction of scenic areas that produce tourism revenue, loss of river species, loss of downstream wetland habitat, and sources of water for major cities and towns. Opponents also point to siltation behind such dams that will mean loss of nutrients for downstream farming and over time is likely to impede the power production potential, as well.

Some environmental advocates face a difficult choice in the case of the Three Gorges project, however, because while they worry about the environmental and human costs the dam may entail, they also wish to see China develop extensive alternatives to the use of high-sulphur coal, which remains a major source of the energy powering China's rapid economic growth, and which contributes to health-threatening air pollution in China and hypothesized global impacts in adding greenhouse gases to the atmosphere.

Trade in Endangered Species. China has been cited by wildlife protection advocates as a major problem in the protection of some key species whose parts are used in China for medicinal and other purposes. It is a major market for these animal parts and is reportedly importing them. Of recent concern are the protection of rhinoceroses and tigers, both highly endangered species. In September 1993, Secretary of the Interior Bruce Babbitt certified China and Taiwan under authority of the Pelly Amendment to the Fisherman's Protective Act (P.L. 92-219), which identified these countries as engaging in illegal trade in these endangered species. Such trade is illegal under the Convention on International Trade in Endangered Species (CITES). After an investigation, the president decided to impose trade sanctions against Taiwan but not China. Some observers felt that it was less the results of wildlife concerns that influenced this decision and more the wish to continue political efforts on human rights and other concerns in U.S. relations with China.

Status of Current Environmental Policies in China. Press reports in Chinese newspapers have focused both on remaining problems and their severity and on efforts by both the national and provincial governments to enact better environmental legislation and improve enforcement. The *China Daily* on March 30, 1994, quoted the vice-director of the National Environmental Protection Agency (NEPA): "The environmental situation in China is more serious than most people might have realized." He stated that "the awareness of environmental laws is low. More often than not, laws are not strictly observed and enforcement is lax."

Press reports in April 1994 announced the introduction of a National "Agenda 21," which responds to the environment and development "action plan" of the 1992 Earth Summit. The plan will have three phases, with sixty-three projects in the first phase; the Chinese government will cover sixty percent of the cost, and will seek the additional forty percent from other sources. In September 1994, a newspaper report indicated China will not only speed up its development of an environmental pollution control industry, but will also improve its legislation on and implementation of environmental laws.[18] This report stated that this effort will focus on revisions of the already extensive array of environmental protection legislation that includes "Environmental Protection Law," "Ocean Environmental Protection Law," "Wildlife Protection Law," "Water Law," "Forest Law," and twenty administrative laws on environmental protection. Press reports over the past year also report extensively on increases in forest cover and tree planting, usually under the auspices of local and provincial governments.

China's Commercial Space Launch Business:
Trade and Foreign Policy Issues

China offers commercial space launch services to put satellites into orbit for paying customers. Since most of these satellites are built in the United States or contain U.S. components, export licenses are required for shipment to China. The United States has used the export license process to influence China over issues such as adherence to the Missile Technology Control Regime (MTCR). From a trade policy perspective, there is concern over whether China is abiding by fair trade practices in offering launch services.

China has been launching satellites since 1970 using Long March space launch vehicles. In 1985, China began marketing space launch services to customers with satellites or experiments requiring transportation to orbit. These services are offered through China Great Wall Industry Corporation (CGWIC). Germany, France, and Sweden have used Chinese rockets to put satellites or experiments (aboard Chinese satellites) in low Earth orbit (LEO). Australia and a company named Asiasat Inc. purchased services to place communications satellites into geostationary orbit (GEO, an orbit 35,800 kilometers above the equator where a satellite maintains a stationary position relative to a point on Earth). Placing satellites in GEO is the most lucrative segment of the launch services market today. Asiasat's satellite was launched in 1990; two Australian satellites (Optus B1 and B2) were launched in 1992, although the second launch was unsuccessful.

The commercial launch services market is highly competitive, with several launch service suppliers, but relatively small demand. In addition to China, two U.S. companies (McDonnell Douglas and General Dynamics), a French company (Arianespace), and several enterprises in Russia offer such services to GEO. Congress has been working for several years to ensure the competitiveness of the U.S. companies, and many members are concerned that the entry of China and Russia into the launch services market will undercut the U.S. companies.

In 1989, the United States and China signed a bilateral agreement on launch services, wherein China agreed, among other things, to offer prices "on a par" with Western companies. The agreement paved the way for issuing export licenses for the two Optus satellites (then called AUSSAT) and Asiasat. However, on June 5, 1989, after the Tiananmen Square uprising, President Bush suspended all exports of items on the Munitions List, including the satellites, to China. Congress included language in the 1990-1991 Foreign Relations Authorization Act (P.L. 101-246, Section 902) prohibiting the export of U.S.-built satellites to China unless the president reported to Congress that (1) China has achieved certain political and human rights reforms, or (2) it was in the national interest of the United States. In December 1989, President Bush notified Congress that export of the satellites was in the national interest and the licenses were reinstated. The language is still in effect.

China's adherence to the 1989 agreement was questioned in 1990 when China agreed to launch an Arabsat Consortium satellite for $25 million, much less than what many consider "on a par" with Western companies. No formal U.S. action was taken, and the contract was later terminated, so this particular case is moot; but the issue of what constitutes "on a par" remains. The Chinese argue that because their costs are so low, they can offer lower prices and still adhere to international norms as to what costs are included in setting the price.

In 1991, the question arose of linking satellite export license approval to the MTCR, designed to stop the proliferation of ballistic missile technology. The Bush White House announced that because of China's ballistic missile proliferation policies, the United States would not approve any further satellite export licenses. The State Department identified CGWIC as one of two Chinese entities engaged in missile technology proliferation activities, and imposed sanctions under the Arms Export Control Act, including denial of export license applications for MTCR items. Although the MTCR does not cover satellites (only launch vehicles), the identification of CGWIC as a cause of concern to the U.S. government complicated China's marketing plans. China subsequently agreed to adhere to the MTCR (although it has not signed the agreement), and the sanctions were lifted. In September 1992, in a move viewed as a conciliatory gesture in the wake of the U.S. decision to sell F-16s to Taiwan, the State Department notified Congress that it was waiving legislative restrictions on U.S. exports for six satellite projects with China: five satellites for launch and satellite technology for China to construct a new type of communications satellite.

In August 1993, however, the United States asserted that China had violated the MTCR by selling missile technology to Pakistan and again imposed sanctions (China claims it did not violate the MTCR). Seven communications satellites being built by Hughes and Martin Marietta for customers who planned to launch them on Chinese launch vehicles are affected. According to the State Department, five of the satellites are governed by the Munitions List, while two are under the jurisdiction of the Department of Commerce's Commerce Control List. The State Department says that export of the five on the Munitions List will not be permitted, and wants permission denied for the two on the CCL as well. The companies involved, backed by the Commerce Department, argue that decisions to deny the export licenses hurt their companies, not the Chinese, and want the decision reversed. The issue is under review by the White House.

The five-year agreement between the United States and China on launch services will expire in 1994, requiring negotiation of a new agreement. The United States recently negotiated such an agreement with Russia that may serve as a model for the China talks. Key points are likely to be how to ensure that China will abide by the terms of any new agreement, and how to define and limit government subsidies and practices meant to induce customers to use Chinese launch vehicles. U.S. policy has to balance the interests of domestic launch services companies (such as McDonnell Douglas and General Dynamics) that would benefit from not having to compete with China, and U.S. satellite manufacturers (such as Hughes, Space Systems Loral, and Martin Marietta) that might be disadvantaged by a cumbersome export process. It also must weigh overall foreign policy interests against the economic health of domestic satellite manufacturers.

Dealing with Beijing's Sinister View of U.S. Policy

Chinese officials and opinion leaders claimed that U.S. actions in the mid-1990s contrary to the interests of the People's Republic of China

(PRC) convinced the Beijing regime that the U.S. government was determined to do what it could to weaken and hold back China's growing power. This PRC view was particularly prominent following the visit of Taiwan's president to the United States in June 1995. Dismissing evidence of often fractious debate over China policy in the United States, Beijing's leaders were said to see a tendency among policymakers in the United States that was directed at working against China's emerging strength and influence in world affairs. U.S. specialists were unsure if Chinese leaders were misguided but sincere in their views, or if Chinese leaders were using anti-U.S. themes for tactical advantage in boosting their political standing at home, in seeking concessions from the United States, or as a defensive strategy to deflect criticism of Chinese actions seen by many international experts as bordering on irresponsible. Regardless of Chinese motives, some Americans urged that the United States make concessions and take steps to reassure Beijing of U.S. intentions and restore the wide range of U.S.-China contacts cut off as a result of U.S.-Chinese friction in mid-1995. Other Americans judged that U.S. interests would be better served by a cautious approach that avoided unilateral gestures toward Beijing. The issue posed the most immediate and difficult problem for U.S. policymakers in the mid-1990s seeking to formulate a coherent U.S. policy that would promote advantageous trends in China's role in world affairs.

The U.S. decision to ignore Chinese warnings and allow Taiwan's president to visit the United States in mid-1995 reinforced a strongly negative view of U.S. policy intentions on the part of Chinese officials, intellectuals, and other opinion leaders.[19] This view of U.S. policy has been widely articulated in private by Chinese government officials, military officers, think tank experts, media persons, and others in recent years.[20] It held that U.S. government officials are basically opposed to the rising power of China under Beijing's communist system and are taking a variety of measures in various policy areas, including Taiwan, in order to "hold back" China's power. Recent events cited by Chinese officials and other opinion leaders to support their view range from recent U.S. statements about the security environment in East Asia and the South China Sea that are seen as directed against China, to the pressure brought by the United States against China's trade practices,

human rights policies, and proliferation of technology for weapons of mass destruction.

In general, Chinese officials and opinion leaders maintained that despite lively debate in the United States over many issues in policy toward China, U.S. policymakers reached a consensus that China's growing power poses a threat to the United States that must be countered by weakening China's strength through security, economic, political, and other measures. Presumably because senior PRC leaders were as yet unwilling to confront the U.S. leadership directly on this question, the top Chinese officials and authoritative government commentary often refrained from directly accusing the United States of this conspiratorial intent. Nevertheless, Chinese officials and intellectuals repeatedly affirmed in private conversations with U.S. observers that senior Chinese leaders did indeed harbor such sinister views of U.S. intentions.

Many Chinese officials and intellectuals trace the alleged U.S. desire to weaken and hold down China at least to the reevaluation of U.S. policy toward China following the 1989 Tiananmen massacre and the concurrent collapse of the Soviet empire and the end of the cold war. At that time, they claim that U.S. leaders took a number of measures in the form of economic, military, and political sanctions against China that were designed to help bring down Beijing's communist system. U.S. leaders at this time were not seen as fearful of China's power under Beijing's communist rule; rather, they expected the Chinese regime in a few years time would be swept away by the same forces of history that had just removed their ideological comrades in Europe and elsewhere.

This did not happen as anticipated and the PRC began to grow at a remarkable rate of economic development beginning in 1992 and continuing until the present. China's economic growth was accompanied by greater military power, successful expansion of China's foreign relations, and greater self-confidence and assertiveness by Chinese leaders both at home and in Asian and world affairs. In response, the Chinese claimed the United States began to step up its efforts in a wide range of areas to curb the growth of China's power. Alleged evidence of such U.S. efforts included:

- stronger U.S. support for Taiwan, Tibet, and Hong Kong as entities separate of PRC control. U.S. support for the Taiwanese president's visit and provisions on Taiwan, Hong Kong, and Tibet in U.S. foreign policy legislation in 1995 (e.g., H.R. 1561, S. 908) were viewed as designed to keep the PRC preoccupied with tasks of protecting China's sovereignty and territorial integrity and less able to exert influence elsewhere;
- pressure on Chinese trade and other economic practices. The period 1994-1995 saw strong U.S. efforts to press Beijing to

observe intellectual property rights, to open its markets to outside goods and services, and to meet strict conditions before gaining entry into the WTO. Chinese leaders apparently saw these steps as being designed to help to keep the PRC economically weaker and less influential that it otherwise would be;

- restrictions against military related and other high technology to China and pressure on China to restrict its sales of technology and equipment that could be used for weapons of mass destruction. For example, the United States maintained its own technology restrictions against China and warned others (e.g., Russia) about the dangers of military or military technology sales to China–steps interpreted by Beijing as designed to keep China from becoming militarily stronger; and

- warnings against Chinese assertiveness in Asia. The Clinton administration's February 1995 statement about the security environment in East Asia[21] was seen in Beijing as implicitly critical of China's assertiveness and lack of transparency in flexing its military power in the region. At the same time, the administration articulated a security approach to the region that gave renewed emphasis to Japan as the center of U.S. attention in the face of regional uncertainties–a statement also viewed with some suspicion in China.[22] In May, the administration came out with a stronger position about U.S. interests in the South China Sea–a statement coming after China had caused serious concerns in the region by taking unilateral military action in South China Sea islands claimed by others. Meanwhile, Congress was considering legislation (H.R. 1561, S. Res. 97) that took aim at China's assertive actions in the South China Sea. Some in Congress added that the United States should move ahead with full diplomatic relations with Vietnam as a way to counter PRC expansion.[23]

U.S. analysts differed on the importance of such a conspiratorial Chinese view for U.S.-China relations. On one side were those who judged that Chinese government leaders were deliberately and cynically manipulating Chinese opinion mainly for other motives. Thus, the critical Chinese line against the United States was seen as part of a broader effort by PRC leaders to use nationalism and nationalistic themes, which enjoy widespread support in China, to fill the ideological void caused by the collapse of world communism and to help shore up the sagging prestige of the PRC leaders in the wake of the Tiananmen massacre. In particular, by associating the policies and practices of the Beijing regime with Chinese nationalism, PRC leaders were able to portray criticism of those policies by the United States and others as affronts to the Chinese nation and the Chinese people. This could have the side effect of alleviating the need to deal with the substance of complaints.

Meanwhile, another perceived ulterior motive of Chinese officials was to put the U.S. side on the defensive. In particular, U.S. officials anxious to restore a meaningful dialogue with China presumably would first be expected to "prove" their intentions with some gestures designed to show the Chinese that their conspiratorial view of U.S. policy was no longer correct. Of course, such gestures would involve unilateral U.S. steps of benefit to China. Chinese leaders were said to have used similar techniques against Japan in the 1970s and 1980s–whipping up sometimes strident campaigns against Japan's alleged "militarist" designs against China and the rest of Asia until Japan agreed to several billions of dollars of grants or low interest loans for China. Once the money was promised, the charges against Japanese "militarism" subsided.[24]

A very different view came from U.S. analysts who saw the Chinese leaders' conspiratorial view of U.S. policy as misguided but genuine. They believed it reflected the mix of U.S. pressures on China, the suspicious view of the outside world of many Chinese leaders, and the pressures of domestic Chinese politics during a period of leadership succession. The latter pressures were thought to incline PRC leaders to adhere to more narrow, somewhat chauvinistic views of foreign powers, especially those like the United States with an ability to threaten Chinese interests. They argued that it had now reached a point where PRC leaders were convinced that the U.S. government was "out to get them" and would almost certainly interpret future U.S. policy actions toward China along those lines.

Many Americans were anxious to restore a constructive dialogue in U.S.-China relations following the suspension of a range of contacts by Beijing as a result of the Taiwanese president's visit to the United States. Smooth running relations between such big powers as the United States and China were deemed of primary importance for U.S. interests in the view of this group. They were inclined to make gestures and take steps designed to reassure China of U.S. intentions. Whether or not the PRC leaders were manipulating Chinese opinion toward the United States or sincerely viewed the United States as conspiring against them might be of secondary importance to the broader goal of getting U.S.-China relations "back on track" after the break in relations caused by the Taiwanese president's visit. Suggested gestures included an easing of U.S. conditions on China's entry into the WTO, a visit to China by Vice President Gore or President Clinton, a muting of criticism of Chinese military intentions in Asia, or some other step long sought by Beijing.

Other Americans judged that unilateral U.S. gestures might do little good and could cause some harm to U.S. interests. Moreover, they tended to calculate that the break in U.S.-PRC communication following the visit of Taiwan's president was not so serious as to warrant unilateral U.S. action. They judged that China's interests in trade and other relations with the United States would eventually prompt Beijing to restore contacts with the United States.

Some averred that if Beijing's hard view of U.S. policy was indeed influenced by the pressures of domestic Chinese politics in a period of leadership transition, the United States might be wise to wait until the passing of Deng Xiaoping and the rise of a successor leadership before making such positive moves. Meanwhile, unilateral U.S. gestures at this time could signal to Beijing and to those in Asia and the world who are watching closely how the United States deals with China, that Washington was now prepared to allow the PRC to have freer rein in such areas as the international trading system, the world weapons proliferation regime, and in the South China Sea.

Notes

1. For background, see among others CRS Issue Brief 94002, replayed on pp. 196-210 in Senate Document 104-3, cited in chapter 1, note1.

2. For background see Robert Sutter, CRS Issue Brief 94002, *China-US Relations*, op. cit., and CRS Issue Brief 94006, *Taiwan*, op. cit. These briefs are replayed respectively on pp. 196-210 and pp. 126-140, in Senate Document 104-3, cited in chapter 1, note 1.

3. *Los Angeles Times,* August 2, 1995.

4. Consultations, Washington, DC, and/or New York, August 23, 25, and 28, 1995.

5. New China News Agency, August 18, 1995.

6. Radio Beijing, August 29, 1995.

7. New China News Agency, August 22, 1995.

8. See for example, "China Bitterly Attacks Critics in U.S.," *Washington Post,* August 24, 1995.

9. Consultations, Washington, DC, August 29, 1995.

10. Consultations, New York, August 8, 1995.

11. This is based on information cited below as well as interviews and consultations with Chinese officials, especially an interview conducted on October 17, 1995. For background on scholarly assessments of Jiang's rising power, see the article by Joseph Fewsmith in *Current History*, September 1995.

12. Consultations with a senior U.S. official recently returned from Beijing, October 10, 1995.

13. See *Financial Times*, October 9, 1995, p. 5.

14. See coverage of Jiang's speech in *Washington Post*, October 9, 1995. The official communist-owned newspaper in Hong Kong, *Ta Kung Pao*, was notably explicit in linking the importance of Jiang's discussion of the so-called twelve great relationships with Mao's discussion in the mid-1950s of the so-called ten great relationships.

15. For background on the PRC stance toward Taiwan, see CRS Issue Brief 94006, *Taiwan*, December 1, 1995; CRS report 95-968 S, *Taiwan-Mainland China Relations*, September 8, 1995; and CRS report 95-727 S, *China Policy*, June 19, 1995.

16. This section is based on syntheses drawn from the CRS issue papers replayed in Senate Document 104-3, listed in chapter 1, note 1. Among works used are those written by Kerry Dumbaugh, Wayne Morrison, Robert Shuey, Shirley Kan, and Robert Sutter.

17. For details see CRS Report 95-46S.

18. *Zhongguo Xinwen She*, September 10, 1994.

19. For details on China's breaking off of contacts with the United States and other reaction to the Taiwanese president's visit, see *China Policy: Managing U.S.-PRC-Taiwan Relations After President Lee's Visit to the U.S.* by Robert Sutter, CRS Report 95-727S, June 19, 1995, p. 5.

20. This finding is based on interviews and in-depth consultations with sixty Chinese specialists during two visits to China in 1994; consultations with thirty Chinese specialists who have visited the United States in 1995; and consultations with twenty-five U.S. specialists who have traveled to Beijing in recent years for consultations on U.S.-China relations. For background, see CRS General Distribution Memorandum *Sino-U.S. Relations: Status and Outlook--Views from Beijing*, August 15, 1994.

21. U.S. Department of Defense, *United States Security Strategy for the East Asia-Pacific Region*, Washington, February 1995, p. 32.

22. *Washington Post*, February 19, 1995.

23. These latter events are reviewed in CRS Issue Briefs 94002 and 93081.

24. See among others, Allen Whiting, *China Eyes Japan*, op. cit.

7

Charting China's Course:
Outcomes and Implications
for U.S. Policy

Looking ahead, there remains much uncertainty about China's future direction, despite the relative consistency of the overall foreign and domestic policy framework of the post-Mao leaders. Prudence requires examination of a range of possible outcomes for China's ongoing transition. Much will depend on a number of critical variables that have determined Beijing's success or failure in recent years and seem likely to remain major determinants for the next few years. As noted above, the most important and most uncertain element determining China's future in world affairs could be the United States, specifically U.S. policy on issues sensitive to China's interests.

Analysis of key determinants shows a wide range of possible outcomes for China over the next decade. A positive scenario posits increasingly effective political administration and eventual democratic reform along with continued successful economic modernization. Alternative outcomes viewed negatively in the West are of two kinds. One sees a series of developments leading to a steady degeneration of government effectiveness and authority, with a number of resulting negative side effects for China's economic and social development. Another sees China successfully developing economic power while retaining strong authoritarian political control. This contemplates an emerging Chinese economic and military superpower, much less interested in accommodation with the outside world and unfettered by the political checks and balances that would accompany a less authoritarian political structure.[1] In many respects, the three outcomes represent extremes. There are many outcomes that fall in between, or contain elements of more than one of these three. Thus, for example, an authoritarian China that is not strongly successful economically would lie somewhere between the outcomes of "degeneration" and "economically powerful authoritarianism" and presumably would have elements of both. Similarly, greater political-economic decentralized decision making need not be accompanied by substantial degeneration, and China would lie somewhere between "transformation" and "degeneration" under these circumstances.

- ***Transformation.*** This scenario assumes that the decentralization of political and economic decision-making power can be managed effectively to favor China's continued development and stability. China may adopt aspects of the federal political system, where the federal and state governments share revenue, power, and the tasks of governance. The revenue base and macroeconomic control of the central government would improve with an overhaul of the financial, taxation, and central bank systems. Price reform and return to private property would stir greater rural and urban productivity. The peaceful transition of power could be institutionalized. The political system could shift to greater liberalization, such as steps towards strengthening the legislature and greater press freedom. Prior to the 1989 crackdown, some officials were beginning to initiate such political reforms. There is also room for reconciliation between the government and society, if human rights are respected and rule of law is established to check arbitrary abuses of power. As economic power of the individual grows in China, the groundwork for a civil society and pluralistic politics is strengthened. The expansion of foreign trade and investment could lead to China's integration with the international community. Such a development would also produce greater consensus on trade, weapons nonproliferation, and other common interests.

- ***Degeneration.*** This scenario posits a leadership in Beijing that could become paralyzed in a prolonged power struggle that cripples the government. The delay in needed economic as well as political reforms could produce greater decay, discontent, and multiplying problems in the longer run. Major economic problems that persist, widening income gaps, and uncontrolled inflation could lead to rampant social instability. The kind of corruption that drains, not fuels, the system could swell to distort development and further breed organized crime. Environmental problems, national disasters, uncorrected infrastructure and energy bottlenecks, and fiscal crises could lead to economic breakdown. Continued repression or brute coercion could contribute to social apathy or anarchism. Weak and divided civilian as well as military authorities could also induce separatist protests in areas like Xinjiang and Tibet, provoking ethnic conflicts and civil war. An insecure Chinese government would be unable to responsibly participate in the United Nations or credibly negotiate international agreements.

- *Economically Powerful Authoritarianism.* This outcome contradicts much social science literature, which holds that continued economic reform will lead to greater political pluralism. It assumes that authorities in China will be successful in modernizing the Chinese economy and use that success to justify and support an authoritarian structure at home. The probable result would be substantial continued political repression and human rights abuses. China's economic power would be of such a scale as to make most foreign powers unwilling to confront Beijing on most issues. Thus, Chinese leaders inclined to more assertive, nationalistic policies would have a freer hand to pursue their objectives, less concerned that important Chinese trading partners would shun economic opportunities in China if Beijing failed to behave according to accepted international norms. Even moderate state direction of the massive Chinese economy would give Beijing strong economic power to manipulate terms of trade and investment in critical economic sectors toward creation of an Asian sphere of influence or other objectives.

Implications for the United States

The rapid growth of China's wealth and power and a prominent role in Asian and world politics have increased the importance of China for American interests.[2] Developments in China will have important implications for long-standing American interests in sustaining influence in Asian and world affairs, assuring smooth access to economic opportunities abroad, and in promoting American values of economic free enterprise and political democracy. In the post-cold war international environment, these American security, economic, and political interests have been closely tied to a number of newly prominent transnational issues (weapons proliferation, trade practices, environmental policies, immigration, and refugees) where China's actions loom large in the American calculus.

Recent practice has made clear that developments in China can have positive or negative implications for American interests. Thus, China's large, current economic market and great potential are a magnet to American exporters, and U.S. importers and consumers benefit from imported Chinese consumer goods. But China's trade and economic practices are major headaches for American firms concerned with intellectual property rights, fair access to the China market, and other issues. Although Beijing has been generally cooperative with the United States and Japan in post-cold war Asia, there is no guarantee that an economically stronger China might not use its influence to adjust the Asian security order contrary to American interests. Meanwhile, the American and Chinese political, social, and economic systems remain fundamentally different. With greater U.S.-Chinese interaction comes greater familiarity with such differences and the rise of friction over what are seen as repeated Chinese affronts to values respected by the United States.

In view of the range of possible developments in China, discussed below are the likely implications of three generic outcomes for U.S. interests:

- *Transformation.* A positive transition process in China would mean that leaders in Beijing would be able to avoid political paralysis, establish leadership consensus on a wide range of policy goals, and implement policies effectively. This context allows policy decisions that could well be compatible with a broad array of U.S. interests and goals. In the economic sphere, these would include pursuing pragmatic, market-oriented economic policies; promoting plans that attract foreign investment; and adopting and enforcing laws that would more effectively curb rampant corruption and the abuse of power by central, regional, and local officials.

Such measures would generally complement U.S. economic interests, and movement toward economic reform could offer some likelihood that China would not be moving toward a stricter authoritarian or even fascist system of government. China's pursuit of market-oriented economic objectives also could offer new opportunities for U.S.-China contact and cooperation, such as in the creation of taxation and banking systems. Consistent enforcement of laws against corruption could do much to relieve growing popular discontent and resentment, which could result in violent clashes, increased instability, and renewed suppression.

The expansion of foreign trade, foreign investment, and other foreign economic contacts that would come with continued reform could also lead to greater consensus and cooperation on strategic and foreign policy issues such as weapons nonproliferation, technology transfer, and regional security. A China focused on domestic stability and economic development would be expected to pursue policies to reduce regional conflicts. The United States could find China to be a cooperative partner on a number of regional problems that are of concern to the United States and over which China has considerable influence. These could include such things as attempting to convince North Korean leaders to comply with international nuclear inspection programs; intervening to moderate North Korea's hostile posture toward South Korea, where thousands of U.S. troops are stationed; and being willing to compromise and negotiate over competing claims in the Spratly Islands, where China is one of the claimants.

Even in a positive transition scenario, China's progress in some areas important to U.S. interests-such as meaningful political reform and human rights assurances-would likely be slower than progress in areas of common interest such as economic and foreign policy issues. China's authoritarian leadership tradition, its cumbersome communist government structure and institutions, and its not unjustified preoccupation with ensuring social stability even if repression is called for, would probably continue to varying degrees even under the best of circumstances. Some Western observers have even argued that continued authoritarian government in China would be necessary for a positive transition, since economic development and growth occur best in a stable environment and interregional stability is not to be assumed.

As in the late 1970s, when the United States was considering normalizing relations with China, U.S. policymakers would have to balance the benefits of having some U.S. policy objectives met against the costs and tradeoffs to other U.S. policy goals over both the short and long terms. To encourage a positive transition, the United States could consider such economic incentives as facilitating China's entry into the WTO or granting MFN status to China on a permanent basis. Some would urge that, in the interim, political and human rights issues could remain important U.S. concerns, but would become less important relative to the entire context of U.S. policy objectives. Others fear this lessening would conduce toward the third generic outcome ("economically powerful authoritarianism") noted below.

- *Degeneration.* Decline and failure in China's administrative structure and paralysis of economic reform efforts could result in economic stagnation and contribute to political paralysis, leading to increased popular resentment with more frequent protests and violence. Fearful central leaders could turn increasingly to coercion in an attempt to maintain stability and re-establish some degree of national control.

A significant escalation of violence or repression could spur an exodus of refugees seeking asylum in other countries, perhaps on a massive scale. Countries near China–such as India, Russia, Mongolia, Japan, and South Korea–may call for U.S. or international assistance to protect their borders and deal with the consequences of Chinese unrest. China's economic stagnation and the political problems that may accompany it could lead to less certain foreign policies and a riskier strategic environment. Chinese leaders may be too preoccupied with internal matters to become engaged in solving regional problems or potential conflicts; or, conversely, a beleaguered Chinese leadership may see the need to adopt a higher state of military readiness in the region to offset domestic difficulties.

In such a scenario, U.S. businesses could suffer financial losses and U.S. economic and trade relations with other countries could be complicated. The United States would find itself with fewer opportunities to cooperate economically with China. At the same time, economic dislocation and popular discontent would raise the visibility of human rights, democratization, and other issues that are important U.S. policy priorities.

Some experts have argued that this kind of a negative transition for China may ultimately be in U.S. interests despite potentially destabilizing effects in Asian and world affairs. They believe it would be most likely to disenfranchise current communist leaders and lead to the collapse of Chinese communism and possibly the development of two, three, or more states. Development of a China-dominated economic zone would be impossible. They emphasize that the United States and China have fundamental underlying conflicts and differing value systems that are unlikely to moderate; the United States and other Western countries should maintain military superiority over China and take no actions that might benefit the current system of government.

- *Economically Powerful Authoritarianism.* The China that emerges in this scenario holds considerable economic opportunity for the United States among others, but poses dangers for U.S. security, political, and longer-term economic interests. Chinese economic prosperity presumably would continue to attract important world attention, including from the United States. But without political reform, Beijing would be less constrained in mobilizing this economic power against American interests.

As far as U.S. values are concerned, Chinese leaders would presumably continue the repressive authoritarian measures of the past, justified in the name of "stability." In international affairs, Beijing would likely be less deferential to U.S. and allied concerns regarding security issues, trade practices, and the like. Aware that foreign countries increasingly "need" access to China for their own economic well being, Beijing could attempt to isolate the United States from its allies or prompt Washington to soft pedal differences with China out of concerns for the American economy. U.S. business interests would likely be split in their political support of China policies. Over the longer term an economically powerful and politically authoritarian China could be diplomatically, technologically, and militarily formidable, possessing sufficient power and differences with the United States to pose the most serious single international threat to U.S. interests in Asian and world stability in the twenty-first century.

Outlook and Tasks for U.S. Policy

There is general agreement in the United States that Washington should use its influence in order to have Beijing conform to international norms and over time to foster changes in China's political, economic, and security systems compatible with American interests. At the same time, there is little agreement in Washington on how the United States should achieve these objectives. As noted in Chapter Five, there are three general approaches influencing current U.S. China policy and little indication as to which approach will ultimately succeed.

First is the approach favored by some in the Clinton administration, the Congress, and elsewhere who argue in favor of a moderate, less confrontational and "engaged" posture toward China. Underlying this moderate approach is a belief by many adherents that trends in China are moving inexorably in the "right" direction. That is, China is becoming increasingly interdependent economically, and is increasingly unlikely to take disruptive action. Greater wealth in China also is seen pushing Chinese society to develop a materially better-off, more educated, and cosmopolitan populace that will over time press its government for greater representation, political pluralism, and eventually democracy.

Second is the tougher approach of some U.S. advocates who have doubts about the interdependence argument. This approach encourages U.S. leaders to be more firm than moderate in dealing with China. The United States is advised to keep military forces as a counterweight to rising Chinese power in Asia; to remain firm in dealing with economic, arms proliferation, and other disputes with China; and to work closely with traditional U.S. allies and friends along China's periphery in order to deal with any suspected assertiveness or disruption from Beijing.

Third is the approach that believes that the political system in China needs to be changed first before the United States has any real hope of reaching a constructive relationship with China. U.S. policy should focus on mechanisms to change China from within while maintaining a vigilant posture to deal with disruptive Chinese foreign policy actions in Asian and world affairs.

Given the continued wide range of opinion in the United States over the appropriate U.S. policy toward China, it appears likely that U.S. policy will continue its recent pattern of trying to accommodate elements of all three approaches. On some issues, like linking MFN treatment and human rights, the U.S. government has seen U.S. interests best served by an approach that meets PRC concerns. On others, like intellectual property rights protection and proliferation of missile technology, it seems prepared to threaten sanctions or to withhold benefits from Beijing until it conforms to norms acceptable to the United States. Meanwhile, although many U.S. officials would see as counterproductive any declaration by the U.S. government that a policy goal was to change China's system of government, there is a widespread assumption that greater U.S. "engagement" will encourage such desirable changes.

Whether the U.S. government policy synthesis of these three tendencies is done smoothly or is accompanied by the often strident policy debates accompanying U.S. China policy decisions in recent years depends partly on U.S. leadership. In this vein, several rules of thumb are suggested that U.S. leaders could consider when determining whether the United States should try to accommodate, confront, or change China on a particular policy issue:

1. How important is the issue at hand for U.S. interests? (In general the more important U.S. interests at stake, the less accommodating and more forceful U.S. leaders should be.);
2. How does the issue at hand fit in with broader U.S. strategic interests in relation with China? (Presumably, some U.S. officials would be inclined to soft pedal relatively minor disputes with China when they are pressing for broader gains elsewhere.);
3. How much leverage does the United States have over the PRC on this issue? (In general, the greater the degree of U.S. leverage, the easer it is for U.S. leaders to press for their demands.);
4. What are the attitudes of U.S. allies and associates? (If they do not support a firm U.S. stance, U.S. efforts to pressure China may be outflanked, quixotic, and counterproductive.); and
5. How sensitive is the issue at hand to the PRC. (Experience has indicated that Beijing has shown less sensitivity and greater flexibility on international economic issues, and has shown more sensitivity and less flexibility on issues involving domestic political control and territorial claims. Many analysts believe that PRC leadership flexibility on sensitive issues will be restricted for a time as a result of the decline of Deng Xiaoping's health and the ongoing leadership succession struggle.)

Other matters of importance in considering specific China policy issues include:

- How does the U.S. stance affect broader U.S. interests in Asian stability and international affairs?
- What is the U.S. "bottom line"? Chinese officials will press for the advantage until they find it.
- Can this matter be effectively pursued in an overall friendly and respectful atmosphere? This reduces suspicions in Beijing regarding the alleged overall hostile intent of U.S. policymakers toward China–suspicions that greatly limit PRC flexibility.
- Can this issue be pursued with the aid of U.S. allies, associates, and other international leaders to create an atmosphere that would prompt Beijing to change in directions favored by the United States? (The United States used this approach in part

to get Beijing to go along with international sanctions and military action against Libya and Iraq; with planned sanctions against North Korea; and with provisions of the 1991 Cambodian peace accord that were opposed by Beijing's former client, the Khmer Rouge.)

Notes

1. Among sources useful for this section, see "China in Transformation," *Daedalus*, (spring 1993); Lowell Dittmer and Samuel Kim, eds., *China's Quest for National Identity*, Cornell, 1993; Arthur Waldron, "The Sino-American Scene," *Wall Street Journal*, May 22, 1992; Roderick MacFarguhar, "Deng's Last Campaign," *New York Review of Books*, December 17, 1992; Anne Thurston, "The Dragon Stirs," *Wilson Quarterly*, (spring 1993); David Shambaugh, "Losing Control," *Current History*, September 1993; Harry Harding, "China in the 1990s: Prospects for Internal Change," *National Bureau of Asian and Soviet Research*, September 1990; Barber Conable and David M. Lampton, "China: The Coming Power," *Foreign Affairs*, (winter 1992/1993); Martin Whyte, "Prospects for Democratization in China," *Problems of Communism*, May-June 1992; and Chong-pin Lin, "The Deng Linchpin Debate," *International Economy*, July/August 1993. See more recently Robert Sutter, *China's Changing Conditions*, CRS Issue Brief 93114 (updated regularly), and the analysis in the Defense Department Net Assessment office's review of China's future, presented at the Heritage Foundation, February 17, 1995, and reported on by the *Washington Times*, February 18, 1995.

2. For background, see discussion in Robert Sutter, Shirley Kan, and Kerry Dumbaugh, *China In Transition: Changing Conditions and Implications For U.S. Interests*, CRS Report 93-1061S, December 20, 1993, p. 23, and Robert Sutter, Shirley Kan, and Kerry Dumbaugh, *China's Changing Conditions*, CRS Issue Brief 93114 (updated regularly).

Appendix

Prominent Leaders In Contemporary China

Jiang Zemin (b. 1926) is a moderate reformer who stepped into the spotlight of Chinese national politics in the aftermath of the Tiananmen massacre in 1989. As Beijing's top party man in Shanghai in 1989, Jiang had dealt firmly with demonstrations in that city, but without having to resort to the massive bloodshed and brute force used in Beijing. He was widely seen as a compromise choice to head a party internally divided over the events at Tiananmen and, more broadly, the course of future reforms. Since being named general secretary of the party in June of 1989, Jiang has acquired the two other top posts in Chinese politics, chairman of the Central Military Commission and president of the PRC.

Jiang is viewed by some in the Western media as an ineffectual and uncharismatic figurehead who is unlikely to last long as leader in the post-Deng era. They view him as a transitional figure between Deng and a future leader, just as Hua Guofeng proved a short-lived transitional leader between the Mao and Deng eras. His detractors point to his lack of a commanding presence and his lack of military ties (despite his position as head of the military).

Reports of Jiang's imminent demise, however, may be exaggerated. He has been assiduously working to shore up his power base. He has lavished praise and funding on the military and has stacked key positions in the military, party, and security apparatus with his supporters. Jiang has now promoted to general twenty-five out of the twenty-nine top military leaders in China. Moreover, Jiang is peppering the department structure of the Central Committee with his former Shanghai associates. Thus, while it may be unlikely that Jiang will serve a long period as the authoritative leader of China, it is not inconceivable that he could retain his titles and play a central role in substantial period of collective leadership.

Qiao Shi (b. 1924) is seen by many as a dark horse candidate to assume power after Deng's death. Some reports say Qiao has played a prominent role in Beijing's security apparatus. Some in China and abroad view Qiao as a closet liberal and an enthusiast for economic reform, while others see him aligned with old guard communists and thus skeptical of Deng's economic reforms. Qiao's control of the party's personnel files is believed by some to be an important source of authority. As chairman of the National People's Congress (NPC), Qiao has been working to transform the NPC from a rubber-stamp body to a genuine power base.

The current leader most widely hailed by the West is Vice-Premier *Zhu Rongji* (b. 1928). Zhu was elevated to the national leadership in the early 1990s from his positions as mayor and top party boss of Shanghai. In 1989 he worked with Jiang Zemin to engineer the firm, but relatively bloodless, suppression of demonstrations in Shanghai. Zhu soon followed Jiang to Beijing, becoming a vice-premier in 1991 and member of the party Politburo Standing Committee in 1992. Zhu is believed to be an ardent economic reformer. He maintains a reputation as a commanding figure with an ability to cut through bureaucracy, although this image has been tarnished by the slowness of economic changes under his leadership. In 1993 Zhu was made senior vice-premier and was placed in charge of reining in China's overheating economy.

The conservative standard bearer on the Politburo Standing Committee is Prime Minister *Li Peng* (b. 1928). Li is believed to be the Standing Committee member most skeptical of fast-paced economic reforms. As prime minister in 1989, Li Peng was widely associated with the bloody suppression of demonstrators at Tiananmen Square in 1989. Mr. Li has survived his domestic and international unpopularity and has not yet been pushed to the political sidelines as economic reforms have accelerated. In addition to his duties as head of the State Council, Li Peng also heads the Foreign Affairs Small Working Group, which essentially makes him China's chief foreign policy architect. Mr. Li reportedly favors a hard line toward the United States concerning human rights.

Other influential communist party members who presently reside at the periphery of Politburo politics could conceivably step forward to assume leadership of the party. Most prominent among these are Yang Shangkun and Zhao Ziyang. *Yang Shangkun* (b. 1907) is a still active party elder with a long military background. Yang has been a close confidant of Deng Xiaoping and helped deliver the loyalty of the armed forces in the tumultuous period of June 1989. Yang preceded Jiang Zemin as PRC president and served as the second ranking official in charge of the military. Mr. Yang appeared to have overreached politically in 1992 when he, and his half-brother Yang Baibing, were removed from their military posts after Deng apparently concluded that they were building up an independent power base that could threaten the position of Jiang Zemin. But Yang has maintained political contacts within the military and elsewhere. In January 1995, he toured China's southern Special Economic Zones and emphasized his support for economic reform. Mr. Yang's age precludes him from becoming a long-term successor to Deng, but he could play a crucial role in any succession struggle given his ties with the military. Mr. Yang is believed to be a committed economic reformer.

Former prime minister and communist party head, *Zhao Ziyang* (b. 1919) was blamed for the events at Tiananmen. Following the massacre he was stripped of his posts and temporarily placed under house arrest. Zhao's longer term disgrace, however, has been relatively mild and he remains popular throughout southern China. His return may entail a reversal of the verdicts surrounding the events at Tiananmen that may alienate some elements in the military and others, notably Li Peng. Mr. Zhao is an ardent economic reformer and, unlike other prominent leaders, he is believed to favor some degree of political reform.

Chronology

1911

October 10:   The 1911 Revolution against the Qing Dynasty began, led by Sun Yat-sen.

1912

February: Infant Emperor Xuantong abdicated the throne, leaving Yuan Shikai, leader of the Beijing Army (the most powerful army of the Qing Dynasty), to establish a republic in Beijing.

1914

                Yuan Shikai suspended the Parliament after power struggles with military governors in the south. China fell under the control of the Japanese military.

1915

                Yuan Shikai declared himself emperor.

1916

                Yuan Shikai was forced to end the monarchy and died later that year.

1916-1927

                Warlord Era. Control of China rested in the hands of a group of warlords, each with independent control over his territory. It was a return to feudal patterns of rule.

1919

May 4:   "May 4th Movement." Beijing students launched mass demonstrations that spread throughout China in protest of agreements reached at the Versailles Conference that failed to return Japanese territorial concessions to China at the end of World War I. This movement expanded to include a "literary and cultural renaissance" among Chinese intellectuals, and Marxism and Leninism caught on at this time.

1921

July 1:   The Chinese Communist party was officially founded in Shanghai by twelve delegates, including Mao Zedong.

1923-1926

                The KMT and the CCP joined in a "united front" in an attempt to deal with the warlords and the Japanese.

1925

                Sun Yat-sen died and Chiang Kai-shek became the KMT leader.

1926

                Chiang Kai-shek led the "Northern Expedition" to gain control of warlord areas in the north.

1927

                The KMT under Chiang Kai-shek was formed.

1927

April: Under Chiang Kai-shek's command, KMT troops launched a surprise attack against Shanghai labor unions and radical activists, killing communist leaders and destroying the CCP-KMT alliance. Chiang, allied with the conservatives, went on to form his own nationalist government in Nanjing.

1931

September: Japan bombarded and gained control of the northeast Chinese city of Shenyang.

1934

Feb./March: Japan completed its occupation of Manchuria and established the puppet state of Manchukuo. The last of the Manchu emperors, Pu Yi, was inaugurated as the provincial dictator.

March 1: Japan installed Pu Yi as the Kangde Emperor.

October: The KMT launched a military offensive in the south against the communists. After the fall of their base at Jiangxi, the CCP retreated to Yan'an in Shaanxi Province in what came to be known as the "Long March."

1937

July: Japanese forces attacked Chinese troops at the Marco Polo bridge outside Beijing and later began a full-scale offensive against China.

September: The CCP and KMT entered into a second united front to fight the Japanese.

1942

February: The United States sent Lieutenant General Joseph Stilwell to act as chief of staff for Chiang, and authorized a $500 million loan to nationalist China.

1943

February: The United States and China under Chiang signed a treaty to relinquish U.S. extraterritorial and related rights to China. The United States promised to ease immigration restrictions on Chinese citizens traveling to the United States.

October 30: According to the "Declaration of Four Nations on Great Security," China, acknowledged as a "great power," had the right to participate with the United States, the USSR, and Great Britain in prosecuting war, organizing peace and establishing a framework for international cooperation.

1944

November: Patrick Hurley arrived in China to take up duties as the first U.S. ambassador there.

1945

March: Chiang Kai-shek announced that a national assembly would be convened to draft a new constitution for the republic. The

CCP was invited but refused. After meeting with U.S. Ambassador Hurley, Chiang and Mao signed the "Double Ten" agreement to decrease hostilities, though battles were still being fought.

1946

November: The national assembly promised by Chiang Kai-shek in 1945 was held in Nanjing. Fighting between KMT and CCP forces resumed by the end of the month.

1947

June: The United States ended its arms embargo on China and began supplying the nationalist forces with over $6.5 million worth of ammunition to aid in their fight against the communists.

November 23: The first elections in China's history ended with the nationalists winning the majority of seats.

December 25: The Chinese National Assembly adopted a new constitution.

1948

September: CCP troops began winning ground with the fall of the city Jinan. Prompted by CCP gains, Chiang Kai-shek asked for additional U.S. aid and sent his wife to the United States to request more support.

1949

October 1: The PRC was formally inaugurated. Mao Zedong was named chairman and Zhou Enlai was named premier and foreign minister. The capital was established in Beijing. The United States withdrew all diplomatic personnel from China.

December: Nationalist forces retreated to Taiwan.

1950

January : The United States cancelled aid to KMT forces on Taiwan.

February: China and the USSR signed a Treaty of Friendship, Alliance and Mutual Assistance.

March: Chiang Kai-shek reclaimed the presidency of nationalist China and continued to build his government from his new base in Taipei.

June 25: North Korean troops invaded South Korea.

June 27: In response to the North Korean invasion, President Truman ordered the U.S. Seventh Fleet to protect Taiwan from possible communist attack, marking an upgrading of U.S. commitment to Taiwan. In response, China began a campaign to "resist America and aid Korea."

June: China passed the Agrarian Reform Law, thus beginning the process of land reform by abolishing "feudal exploitation" by the landowning class and by distributing land to peasants.

These drives to collectivize agriculture continued throughout the 1950s.

August: Communist forces invaded Tibet.

Oct./November: The Chinese military crossed into North Korea and attacked South Korean troops.

December: The United States enacted an "informal" embargo of all U.S. exports to China that remained in place for the next twenty-one years.

1951

March: The invasion by communist forces into Tibet ended and the PRC claimed control over the region.

April: The United States resumed aiding Taiwan's government with the appointment of a 100-man Military Assistance and Advisory Group.

1953

February: President Eisenhower declared that the U.S. Seventh Fleet would no longer "protect" communist China from the nationalist forces on Taiwan.

February 4: The Chinese government declared that the country's post-civil war recovery was complete and took steps to begin a five-year plan to develop the Chinese economy along the Soviet model. Soviet advisors and aid were provided to help the Chinese.

July: North and South Korea agreed to an armistice to end the Korean War. China reportedly suffered one million casualties during the war. Due to foreign involvement, the war reinforced China's negative perceptions of the West and made the United States the prime enemy.

1954

September 3: PRC forces began shelling the nationalist-held island of Quemoy.

September 4: U.S. Secretary of State John Foster Dulles ordered the Seventh Fleet to recommence patrolling the Taiwan Strait.

September 7: The nationalist forces of Taiwan began air strikes against the mainland.

September: The Chinese People's Political Consultative Conference adopted a formal constitution establishing the National People's Congress.

December 2: The United States and Taiwan signed a Mutual Defense Treaty stipulating that the two would develop and maintain their collective capacity to resist armed attack by "Communist subversion from without;" cooperate in economic development; consult on implementation of the treaty; and jointly meet an armed attack of either in the West Pacific.

1955
April: Chinese Premier Zhou Enlai addressed delegates from Asian and African countries at the Bandung Conference in Indonesia, marking the beginning of the "Bandung phase" of Chinese foreign policy in which China sought to ease tensions along its border and increase its contacts with African and Asian countries.

1956
May: Mao launched what came to be known as the "Hundred Flowers Movement," suggesting that the Chinese people voice their criticisms of the Communist party in order to strengthen it.

September: The 8th Party Congress adopted measures to shift emphasis away from sole leadership by Mao Zedong to a more collective leadership, giving Liu Shaoqi and Deng Xiaoping larger roles.

1957
October 10:   The PRC and the USSR signed a secret agreement promising that the USSR would help China develop its nuclear capacity.

1958
July: China announced that it would begin a campaign to "liberate" Taiwan. The nationalists, in response, ordered a state of emergency on the islands of Matsu and Pescadores.

August: The communist Chinese forces began shelling Quemoy and the Tan Islands.

September: The nationalists claimed 3,000 civilian and 1,000 military casualties as a result of the shelling from the communist Chinese.

Sept./October: U.S. and Chinese ambassadors to Poland met in Warsaw to discuss the Taiwan Strait crisis. On October 6, China declared a one-week cease-fire and on October 25, the Chinese announced there would be a cease-fire every other day.

December 17:   Mao announced that he would resign as chief of state in January 1959 to devote his energies to being chairman of the Communist party.

1959
March 10:   Riots broke out in the Lhasa, Tibet. One week later, after Chinese troops fired on the crowd, Tibetan spiritual leader, the Dalai Lama, fled to India.

June: The USSR secretly announced that it would withdraw nuclear assistance to China.

1960
February 24:   China warned that U.S. involvement in South Vietnam was a direct threat to North Vietnam and that it also affected the security of China and Asia.

Oct./November: Fighting along the Sino-Indian border erupted into full-scale war when China opened an offensive and drove Indian troops across the border.

November 20: China cleared the disputed territory of all Indian troops. A cease-fire was declared and Chinese troops were moved to a position behind the original border line.

December: China signed a Treaty of Friendship and Mutual Non-aggression with Cambodia, and later began to supply the country with arms in support of its battle with Vietnam. China and Cambodia established diplomatic relations as part of China's attempt to counteract what it saw as growing ties between the USSR and Vietnam.

1963

October 28: Chinese Foreign Minister Chen Yi made China's first official statement regarding its nuclear program, stating that it would be several years before China could test its nuclear weapons.

December 14: Zhou Enlai and Chen Yi toured Africa and stressed the importance of relations between China and African countries. These anti-colonial states in Asia, Africa, and Latin America.

1964

January 27: France formally recognized the PRC.

February 10: In response to France's recognition of China, Taiwan broke relations with France.

October 16: China detonated its first nuclear bomb.

1965

January: President Johnson announced that aid to Taiwan had been a success and was no longer needed.

Feb./March: China announced that if U.S. troops crossed the 17th parallel into North Vietnam, China would join the fighting.

June 30: The U.S. Agency for International Development announced the termination of non-military aid to Taiwan.

July: China and North Vietnam concluded an agreement in which China promised to supply "equipment, whole sets of installations, and defensive and economic supplies" to North Vietnam.

1966

July 28: All Universities and schools were closed to give students the opportunity to participate in the Cultural Revolution.

July: The Chinese government closed the country to foreign visitors and suspended issuance of most visas.

August 8: The CCP Central Committee released a statement asserting that certain members of the party had taken the "capitalist road" and had to be removed. It called upon the masses to

| | establish "cultural revolutionary" groups to attack what it labeled "anti-party, anti-socialist rightists." |
| October 27: | China successfully conducted a launch of its first atomic missile. |

1967

January:	Announcements were made calling for extending the Cultural Revolution into factories. Workers, however, resisted the directive.
January 22:	An editorial appeared calling on the Red Guards to "seize power." The army was later brought in to ensure that the Red Guards were able to carry out their activities.
June 16:	The Central Committee, State Council, Military Affairs Committee, and Cultural Revolution Group issued a joint order to curb the anarchy caused by the Red Guards.

1968

| July 1: | Sixty-two countries including the United States, the USSR, and Great Britain signed the Nuclear Non-proliferation Treaty (NPT). The PRC refused to sign it because of the UN's unwillingness to recognize it as the legitimate government of China. |
| October 4: | Mao ordered urban youth to go to the countryside to "learn from the masses." Known as the Xiafang Movement, an estimated 15 million youths were affected by the campaign. |

1969

March:	Fighting broke out among Chinese and Soviet troops along the border near the disputed Zhenbao Island in the Ussuri River.
May:	The Chinese government announced that it could accept the status of the Ussuri River boundary as long as conflict with the USSR could be avoided.
May:	China began to end its isolation from the rest of the world in May by appointing its first ambassador since the start of the Cultural Revolution.
September 23:	China conducted its first underground nuclear test.
November 7:	The United States ended the Seventh Fleet's nineteen-year presence in the Taiwan Strait. The decision was said to have been precipitated by China's willingness to reopen the Warsaw Talks, which had been a forum for discussions of the U.S. and Chinese positions regarding Taiwan but had reached a stalemate.

1970

| February 1: | In its first official statement of foreign policy since 1967, the Chinese government expressed its support of Arab countries in their disagreements with Israel. |
| April 24: | China launched its first satellite. |

May:	More than a week after U.S. forces moved into Cambodia, the *Beijing Review* condemned the invasion. Analysts of China argued that the delay in publishing the criticism and the relative mildness of the statement suggested China's unwillingness to jeopardize improving U.S.-Sino relations.
October 12:	Canada officially recognized the PRC. The two countries signed a joint communiqué reaffirming their belief that Taiwan was an "inalienable part of the territory of China."

1971

February:	China responded to the U.S.-assisted South Vietnamese invasion of Laos by calling it a "rabid act" and "grave provocation." The official criticism of the United States was considered mild.
March/April:	The U.S. State Department announced the removal of restrictions on the use of U.S. passports for travel in China.
June 10:	The White House announced a full relaxation of the twenty-one year embargo on U.S. trade with China. Chinese exports to the United States were henceforth to be under the same restrictions as those from USSR and Eastern Europe.
July:	President Nixon announced that National Security Advisor Kissinger had returned from a secret visit to China during which he arranged for the president to make an official visit to Beijing in 1972.
Oct./November:	The PRC was given Taiwan's seat in the UN.

1972

February:	President Nixon became the first U.S. head of state to visit the PRC. At the end of Nixon's visit, the two countries issued the Shanghai Communiqué and pledged to work toward normalization.
March:	China and Great Britain reopened relations after a twenty-two year hiatus. In their joint communiqué, Britain acknowledged China's claim to sovereignty over Taiwan.
September 29:	During a visit to China by Prime Minister Kakuei Tanaka, Japan and China released a communiqué affirming Japan's recognition of the PRC as the sole legitimate government of China.
December:	Japan opened the Japan Interchange Association in Taipei in an attempt to maintain unofficial relations with Taiwan. This arrangement came to be known as the "Japanese Solution."

1973

January:	The United States, North Korea, South Korea, and the Vietcong signed an agreement that called for a cease-fire in Vietnam, but that did not end the fighting in Cambodia. China's reaction was favorable, noting that the U.S. presence

in Vietnam had been a major source of tension in Sino-American relations.

May 1: Liaison offices were opened in Beijing and Washington to expand trade and deepen scientific and cultural relations. The opening of these facilities signified a major concession by the Chinese, who had insisted that they would not establish a mission in any country that recognized Taiwan.

1975

January 19: South Vietnam and China began a two-day war over the uninhabited but oil-rich Paracel Islands. The Vietnamese were ousted from the islands, but moved to occupy many of the Spratly Islands. China lodged verbal complaints but did not send troops.

April 5: Chiang Kai-shek died at the age of eighty-eight in Taipei. His son, Chiang Ching-kuo, was later named to succeed him.

September: China and the European Economic Community opened formal relations.

December 5: President Ford completed a five-day cordial visit to China. Deng Xiaoping would later claim that Ford agreed to accept China's three demands for normalization during the trip.

1976

January 8: Premier Zhou Enlai died of cancer at the age of seventy-eight. His death was considered a gain for the radical faction of China's leadership.

April 7: The Central Committee chose Hua Guofeng to replace Zhou Enlai as premier and stripped Deng Xiaoping of all his positions although he was allowed to remain in the party.

April 15: China and India announced that they would exchange ambassadors.

September 9: Chairman Mao died at the age of eighty-two. His death was followed by the arrest of the radical groups in charge of many of the policies implemented during the Cultural Revolution (later known as the Gang of Four). Hua Guofeng was named to succeed Mao as chairman of the party and of the Military Commission.

1977

July/August: Hua Guofeng was formalized as chairman, and Deng Xiaoping was restored once again to his posts.

1978

July: Vice Premier Li Xiannian announced that China would reverse its policy of not accepting foreign capital.

August 12: China and Japan signed a treaty of peace and friendship.

December 15: The United States and Chinese governments announced that diplomatic relations would be restored as of January 1, 1979. The United States promised to recognize the PRC as the sole legitimate government of China and acknowledged Beijing's position that Taiwan was part of China.

1979

January 1:   The PRC announced that it had stopped bombarding the nationalist islands of Matsu and Quemoy. Beijing also proposed talks with Taiwan to end the military confrontation and removed troops from the area. The U.S. Mutual Defense Treaty with Taiwan was abrogated.

January 28:   Vice Premier Deng Xiaoping arrived in the United States for a nine-day visit, during which President Carter and Deng signed an agreement to establish a framework for a "new and irreversible course" in Sino-American relations and made plans for the opening of consulates in each country.

February 15:   Taiwan created the Coordination Council for North American Affairs to act as the unofficial diplomatic counterpart to the newly established American Institute in Taiwan.

February/March: China invaded Vietnam on February 17 as a counterattack brought about by repeated Vietnamese border incursions. China and Vietnam entered negotiations on March 2 and hostilities ended March 5. China formally withdrew from Vietnam on March 16.

April 10:   President Carter approved the TRA, which legalized America's new relationship with Taiwan. In effect, the bill approved treatment of Taiwan as an independent state to which the United States would sell arms, lend money, and grant diplomatic immunity.

May 14:   China and the United States signed a trade agreement, paving the way for the United States to grant MFN trade status.

October 4:   The first Sino-American joint venture contract was signed by the E-S Pacific Development Company of San Francisco and the China International Travel Service to build the Great Wall Hotel in Beijing.

November 19:   Vice Premier Chen Muhua announced that China would work to control its rapid population growth and set a goal of bringing the rate of growth to zero by the year 2000.

1980

January 8:   U.S. Secretary of Defense Harold Brown in a visit to China announced that the United States was willing to sell certain nonoffensive military equipment and high technology to China.

March 14:   Deng Xiaoping set forth two of the country's key foreign policy goals in the coming years: to contain Soviet expansionism and to work for the reunification of China.

April/May: The PRC was formally readmitted to the IMF in April and to

	the World Bank in May, and because of this Taiwan lost its standing within these lending institutions.
May 18:	China announced the successful launch of China's first multistage intercontinental ballistic missile (ICBM).
May 21:	In an attempt to emphasize ownership of the islands, China warned the USSR and Vietnam against conducting oil or gas exploration near the Paracel and Spratly Islands. This created deeper tensions in Sino-USSR relations.
September:	At the 3rd session of the 5th National People's Congress, Wang Zhen and Xu Xiangqian resigned their State Council positions, citing old age. Ye Jianying was named NPC chairman and Zhao Ziyang replaced Hua Guofeng as premier. The one child policy went into effect. An amendment to the constitution was passed suggesting that Chinese citizens no longer had the inherent right to express themselves freely.

1981

February 28:	The Chinese government announced plans to slow down economic growth and contract output.
March:	The IMF approved a $550 million loan to China to help finance its balance of payments deficit and stabilize the economy.
May 9:	China offered arms and other weapons to help the Cambodian forces to strengthen its opposition to the presence of Vietnamese forces in Cambodia and Soviet support for those forces.
June:	U.S. Secretary of State Alexander Haig visited Beijing and renewed promises to supply military equipment to China, signed cultural agreements, and made arrangements to open more consulates.
October 2:	Deng Xiaoping voiced support for a proposal presented by Ye Jianying on the question of relations between Taiwan and the mainland. The proposal called for eventual reunification, and focused on the economic benefits of reunification. Taiwan dismissed the proposal.
November 30:	The 4th session of the 5th National People's Congress further reformed the economy and emphasized opening China's economy to the outside world.

1982

February:	The China National Offshore Oil Corporation (CNOOC) was established, and it extended invitations to foreign companies to bid on oil exploration along China's continental shelf, including the Spratly Islands.
May 31:	General Secretary Zhao Ziyang began an official visit to Japan signaling closer relations between the two nations.
September 1:	The 12th CCP Congress opened, and Deng stepped down as

party leader and named Hu Yaobang to replace him. The party outlined the three major tasks for the 1980s as modernization, reunification with Hong Kong and Taiwan, and carrying out an independent foreign policy.

September: British Prime Minister Margaret Thatcher visited Beijing and promised to continue talks regarding the status of Hong Kong. It was agreed that formal talks begin in July 1983.

October 5: China and the USSR opened negotiations to improve bilateral relations, the first such talks in three years.

1983

April: China and India agreed to renew diplomatic ties, which had been broken since border clashes in 1968, as part of Chinese strategy of securing its borders in order to better deal with what it saw as the Soviet threat.

April 10: The USSR and China signed a barter trade agreement, but normalization talks broke off due to Soviet insistence that third-country issues (namely Vietnam) not be a subject of discussion.

July: The first volume of Deng Xiaoping's selected works was published signaling Deng's successful consolidation of power within the party.

July 23: Vietnam accused China of sending raiding parties, and Chinese fishing boats were charged with violating Vietnam's territorial waters.

October: China was admitted into the International Atomic Energy Agency (IAEA). As a member, China had to agree to allow inspection of its nuclear sites to verify that they were being used for peaceful purposes.

December: After almost two years of diplomatic pressure from China and the downgrading of relations between the two countries, the Dutch decided not to sell submarines to Taiwan.

1984

January 10: At the invitation of President Reagan, Chinese Premier Zhao Ziyang made an official visit to the United States. Zhao also made an official visit to Canada.

March 26: China opened fourteen coastal cities to foreign investment and offered such incentives as tax breaks.

April: President Reagan made an official visit to China, during which the two countries agreed to avoid double taxation of U.S. companies operating in China, and signed agreements on the peaceful uses of nuclear energy and on cultural exchange.

September: British and Chinese signed a joint communiqué regarding the status of Hong Kong after 1997. Hong Kong was to retain its economic and social system for at least fifty years after its reversion to Chinese rule.

October 20:	The Central Committee passed its "Decision on the Reform of the Economic Structure," involving a mixed economy maintaining a state planning function that would concentrate on regulation.
December 21:	Soviet Deputy Prime Minister Ivan Arkhipov became the highest ranking Soviet official to visit Beijing since the Sino-Soviet split.

1985

January 7:	The first of many student protests during the year took place on Beijing University campus.
March 10:	The PRC was formally admitted in to the Asian Development Bank (ADB) as the result of a compromise in which Taiwan would remain in the ADB under the name of Taipei, China.
March 27:	The third session of the sixth National People's Congress adopted plans to move the country towards price reform.
May 6:	Deng Xiaoping confirmed plans to reduce the size of the PLA in order to modernize and improve it.
May 18:	A scheduled visit of U.S. warships to the port of Shanghai was canceled because of a dispute over the ships' nuclear capacity.
July 22:	President Li Xiannian visited the United States, the first communist head of state to do so. During the visit, the two countries agreed to an accord on the peaceful use of nuclear technology.
October 2:	A Soviet delegation in China agreed to begin the process of normalization between China and the USSR.
December:	Students marched on Tiananmen denouncing closer Sino-Japanese ties. A few days later, other students rallied in Beijing to support Deng Xiaoping's program for greater opening to the world.

1986

April:	China signed an agreement with Sweden to launch a Swedish satellite in 1991 using China's Long March 2 rocket. The agreement was the first involving the launch of a foreign satellite by the Chinese.
June 9:	Communist party General Secretary Hu Yaobang toured Western Europe in a trip heralded as "a new stage in China's friendly cooperation with Western Europe."
July 28:	Soviet President Mikhail Gorbachev made a speech that signalled a shift in Soviet policy from one of opposition to one of accommodation, compromise, and renewed friendship with China.
September 26:	The first stock market in China opened in Shenyang, Liaoning Province.
October 1:	Labor contracts were introduced in China.

December:	The National People's Congress announced the establishment of the Ministry of Supervision, created to oversee the proper functioning of the government and to handle corruption within the bureaucracy.
December 19:	Student demonstrations began in Shanghai and spread to Beijing and other cities over the next few weeks.

1987

April 13:	China and Portugal signed a joint declaration that Portugal would cede control of Macao to China in 1999, with Macao to retain its economic and political system for at least fifty years thereafter.
September 11:	The Asian Development Bank issued its first loan to China for $100 million.
October:	After months of riots in Lhasa, the Chinese Foreign Ministry announced that Tibet would be closed to foreign tourists for an unspecified amount of time.
November:	Zhao Ziyang was elected general secretary of the Chinese Communist party, replacing Hu Yaobang. Deng Xiaoping resigned from the Central Committee, and Li Peng was approved as acting premier.
November 30:	China and Laos agreed to renew diplomatic relations, which had broken off in 1978 due to Laotian support of Vietnam and Chinese support of Laotian rebels.

1988

January 1:	The State Council published the first set of regulations for private enterprises in China.
January 14:	President of Taiwan Chiang Ching-kuo died in Taipei. Lee Teng-hui was later named Chiang's successor.
March:	Yang Shangkun, vice chairman of the Central Military Commission, announced plans to reform the armed forces.
June 3:	One thousand Beijing students conducted a protest march in front of the Ministry of Public Security to criticize the government's handling of a crime within the city.
November:	China and Mongolia signed a border treaty in Beijing after announcements of Soviet troop cutbacks.

1989

February 10:	New riots broke out in Lhasa, Tibet. The Tibetan Military Region was sent in to quell the disorder.
April 15:	Hu Yaobang, former party general secretary, died.
April 22:	On this official day of mourning for Hu Yaobang, University students gathered in Tiananmen Square to protest against poor student living standards. Hu had been a symbol of support for the student movement since his actions during the 1986 student protests.
May 18:	Soviet President Gorbachev ended his official visit to China,

	and during his stay he formally re-established diplomatic relations.
May 20:	As a result of continued student protests martial law was proclaimed by Li Peng. Despite the proclamation, the students remained.
June 4:	Deng Xiaoping, having exhausted all attempts to persuade the students to leave Tiananmen Square, ordered military troops into Beijing. The Chinese government reported 300 deaths, but non-Chinese sources reported 1,000 deaths in Beijing and 300 deaths in Chengdu.
June 23:	Zhao Ziyang was replaced as general secretary by Jiang Zemin.
November 12:	Deng Xiaoping resigned as chairman of the CCP Central Military Commission, and Jiang Zemin took his place. Deng no long held any formal positions within the party or government.

1990

January 1:	The British government gave full British citizenship to 50,000 select Hong Kong residents, giving them the right to emigrate to Britain. China protested, contending that this action interfered in its internal affairs, since the ruling would remain in effect after 1997.
January 11:	The state of martial law in Beijing was lifted.
April 4:	Leadership changes were made in light of Deng Xiaoping's retirement in November 1989. Jiang Zemin was formally named chairman of the Central Military Commission.
April 23:	Li Peng during a visit to the USSR signed six agreements concerning trade, scientific exchange, border issues, and periodic consultations.
May 1:	Beijing decided to lift martial law in Tibet.
May 25:	Dissident Scientist Fang Lizhi, accused by the Chinese government of inciting the spring 1989 protests, was allowed to leave China.
June 11:	Jiang Zemin asserted China's policy toward Taiwan was to establish "one China, with two systems."
September 22:	Beijing hosted the eleventh Asian Games with a delegation from Taiwan hoping it would help in the country's bid to host the 2000 Olympics.

1991

March 12:	China formally acceded to the Nuclear Non-proliferation Treaty (NPT), which stipulates that member states will not transfer nuclear devices to countries without nuclear arsenals or help such countries achieve nuclear capability.
July 21:	Qian Qichen attended the twenty-fifth ASEAN foreign ministerial meeting in Manila. He insisted that China had no

intention of seeking to fill the "vacuum" that had emerged in Southeast Asia in the wake of the ending of the cold war.

November: The State Council issued a White Paper on China's human rights practices, emphasizing that different interpretations of human rights exist in different countries.

December: China formally recognized eleven states within the Commonwealth of Independent States (CIS).

1992

July: Disagreements continued between British and Chinese officials over the construction of the new Hong Kong airport.
The announcement that American F-16 fighter aircraft were to be sold to Taiwan elicited an angry response from China.

August 8: The Ukrainian trade minister signed an agreement with China on economic and trade cooperation–the first such between China and Ukraine.

August 24: China and South Korea restored diplomatic relations.

August: Chinese Defense Minister Qin Jiwei traveled to Moscow and met with Russian Deputy Minister Pavel Grachev.
Malaysian Minister of Defense Mohamad Najib Razak visited China and had talks with Li Peng on the issue of the Spratly Islands.

September 8: Qian Qichen arrived in Bangkok to attend the fourth APEC ministerial conference.

September 9: Iranian President Hashemi Ali Akbar Rafsanjani arrived in Beijing and spoke with senior Chinese officials.

September: The State Price Administration lifted price controls on 593 items and materials allowing prices to be determined according to market conditions.
Moscow and Taipei announced mutual establishment of economic, cultural, and trade coordinating committees. President Yeltsin reaffirmed Russia's "one China" policy. Spokesperson from the Chinese Foreign Ministry reiterated that they had no objection to the establishment of "pure, non-governmental exchanges" between Taiwan and other countries.
Qian Qichen arrived in Tel Aviv for the first visit to Israel ever made by a Chinese foreign minister.

October 4: President of the African National Congress Nelson Mandela paid his first visit to China.

October 7: Hong Kong Governor Christopher Patten announced plans to increase the voting rights of Hong Kong's citizens before Hong Kong's return to China in 1997. Beijing rejected Patten's plans.

October 20: Hong Kong Governor Patten met with Lu Ping (director of

HKMAO) to discuss the problems affecting relations between British Hong Kong and Chinese authorities.

October 23: Japanese Emperor Akihito and Empress Michiko arrived to begin their six-day visit to China.

October: The fourteenth party congress adopted the principle of a "Socialist market Economic System" for China, thereby supporting Deng Xiaoping's economic reform program.

Relations between Hong Kong and China deteriorated badly in the wake of Hong Kong Governor Patten's first annual address to the Legislative Council that contained significant constitutional proposals relating to elections in 1995.

October 28: Talks between the representatives of the PRC Association for Relations Across the Taiwan Straits (ARATS) and Taiwan's Straits Exchange Foundation brought progress on the issue of document verification and the question of formulating a "one China" principle.

November 30: Li Peng met with his Vietnamese counterpart, Vo Van Kiet, in Hanoi, and later announced that the two sides had agreed to seek a negotiated settlement in the Spratly Island issue.

December 19: Russian President Boris Yeltsin completed a trip to China during which he signed a joint declaration on border questions.

December: American Secretary of Commerce Barbara Franklin traveled to Beijing to attend the seventh session of the Sino-U.S. Joint Commission on Commerce and Trade (JCCT). Chinese sources saw the JCCT talks as a sign of improving trade relations between China and the United States.

1993

January: Lu Ping (director of the State Council's Hong Kong and Macao Affairs) announced again that the basic condition for improved relations with the British and Hong Kong governments was the total withdrawal of Patten's constitutional package.

March: The National People's Congress elected Jiang Zemin to be China's president.

March 1: Sino-American consultations on the resumption of China's contracting status in GATT reopened after being suspended for almost four years.

April 29: The first high-level talks between China and Taiwan ended in Singapore. The two groups signed agreements on trade and communications as well as on logistical issues.

April 4: President Fidel V. Ramos of the Philippines traveled to Beijing for a five-day state visit to China. Jiang Zemin and the Philippines president agreed that in view of the sensitivity of the territorial principles involved, discussions on the Spratly Islands should be set aside.

April 13: A joint Sino-British statement was issued announcing that the two sides had agreed to begin a dialogue on 1994-1995 electoral arrangements for Hong Kong.

April 22: The first round of talks between Chinese and British officials was held.

April: A Thai source quoted Qian Qichen to the effect that China would be prepared to host the next meeting of Cambodia's Supreme National Council at the end of April.

May 15: New Zealand Prime Minister James Bolger arrived in Beijing and met with Chinese leaders and senior officials.

May 16: Vice-Premier Zhu Rongji arrived in Vancouver on the first official visit to Canada since 1989, marking the full resumption of normal relations between China and Canada.

May 19: Israeli Foreign Minister Shimon Peres arrived in Beijing. During talks, Qian Qichen promised that the Chinese government would no longer sell missiles to Iran or Syria.

May 23: Following the twenty-second anniversary of the "liberation" of Tibet by Chinese forces, there were reports that protests and rioting had taken place in Lhasa.

May 28: President Clinton requested authority to renew China's MFN status for another year, but indicated that he would consider new human rights criteria in considering the MFN renewal in 1994.

A Chinese consular office opened in Hanoi.

May: China rejected the report in the *New York Times* that suggested that China was shipping M-11 missiles to Pakistan. Qian Qichen traveled to Seoul for talks with his counterpart, Han Sung-chu. Talks focused on a shipping agreement and the North Korean nuclear issue, in which the two sides agreed to increase their cooperation.

June 2: Head of State and Chairman of the Supreme Soviet of the Republic of Georgia Eduard Shevardnadze arrived in Beijing at the invitation of Jiang Zemin. The two signed a joint declaration setting down the basic principles that should guide their relations.

June 23: Australian Prime Minister Paul Keating began an official visit to China.

June: A Chinese Foreign Ministry spokesman criticized the attempt to introduce a bill to the U.S. Congress that sought to attach conditions to China's MFN trading status.

July 29: In his address to ASEAN foreign ministers, Qian Qichen reaffirmed his government's determination to pursue a peaceful foreign policy.

August 6:	A report showed that China had become South Korea's third-biggest trading partner.
August 8:	Beijing lodged a strong protest accusing Washington of harassing a Chinese ship, the Yinhe. Washington said the ship was believed to be carrying chemical weapons bound for Iran.
August 23:	He Zhenliang (vice-minister for the State Physical Culture and Sports Commission), the most senior official to travel from the Chinese mainland to Taiwan since 1949, arrived in Taipei.
August 24:	The United States announced it would impose on China the sanctions required by U.S. law because of China's sale of missile technology to Pakistan. The Chinese government lodged a strong protest.
	The first round of territorial border talks between Chinese and Vietnamese officials took place in Beijing for five days.
September 4:	A U.S.-observed inspection of the Chinese ship the Yinhe revealed no chemical weapons ingredients on board. The Chinese filed another strong protest after the search.
September 23:	The International Olympics Committee rejected Beijing's bid for the 2000 Olympics in favor of the bid of Sydney, Australia.
September 25:	National Security Advisor Anthony Lake met China's ambassador to the United States, Li Daoyu, to initiate efforts to restore high-level U.S.-China contacts across the board.
October 1:	Qian Qichen's talk with British Foreign Secretary Douglas Hurd over Hong Kong met with no positive results.
October 5:	China conducted an underground nuclear test, despite a U.S. call in July for an informal ban on such testing.
October 10:	Israeli Prime Minister Yitzhaq Rabin visited China and with Li Peng pledged their determination to promote the development of friendly and cooperative relations.
October 12:	Assistant Secretary of State for Human Rights John Shattuck visited Beijing to initiate a dialogue on human rights issues.
October 15:	Secretary of Agriculture Mike Espy went to Beijing to discuss China's purchases of U.S. grains, especially wheat.
October 22:	The World Bank issued an "Economic Note" in support of strong Chinese anti-inflationary measures begun in July 1993.
November 1:	Assistant Secretary of Defense Charles Freeman began two days of talks in Beijing; they were the highest level military talks between the two countries since the Tiananmen Square incident in 1989.
November 3:	U.S.-China military talks in Beijing concluded with an agreement to a "modest" agenda of future dialogue and professional exchanges on such topics as international peacekeeping operations and conversion of defense industries to civilian use.

November 12:   It was reported that foreign-funded enterprises now account for thirty-five percent of China's burgeoning foreign trade.

November 14:   At a Chinese party plenary meeting, it was decided to push forward greater growth and reform and to moderate the July 1993 plan to dampen growth and inflation.

November 17:   Two hundred and seventy members of the House of Representatives signed a letter to President Clinton expressing their concern over China's lack of progress in meeting human rights objectives.

November 18:   Secretary of State Christopher announced the United States was dropping its opposition to the sale of $8 million Cray supercomputer to China.

November: Jiang Zemin went to the United States to attend an Asia Pacific Economic Cooperation (APEC) meeting in Seattle.

December 9:   The International Maritime Bureau reportedly certified nearly fifty cases in 1993 of alleged piracy by Chinese official ships against foreign vessels in waters off the South China coast.

December 15:   The World Bank was reported to have found China to have been the largest recipient of foreign funds (amounting to $27 billion) in 1993.

December 20:   A press report about a draft Chinese "Eugenics" law prompted negative comment in the West.

December 21:   The city of Beijing imposed price controls on rice, pork, and other staple foods–a sign of official concern over rising inflation.

December 26:   The one-hundreth anniversary of Mao Zedong's birth was celebrated throughout China.

1994

January 6:   The United States announced it would slash China's textile quotas by twenty-five to thirty percent in retaliation for China's illegal textile shipments.

January 12:   A joint communiqué issued by the French and Chinese confirmed France's recognition of the PRC as the sole legal government of China and recognized Taiwan as an integral part of Chinese territory.

January 17:   Norodom Ranariddh and Hun Sen (respectively, first and second prime ministers of Cambodia) began a five-day official visit to China–the first such visit to take place since the re-establishment of peace in Cambodia.

January 24:   Coincident with senior-level meetings with U.S. officials in January (Secretary Christopher in Paris; Secretary Bentsen in Beijing; congressional-delegated Gephardt and Johnston in Beijing), Chinese leaders released some dissidents, began talks

	on opening their prisons to Red Cross inspections, and agreed to discuss the cases of 235 prisoners with U.S. officials.
January:	A report stated that the value of Sino-Russian trade in 1993 was US$7.68 billion, an increase of thirty percent on the level of the previous year.

Tsutomu Hata, Japan's foreign minister and deputy-prime minister, told Qian Qichen that Japan expected greater "transparency" in China's military affairs and an active role in resolving the North Korean nuclear issue.

Lloyd Bentsen (U.S. secretary of the treasury) was in Beijing to consult senior Chinese government officials and to co-chair the eighth meeting of the Sino-U.S. Joint Economic Commission (JEC).

February 9: Deng Xiaoping appeared on television for the first time in a year.

February 20: Asia Watch issued a report on over 1,000 cases of political/religious imprisonment in China.

February 24: China's Foreign Ministry pledged to replace Hong Kong's democratic institutions after China takes power in 1997.

February: Vice-Premier Zhu Rongji made an official good will visit to Japan.

March 10: Li Peng told the National People's Congress that China should strive for nine percent growth in 1994, in contrast with the 13.4 percent growth rate of 1993. He noted that foreign trade grew eighteen percent in 1993, to $195.8 billion.

The annual session of the People's Congress and the concurrent March 10-13 visit of Secretary of State Christopher saw a crackdown on recently active political dissidents, seriously complicating U.S. relations with China.

March 11: Secretary of State Warren Christopher arrived in Beijing for three days of talks about human rights and China's MFN status.

March 23: In an internal government report likely to prompt heightened leadership concern over social-political stability, the Academy of Social Sciences warned of a potentially explosive mix of inflation, rural and urban labor unrest, and ethnic discord during the period ahead.

March: Prime Minister Hosakawa traveled to Beijing for more talks with Chinese leaders.

April 9: Both the *New York Times* and the *Economist* reported growing official concern in Beijing and other cities, and in rural areas, over signs of popular discontent (e.g., strikes, demonstrations) and over a reported increase in active political dissidents.

April 10: Sino-Russian consultations on bilateral and international

	questions were conducted by Qian Qichen and Alexander Panov, the Russian vice-foreign minister, in Beijing for three days.
May 26:	President Clinton announced that he was recommending the renewal of China's MFN status, "de-linking" it from China's human rights record, and imposing an embargo on arms imports from China.
	President Clinton's extension of MFN tariff treatment for Chinese exports was welcomed by Chinese and foreign officials and entrepreneurs in China.
May 27:	The Chinese Foreign Ministry welcomes the American decision to extend China's MFN status for 1994-1995 and to break the link between the annual MFN review process and human rights issues.
May 28:	The arms import embargo against China went into effect.
May:	Vice-Foreign Minister Tian Zengpei protested the U.S. Foreign Relations Act (passed by the U.S. Congress in April 28) for referring to Tibet as a "country" and for what the minister saw as a deliberate attempt to create "one China, one Taiwan."
June 10:	China conducted an underground nuclear weapons test. The United States expressed regret.
June:	In response to North Korea's refusal to allow full IAEA inspection of its nuclear facilities, Qian Qichen spoke of China's support for the de-nuclearization of the Korean Peninsula and the maintenance of peace and stability throughout the region. He also urged North Korea to seek a settlement on the basis of consultation.
August 9:	The House passed legislation extending MFN to China and de-linking it from human rights, and rejected a bill by Representative Pelosi to limit the extension of MFN to China.
August 17:	Secretary of Defense Perry met with a visiting deputy chief of staff of the Chinese Army.
August 26:	A delegation of more than fifty senior executives, headed by U.S. Secretary of Commerce Ron Brown, visited China. Wu Yi, the minister of foreign trade and economic cooperation, in a meeting with Brown insisted that China deserved to enjoy the rights of full membership of both GATT and the WTO.
September 2:	Secretary of Commerce Brown left China after a visit marked by the signing of over $5 billion worth of contracts involving U.S. business.
September 7:	The Clinton administration disclosed a Taiwan policy review that promised modestly increased contacts with Taiwan. Beijing issued an official protest.

September:	A PRC Foreign Ministry spokesman warned Japan that "serious political trouble" would follow if Taiwan president Lee Teng-hui attended the opening ceremony of the Asian Games in Hiroshima.
	Liu Huaqiu, Chinese vice-foreign minister, protested Washington's decision to "upgrade" its relations with Taiwan. The act was perceived by the Chinese as a violation of the principles contained in the three Sino-American joint communiqués.
	A Chinese delegation attended the 38th conference of the International Atomic Energy Agency (IAEA) in Vienna and signed the IAEA Convention on Nuclear Safety.
October 4:	The United States and China signed an agreement allowing the export of U.S. high technology satellites to China that were halted as an August 23, 1993, sanction against Beijing's secret transfer of missile components and technology to Pakistan. China agreed that once the sanctions are waived, it will abide by the rules of the International Missile Technology Control Regime (MTCR).
	China agreed to work toward a ban on producing fissile material for nuclear weapons.
October 7:	China conducted a nuclear weapons test, its second in 1994.
October 19:	Defense Secretary Perry ended four day of talks in Beijing.
October 31:	Li Peng visited South Korea–the first such visit ever to have been undertaken by a Chinese prime minister. In talks with South Korean President Kim Young-sam, Li and Kim hailed the recent nuclear agreement reached by the United States and the DPRK, and undertook to assist in its implementation.
October:	China made clear its intention to dissolve the political framework that would exist in Hong Kong on the eve of the retrocession of sovereignty.
	A Chinese Foreign Ministry spokesman expressed concern about Vietnamese oil-prospecting activities in waters off the Spratly Islands.
	A meeting was held in Singapore between two state-run oil companies from the PRC and Taiwan on joint exploration in the East China and South China Seas.
November 3:	Qian Qichen met with President Clinton and delivered a letter from Jiang Zemin that expressed satisfaction with the recent development of bilateral relations.
November 4:	Following thirty months of negotiations, China and Britain signed an agreement on a new airport at Chek Lap Kok.
November 11:	Senior Chinese officials, including Jiang Zemin, Qian Qichen, and Wu Yi, attended the sixth meeting of the Asia-Pacific

Economic Cooperation (APEC) Forum in Jakarta. Qian expressed China's support of the long-term goal of trade and investment liberalization for the Asia-Pacific region.

November 14: President Clinton held an official meeting with China's President Jiang Zemin at the APEC leaders' meeting in Indonesia.

November: A report stated that Taiwan had become China's second-largest source of foreign investment after Hong Kong.

December 4: Qian and Christopher signed two joint declarations, one on the cessation of production of fission materials used in the production of nuclear weapons, the other relating to the proliferation of guided missiles.

December 7: *Los Angeles Times* reported that China had threatened to end commercial agreements with the United States if the Clinton administration did not acquiesce in China's entry into GATT by year's end.

December 14: Press reports said Beijing had canceled Secretary Pena's planned visit to China on account of his visit to Taiwan earlier in the month.

December: William Perry traveled to Beijing at the head of a fifty-strong military delegation for a four-day official visit, marking the resumption of high-level military relations between the two countries.

1995

January 12: Deng Xiaoping's daughter told the *New York Times* that the Chinese leader's health had declined significantly in recent months.

January 15: Assistant Secretary Shattuck left Beijing after fruitless talks on human rights.

February 1: The U.S. trade deficit with China grew in 1994 to almost $30 billion on the basis of total annual trade of about $39 billion.

February 4: The United States imposed trade sanctions worth over $1 billion because of an intellectual property rights dispute with China; China immediately announced comparable sanctions against the United States.

February 9: The *Wall Street Journal* reported that China had purchased four modern diesel-powered submarines from Russia in a deal worth $1 billion.

February 16: A senior Chinese official briefed Western reporters on China's strong opposition to a U.S.-backed theater missile defense system in Asia.

February 20: Energy Secretary O'Leary oversaw the signing of agreements valued at $2 billion during a visit to China.

February 22: China protested U.S. support for a UN resolution critical of Chinese human rights conditions.

February 26:	A U.S.-Chinese agreement on intellectual property rights disputes was signed, averting a U.S.-China trade conflict threatening $2 billion in annual trade.
March 5:	Premier Li Peng told the National People's Congress that Beijing would focus in 1995 on cooling economic growth from the 1994 level of 11.8 percent to a level of eight percent to nine percent in 1995, and on reducing inflation from the level of 21.7 percent in 1994 to a level of fifteen percent in 1995.
March 12:	The United States and China signed an eight-point agreement to assist China's entry into the World Trade Organization; China agreed to open its markets to U.S. farm products and hold talks on allowing in more U.S. telecommunications and insurance services. Separately, China agreed to conduct no more than eleven commercial-satellite launches over the next seven years and promised not to undercut Western bids for launches by more than fifteen percent.
March 22:	A U.S. warship visited China for the first time in six years.
March 27:	Clinton administration efforts to come up with a code of conduct for U.S. firms doing business in China and elsewhere were criticized by congressional and other U.S. human rights advocates.
March 29:	Press reports noted possible signs of an incipient power struggle in Beijing, including a spate of attacks against high-level official corruption, overt dissent in China's National People's Congress, and prominent activity promoting leaders thought earlier to have been retired from politics.
April 10:	Chen Yun, China's most senior statesman after Deng Xiaoping and a frequent critic of Deng's free-wheeling market reforms, died.
April 27:	Beijing's communist party secretary, a Politburo member, was forced to resign as a result of a corruption scandal.
May 10:	The Clinton administration publicly expressed concerns about any disruption of maritime activity caused by the territorial dispute in the South China Sea.
May 22:	President Clinton agreed to allow Taiwan's president to make a private visit to the United States. Beijing protested strongly.
May 26:	China postponed the planned visit of its defense minister to the United States.
May 30:	China reportedly tested a newly developed road mobile ICBM with a range capable of hitting targets throughout Europe and the western United States.
June 2:	President Clinton decided to renew MFN tariff treatment for China for another year.
June 4:	The anniversary of the Tiananmen massacre passed quietly in Beijing amid tight security measures.

June 4:   The anniversary of the Tiananmen massacre passed quietly in
            Beijing amid tight security measures.
June 16:   China withdrew its ambassador from the United States in
            protest over Taiwan's president's visit to the United States.

Bibliography

Adie, Ian W. A. C., 1993. "China and the 'Springtime of Nations': Next Steps?" *International Relations*, 11 (August): 435-449.

After Tiananmen Square: Challenges for the Chinese-American Relationship. 1990. Washington: Brassey's, p. 124.

Ai, Wei, 1990. "Economic and Trade Relations Between the United States and Mainland China in the Past Decade." *Issues & Studies*, 26 (April): 63-82.

"America's China Policy." 1991. *Proceedings of the Academy of Political Science,* 38 (21): 149-189.

Anwar, Dewi Fortuna, 1990. "Indonesia's Relations with China and Japan: Images, Perception and Realities." *Contemporary Southeast Asia* 12 (December): 225-265.

Appleton, Jack and Bruce Sun, 1994. "A Theory of Chinese Middle Management." *Journal of Contemporary China*, (spring): 78-87.

Armstrong, Wil. 1989. "The Development of Commercial Law for Foreign Investment in China." *Houston Journal of International Law*, 12 (fall): 55-75.

Arnold, Walter. 1989. "Political and Economic influences in Japan's Relations with China Since 1978." *Millennium*, 18 (winter): 415-434.

Ash, Robert F. 1992. "The Agricultural Sector in China: Performance and Policy Dilemmas during the 1990s." *China Quarterly*, 131 (September): 545-576.

"Asia in the Twenty-First Century: JILP Annual Symposium." 1992. *New York University Journal of International Law and Politics,* 24 (spring).

Bachman, David M. 1991. *Bureaucracy, Economy, and Leadership in China: the Institutional Origins of the Great Leap Forward.* Cambridge, New York. p. 262.

————. 1992. "Fourteenth Congress of the Chinese Communist Party." *Asia Society.*

————. 1994. *Influencing China.* Washington, National Bureau of Asian Research, p. 13.

Bailey, S. F. 1991. "Hong Kong and China: A Difficult Combination." *Contemporary Review*, 258 (March): 113-119.

Baldinger, Pamela. 1992. "The Birth of Greater China." *China Business Review*, 19 (May-June): 13-15, 17-20, 22.

Barnathan, Joyce. 1994. "China: Is Prosperity Creating a Freer Society?" *Business Week,* 3375 (June 6): 94, 96-99, 102.

Barnathan, Joyce and Pete Engardio. 1993. "China: The Emerging Economic Powerhouse of the 21st Century." *Business Week*, 3312 (May 17): 54-60, 64, 68-69.

Barnett, A. Doak. 1977. *China and the Major Powers in East Asia.* Washington, Brookings.

Baum, Julian. 1993. "Taiwan: Divided Nations." *Far Eastern Economic Review*, 156 (September 16): 10-11.

Bean, R. Mark. 1990. *Cooperative Security in Northeast Asia.* Washington, National Defense University, p. 198.

"Beijing Takes Cautious Stance on Russian Political Crisis." 1993. *FBIS Trends,* (October 6): 25-40.

"Beijing Takes More Optimistic View of Sino-U.S. Ties." 1993. *FBIS Trends,* (October 27): 3-5.

Beller, Richard D. 1994. " Analyzing the Relationship Between International Law and International Politics in China's and Vietnam's Territorial Dispute over the Spratly Islands." *Texas International Law Journal,* 29 (spring): 293-320.

Berkeley, Gerald W. 1992. "China as a Member of the GATT: Historical and Contemporary Issues." *Asian Profile,* 20 (August): 269-280.

Bert, Wayne. 1990. "Chinese Policy Toward Democratization Movements: Burma and the Philippines." *Asian Survey,* 30 (November): 1066-1083.

Betts, Richard K. 1993-1994. "Wealth, Power, and Instability: East Asia and the United States After the Cold War." *International Security,* 18 (winter): 34-77.

Bitzinger, Richard A. 1992. "Arms to go: Chinese Arms Sales to the Third World." *International Security,* 17 (fall): 84-111.

———. 1991. *Chinese Arms Production and Sales to the Third World.* Santa Monica: Rand Corporation, p. 46.

Bobrow, Davis B. 1989. "The Continuing Challenge: Balancing Autonomy and Interdependence." *Issues & Studies,* 25 (April): 36-56.

Bohnet, Armin; Hong, Zhong, and Frank Muller. 1993. "China's Open-Door Policy and its Significance for Transformation of the Economic System." *Intereconomics,* 28 (July-August): 191-197.

Brahm, Laurence J. 1992. "The Emergence of China's Securities Markets." *Asia Money & Finance,* 3 (February): 39-41.

Brick, Andrew B. 1991. "The Asian Giants: Neighborly Ambivalence." *Global Affairs,* 6 (fall): 70-87.

———. 1992. "Chinese Water Torture: Subversion Through Development." Washington, Heritage Foundation, p. 5.

Brick, Andrew B., ed. 1991. *America's China Policy and the Role of the Congress, the Press, and the Private Sector.* Heritage Foundation, p. 42.

Brockway, George P. 1994. "The Dismal Science: Playing the China Card." *New Leader,* 77 (July 4-18): 11-12.

Brodsgaard, Kjeld Erik. 1991. "China's Political Economy in the Nineties." *China Report,* 27 (July-September): 177-196.

Brown, David G. 1986. *Partnership with China: Sino-Foreign Joint Ventures in Historical Perspective.* Boulder, Westview Press, p. 175.

———. 1991. "Security Issues in Southeast Asia." *Proceedings of the Academy of Political Science,* pp. 120-130.

Building Sino-American Relations: An Analysis for the 1990s. 1991. New York: Paragon House.

Bullard, Monte R. 1993. "U.S.-China Relations: The Strategic Calculus." *Parameters*, 23 (summer): 86-95.

Bush, Richard. 1993. "Clinton and China: Scenarios for the Future." *China Business Review*, 20 (January-February): 16-20.

Cable, Vincent and Peter Ferdinand. 1994. "China as an Economic Giant: Threat of Opportunity?" *International Affairs,* 70 (April): 243-261.

Cai, Wenguo. 1992. "China's GATT Membership: Selected Legal and Political Issues." *Journal of World Trade,* 26 (February): 33-61.

Calabrese, John. 1990 "From Flyswatters to Silkworms: The Evolution of China's Role in West Asia." *Asian Survey*, 30 (September): 862-876.

Carlson, Paul. 1988. "U.S. Trade Policy and the Hong Kong Agreement." *Journal of Legislation*, 15 (1): 59-72.

Chanda, Nayan and Rigoberto Tiglao. 1995. "Territorial Imperative." *Far Eastern Economic Review*, 158 (February 23): 14-16.

Chang, Maria Hsia. 1992. "Taiwan and the Mainland: A Shifting Competition." *Global Affairs,* 7 (summer): 14-28.

Chang, Pao-Min. 1990. "A New Scramble for the South China Sea Islands." *Contemporary Southeast Asia*, 12 (June): 20-39.

Chang, Teh-Kuang. 1991. "China's Claim of Sovereignty Over Spratly and Paracel Islands: A Historical and Legal Perspective." *Case Western Reserve Journal of International Law*, 23 (summer): 399-420.

"The Changing World Order." 1990. *Survival*, 32 (March-April): 99-172.

Chen, Frederick Yen-Ching. 1990. "Reconsidering U.S. Policy Toward China in the Post-Tiananmen Era." *International Review,* 12 (summer): 41-43.

Chen, Jie. 1994. "China's Spratly Policy." *Asian Survey*, 34 (October): 893-903.

———. 1992. *Ideology in U.S. Foreign Policy: Case Studies in U.S. China Policy.* Westport, Conn.: Praeger.

Chen, Kathy. 1994. "Soldiers of Fortune: Chinese Army Fashions Major Role for Itself as a Business Empire-Skirting Taxes and Tariffs, Military-Run Companies Turn Power into Profit." *Wall Street Journal,* (May 24): A1, A9.

Chen, Qimao. 1993. "New Approaches in China's Foreign Policy." *Asian Survey*, 33 (March).

Chen, Wen-Tsung. 1990. "Worried About 1999." *Free China Review*, 40 (March): 54-61.

Cheng, Chu-yuan. 1990. "Peking's Economic Reform and Open-Door Policy after Tienanmen Incident." *Issues & Studies*, 26 (October): 43-64.

Cheung, Tai Ming. 1988. "Disarmament and Development in China: The Relationship Between National Defense and Economic Development." *Asian Survey*, 28 (July): 757-774.

Chiang, Chen-ch'ang. 1989. "The Social Aftermaths of Mainland China's Economic Reform." *Issues & Studies*, 25 (February): 26-46.

"China, 1991." 1991. *Current History*, 90 (September).

"China." 1993. *Current History*, 92 (September).

"China." 1994. *Current History*, 93 (September).

"The China Challenge: American Policies in East Asia." 1991. New York, Academy of Political Science.

"China: The Coming Changes." 1991. *American Enterprise*, 2 (January-February): 18-25.

"China and Japan: History, Trends and Prospects." 1990. *China Quarterly*, 124 (December).

China in the Near Term; Under Secretary of Defense (Policy) 1994 Summer Study; 1-10 August 1994, Newport, Rhode Island. 1994. Washington: U.S. Department of Defense, p. 72.

"China in Transformation." 1993. *Daedalus* (spring).

"China in Turmoil: Future is Uncertain." 1989. *World Focus*, 10 (August).

"China Policy: Fostering U.S. Competitiveness and the Bilateral Relationship." 1993. *China Business Review*, 20 (January-February): 10-15.

Chiu, Hungdah. 1991. "Recent Chinese Communist Policy Toward Taiwan and the Prospect for Unification." *Issues & Studies,* 27 (January): 13-30.

Chou, David S. 1990. "The Prospects for Peking-Seoul Relations: A Taiwan Perspective." Issues & Studies, 26 September): 43-57.

Chung, Jae Ho. 1990. "Sino-South Korean Economic Cooperation: An Analysis of Domestic and Foreign Entanglements." *Journal of Northeast Asian Studies*, 9 (summer): 59-79.

Cline, Ray S. 1992. *Foreign Policy Failures in China, Cuba, and Nicaragua: A Paradigm.* Washington, U.S. Global Strategy Council.

———. 1989. "New realities for America's China Policy." *Strategic Review*, 17 (fall): 31-35.

Cloughy, B. W. 1987. "Sino-Indian Border: Talks Scheduled by Conflict Possible." *Pacific Defence Reporter*, p. 38. Kunyung: Victoria, Australia.

Conable, Barber and David M. Lampton. 1992-1993. "China: The Coming Power." *Foreign Affairs* (winter).

Copper, John Franklin. 1992. *China Diplomacy: The Washington-Taipei-Beijing Triangle.* Boulder, Colo.: Westview Press.

Cormac, Susan Mac. 1993. "Eyeing the GATT." *China Business Review*, 20 (March-April): 34-38.

Cossa, Ralph. 1994. "China and Northeast Asia: What Lies Ahead?" *Pacific Forum*, CSIS (February).

Costa, Christopher K. 1993. "One Country-Two Foreign Policies: United States Relations With Hong Kong After July 1, 1997." *Villanova Law Review*, 38 (3): 825-870.

Craddock, Percy. 1994. "China, Britain and Hong Kong: Policy in a Cul-de-Sac." *World Today*, 50 (May): 92-96.

Crane, George T. 1993. "China and Taiwan: Not Yet 'Greater China.'" *International Affairs* (London), 69 (October): 705-723.

Cranford, John R. 1990. "Trade and Foreign Policy: The Ties that Bind." *Congressional Quarterly Weekly Report* (June 9): 1773, 1778.

Deadlock over China Policy: Is a New Consensus Possible? Report of the Thirty-Second Strategy for Peace, U.S. Foreign Policy Conference. 1991. Muscatine, Iowa, Stanley Foundation, p. 20.

Delfs, Robert and Michael Vatikiotis. "Burying the Past: China and Indonesia Resume Ties After 23 Years." *Far Eastern Economic Review*, 149 (July 12): 10-11.

Deliusin, Lev. 1991. "The Influence of China's Domestic Policy on its Foreign Policy." *Proceedings on the Academy of Political Science*, 38 (2): 53-62.

Deng, Yong. 1992. "Sino-Thai Relations: From Strategic Co-operation to Economic Diplomacy." *Contemporary Southeast Asia*, 13 (March): 360-374.

Ding, Arthur S. 1991. "Peking's Foreign Policy in the Changing World." *Issues & Studies*, 27 (May): 78-102.

Dittmer, Lowel, and Samuel Kim. 1993. *China's Quest for National Identity.* Cornell University Press.

Drisnan, Robert F. and Teresa Kuo. 1992. "The 1991 Battle for Human Rights in China." *Human Rights Quarterly*, 14 (February): 21-42.

Dreyer, June Teufel. 1991. "U.S.-China Military Relations: Sanctions or Rapprochement?" *In Depth*, 1 (spring): 8-24.

Dreyer, June Teufel , ed. 1989. *Chinese Defense and Foreign Policy.* Paragon House.

Dumbaugh, Kerry. "China Policy Dilemmas." 1992. *CRS Review*, 13 (January): 8.

——. 1992. "The Making of China Policy Since Tiananmen." China Business Review, 19 (January-February): 16-19.

Eikenberry, Karl W. 1995. "Does China Threaten Asia-Pacific Regional Stability?" *Parameters*, 25 (spring): 82-103.

Elliott, Kimberly and Gary C. Hugbauer. 1994. "China Sanctions: Would they Work?" *International Economic Insights*, 5 (May-June): 31-32.

Fairbank, John King. 1966. *China Perceived.* Harvard Universitiy Press, p. 56.

——. 1979. *The United States and China.* Harvard University Press, pp. 158-161.

Farley, Maggie. "China Makes Itself at Home in Hong Kong." 1995. *Los Angeles Times,* (May 2): C1, C4, C5.

Feinerman, James V. 1992. "The Quest for GATT Membership: Will Taiwan be Allowed to Enter Before China?" *China Business Review*, 19 (May-June): 24-27.

Feldman, Harvey J. 1991. "Taiwan and future Sino-American Relations." *In Depth*, 1 (spring): 216-229.

Fewsmith, Joseph. 1994. *Dilemmas of Reform in China: Political Conflict and Economic Debate*. M.E. Sharpe.

Fifoot, Paul. 1994. "One Country, Two Systems--Mark II: From Hong Kong to Macao." *International Relations*, 12 (April): 25-58.

Floum, Joshua R. 1994. "Counterfeiting in the People's Republic of China: The Perspective of the 'Foreign' Intellectual Property Holder." *Journal of World Trade*, 28 (October): 35-59.

Foot, Rosemary. 1995. *The Practice of Power: American Relations with China Since 1949*. Oxford: Clarendon Press.

Funabashi, Yoichi. 1994. *Emerging China in a World of Interdependence*. Trilateral Commission.

Gallagher, Joshua P. 1987. "China's Military Industrial Complex." *Asian Survey*, 27 (September): 991-1002.

Gao, Shiguo. 1994. "The South China Sea: From Conflict to Cooperation?" Ocean Development and International Law, 25 (July-September): 345-359.

Gardner, Hall. 1990. "China and the World After Tiananmen Square." *SAIS Review*, 10 (winter-spring): 133-147.

Garver, John W. 1991. "China-India Rivalry in Nepal: The Clash Over Chinese Arms Sales." *Asian Survey*, 31 (October): 956-975.

------. 1992. "China's Push Through the South China Sea: The Interaction of Bureaucratic and National Interests." *China Quarterly*, 132 (December): 999-1028.

------. 1993. *Foreign Relations of the People's Republic of China*. Prentice Hall.

------. 1991. "The Indian Factor in Recent Sino-Soviet Relations." *China Quarterly*, 125 (March): 55-85.

Gelber, Harry G. 1990. "China's New Economic and Strategic Uncertainties and the Security Prospects." *Asian Survey*, 30 (July): 646-668.

Gerstenzang, James and Jim Mann. 1992. "China Gets Chilly Welcome Back into World Arena." *Los Angeles Times*, (February 2): A3, A7.

Gibert, Stephen P. 1989. "Safeguarding Taiwan's Security." *Comparative Strategy*, 8 (4): 425-446.

Gill, R. Bates. 1991. "China Looks to Thailand: Exporting Arms, Exporting Influence." Asian Survey, 31 (June): 526-539.

Giunta, Tara Kalagher and Lily H. Shang. 1993-1994. "Ownership of Information in a Global Economy." *George Washington Journal of International Law and Economics*, 27 (2-3): 327-358.

Glaser, Bonnie S. 1993. "China's Security Perceptions: Interests and Ambitions." *Asian Survey*, 33 (March).

Godwin, Paul and John Schulz. 1993. "Arming the Dragon for the 21st Century." *Arms Control Today* (December).

Goldberg, Morton David and Jesse M. Feder. 1991. "China's Intellectual Property Legislation: New Copyright Regulations Leave Much to be Desired." *China Business Review*, 18 (September-October): 8-11.

Goldman, Marshall I. and Merle Goldman. 1989. "When Communism's Reformers Meet." *World Monitor*, 2 (May): 44-47.

Goldstein, Steven M. 1992. *China at the Crossroads: Reform after Tiananmen.* Ithaca, NY: Foreign Policy Association, p. 127.

Gong, Gerrit W. 1994. "China's Fourth Revolution." *Washington Quarterly*, 17 (winter): 29-43.

———. 1990. "U.S.-China Relations in the Post-Deng Era." *World & I*, 5 (August): 143-149.

Goodlad, Alastair. 1994. "Hong Kong: Britain's Legacy, China's Inheritance." *World Today*, 50 (June): 112-115.

Goodman, David S. G., and Gerald Segal, eds. 1994. *China Deconstructs: Politics, Trade and Regionalism.* London; New York, Routledge, Grant.

Grant, Richard L. 1994. "China and its Asian Neighbors: Looking toward the Twenty-First Century." *Washington Quarterly*, 17 (winter): 59-69.

"Greater China." 1993. *China Quarterly*, 136 (December): 653-948.

Gregor, A. James. 1991. "'Links' and 'Exchanges': The Mainland Policy of the ROC." *Global Affairs*, 6 (winter): 54-73.

Guo, Simian. 1991. *China's Peripheral Situation in the 1990s.* Cologne, Bundesinstitut fur Ostwissenschaftliche und Internationale Studien, p. 37.

Gurtov, Melvin and Byong-woo Hwang. 1980. *China Under Threat*, p. 118. Johns Hopkins University Press.

Han, Guojian. 1993. "ROK Traders Pour into China." *Beijing Review*, 36 (June 21-27): 23-25.

Han, Yong-Sup. 1994. "China's Leverages Over North Korea." *Korea & World Affairs*, 18 (summer): 233-249.

Han, Xiaoxing. 1993. "Sino-Israeli Relations." *Journal of Palestine Studies*, 22 (winter): 62-77.

Handke, Werner. 1989. "China is Different: Economic Reform-Democracy-Opening." *Aussenpolitik*, 40 (2): 129-138.

Hao, Yufan and Guocang Huan. 1989. *The Chinese View of the World.* Pantheon.

Harding, Harry. 1994. *Beyond MFN: A Comprehensive American Policy Toward China.* Washington, National Bureau of Asian Research, p. 12.

———. 1983. "Change and Continuity in Chinese Foreign Policy." *Problems of Communism*, Washington: pp. 17-18.

———. 1984. *China's Foreign Relations in the 1980's.* Yale.

———. 1990. *China in the 1990s: Prospects for Internal Change.* National Bureau of Asian and Soviet Research.

———. 1992. *A Fragile Relationship: The United States and China Since 1972.* Washington: Brookings Institution.

——. 1992. "Neither Friend Nor Foe: A China Policy for the Nineties." *Brookings Review*, 10 (2): 6-11.

——. 1994. "On the Four Great Relationships: The Prospects for China." *Survival* (summer).

Harland, Bryce. 1994. "For a Strong China." *Foreign Policy*, 94 (spring): 48-52.

Harris, Lillian Craig. 1993. "Xinjiang, Central Asia and the Implications for China's Policy in the Islamic World." *China Quarterly*, 133 (March): 111-129.

He, Liping. 1991. "The Economic Foundation of China's Foreign Policy." *Cambridge Review of International Affairs*, 5 (spring): 32-39.

Heinzig, Dieter. 1989. "China Between the Superpowers." *Asian Thought and Society*, 14 (January): 47-52.

Hermann-Pillath, Carsten. 1994. "Growth and the Claim to Big-Power Status in China." *Aussenpolitik*, 45 (4): 374-382.

Hickey, Dennis Van Vranken. 1991. "Will Inter-China trade change Taiwan or the Mainland?" *Orbis*, 35 (fall): 517-531.

Hood, Steven J. 1990. "Beijing's Cambodia Gamble and the Prospects for Peace in Indochina: The Khmer Rouge or Sihanouk?" *Asian Survey*, 30 (October): 977-991.

Hornik, Richard. 1994. "Bursting China's Bubble." *Foreign Affairs*, May-June.

Hu, Weixing. 1993. "Beijing's New Thinking on Security Strategy." *Journal of Contemporary China*, 3 (summer): 50-65.

Hua, Di. 1992. *Recent Developments in China's Domestic and Foreign Affairs.* Canberra, Strategic and Defense Studies Centre, Australian National University, p. 24.

Huan, Guocang. 1992. "Taipei-Beijing Relations." *World Policy Journal*, 9 (summer): 563-579.

Huang, Chih-lien. 1991. "China's Foreign Policy: Onto the Twenty-First Century." *China Report*, 27 (October-December): 299-308.

Humble, Ronald D. 1992. "Science, Technology and China's Defence Industrial Base." *Jane's Intelligence Review*, 4 (January): 3-11.

Hunt, Michael. 1984. "Chinese Foreign Relations in Historical Perspective," in Harry Harding, ed., *China's Foreign Relations in the 1980s*, pp. 6-7. Yale.

"It's Already 1997 in Hong Kong." 1993. *Economist*, 329 (December 17): 36-38.

Jia, Qingguo. 1992. "Changing Relations Across the Taiwan Strait: Beijing's Perceptions." *Asian Survey*, 32 (March): 277-289.

——. 1994. "Toward the Center: Implications of Integration and Democratization for Taiwan's Mainland Policy." *Journal of Northeast Asian Studies*, 13 (spring): 49-63.

Japan Forum on International Relations. 1995. "The Policy Recommendations on the Future of China in the Context of Asian Security." *The Forum*, Tokyo. 2 volumes.

Jayawickrama, Hihal. 1991. "Hong Kong: The Gathering Storm." *Bulletin of Peace Proposals*, 22 (June): 157-174.

Joffe, Ellis. 1991. *China After the Gulf War.* Taiwan, Sun Yat-Sen Center for Policy Studies, p. 9.

Johnson, Chalmers. 1991. "Where Does Mainland China Fit in a World Organized into Pacific, North American, and European Regions?" *Issues & Studies*, 27 (August): 1-16.

Kaye, Lincoln. 1994. "Learning to Bow." *Far Eastern Economic Review*, 157 (January 27): 12-14.

Kesavan, K. V. 1990. "Japan and the Tiananmen Square Incident: Aspects of the Bilateral Relationship." *Asian Survey*, 30 (July): 669-681.

Keum, Hieyeon. 1991. "Lukewarm Marriage: Political and Economic Components of Peking-Tokyo Relations." *Issues & Studies*, 27 (July): 30-60.

————. 1989. "Recent Seoul-Peking Relations: Process, Prospects, and Limitations." *Issues & Studies*, 25 (March): 100-117.

Kim, Hong Nack. 1989. "Sino-Soviet Rapprochement and its Implications for South Korea's Northern Policy." *Korea and World Affairs*, 13 (summer): 297-316.

Kim, Samuel S. 1990. "Chinese Foreign Policy After Tiananmen." *Current History*, 89 (September): 245-248, 280-282.

————. 1991. "Peking's Foreign Policy in the Shadows of Tiananmen: The Challenge of Legitimation." *Issues & Studies*, 27 (January): 39-69.

————. 1989. *The Third World in Chinese World Policy.* Princeton: Center of International Studies, Princeton University, p. 67.

Kim, Won Bae. 1994. "Sino-Russian Relations and Chinese Workers in the Russian Far East: A Porous Border." *Asian Survey*, 34 (December): 1064-1076.

Klintworth, Gary. 1989. "China's Indochina Policy." *Journal of Northeast Asian Studies*, 8 (fall).

Kraar, Louis. "The Risks are Rising in China." *Fortune*, 131 (March): 179-180.

Kreisberg, Paul H. 1991. "China's Asia Policies." *Proceedings of the Academy of Political Science*, 38 (2): 75-86.

Kristof, Nicholas D. 1992. "As China Looks at World Order, It Detects New Struggles Emerging." *New York Times*, April 21: A1, A10.

————. 1993. "The Rise of China." *Foreign Affairs*, 72 (November-December): 59-74.

Kuan, Hsin-chi. 1990. *Hong Kong After the Basic Law.* Halifax, N.S., Institute for Research on Public Policy, p. 36.

Kuo, Cheng-Tian. 1992. "The PRC and Taiwan: Fujian's Faltering United Front." *Asian Survey*, 32 (August): 683-695.

Lachia, Eduardo. 1983. "China Tops List with 10 Border Disputes." *Asian Wall Street Journal*, p. 3.

Lardy, Nicholas R. 1994. *MFN Denial: the Economic Consequences.* Washington: National Bureau of Asian Research, p. 9.

Lasater, Martin L. 1989. *Policy in Evolution: The U.S. Role in China's Reunification.* Boulder, Colo.: Westview Press.

Lawrence, Susan V. 1992. "Pointing the Way." *U.S. News & World Report,* 113 (August 3): 36-39.

Lee, Alissa. 1992. "Queen Sacrifices Pawn: Hong Kong Braces Itself for 1997." *Harvard International Review,* 15 (fall): 44-45, 59.

Lee, Deng-ker. 1990. "Communist China's Foreign Policy Since June 4, 1989." *Issues & Studies,* 26 (May): 83-99.

Lee, Dinah. 1991. "China's Ugly Export Secret: Prison Labor." *Business Week,* 3210 (April 22): 42-43, 46.

Lee, Jane C. Y. 1993. "The Exercise of PRC Sovereignty: Its Impact on Hong Kong's Governing Process in the Second Half of the Political Transition." *Issues & Studies,* 29 (December): 88-111.

Lee, Teng-hui. 1993. *Creating the Future: Towards a New Era for the Chinese People.* Taipei: Government Information Office, p. 177.

Levine, Steven I. 1992. "China and America: The Resilient Relationship." *Current History,* 91 (September): 241-246.

———. 1989. "The Uncertain Future of Chinese Foreign Policy." *Current History,* 88 (September): 261-264, 295-296.

Li, Shaomin. 1989. "What China Can Learn From Taiwan." *Orbis,* 33 (summer): 327-340.

Lilley, James R. and Wendell L. Willkie II, eds. 1994. *Beyond MFN: Trade with China and American Interests.* Washington: AEI Press, p. 171.

Lin, Bih-jaw. 1991. "Current Situation in Mainland China and Cross-Strait Relations." *Issues & Studies,* 27 (March).

Lin, Chong-pin. 1993. "Beijing and Taipei: Dialectics in Post-Tiananmen Interactions." *China Quarterly,* 136 (December): 70-804.

———. 1994. "China Military Modernization: Perceptions, Progress and Prospects." *Security Studies* (summer).

———. 1992. "The Coming Chinese Earthquake." *International Economy,* May-June.

———. 1993. "The Deng Linchpin Debate." *International Economy,* July-August.

———. 1994. "The Stealthy Advance of China's People's Liberation Army." *American Enterprises,* January-February.

Lin, Yu-siang. 1989. "China's Reunification and Tiananmen." *Global Affairs,* 4 (fall): 6-56.

Lippencott, Brent C. 1994. *Ending the Confusion in U.S. China Policy.* Washington: Heritage Foundation, p. 15.

Lo, Shiu-Hing. 1994. "An Analysis of Sino-British Negotiations over Hong Kong's Political Reform." *Contemporary Southeast Asia,* 16 (September): 178-209.

——. 1991. "The Problem of Perception and Sino-British Relations Over Hong Kong." *Contemporary Southeast Asia*, 13 (September): 200-219.

Lu, Ping. 1992. "Hong Kong and Free Enterprise: British to Chinese Rule." *Vital Speeches of the Day*, 48 (February 1): 232-235.

MacFarquhar, Roderick. 1992. "Deng's Last Campaign." *New York Review of Books* (December 17).

Malik, J. Mohan. 1991. "Peking's Response to the Gulf Crisis." *Issues & Studies*, 27 (September): 107-128.

Manning, Robert A. 1994. "Burdens of the Past, Dilemmas of the Future: Sino-Japanese Relations in the Emerging International System." *Washington Quarterly*, 17 (winter): 45-58.

——. 1994. "Clinton and China: Beyond Human Rights." *Orbis*, 38 (spring): 193-205.

——. 1994. *Starting Over: From MFN to a China Policy for the Future.* Washington: Progressive Policy Institute, p. 21.

Martin, Keith. 1994. *China and Central Asia: Between Seduction and Suspicion.* Radio Free Europe/Radio Liberty Research Report, 3 (June 24): 26-36.

May. Ernest R. and Jon K. Fairbank, eds. 1986. *America's China Trade in Historical Perspective: The Chinese and American Performance.* Cambridge: Harvard University Press, p. 388.

McNamara, Robert. 1994. *Sino-American Military Relations: Mutual Responsibilities in the Post-Cold War Era.* National Committee on U.S.-China Relations (November).

McNaugher, Thomas. 1994. "A Strong China: Is the U.S. Ready?" *Brookings Review*, 12 (fall): 14-19.

"MFN Status, Human Rights, and U.S.-China Relations." 1994. *NBR Analysis*, 5 (July).

Milivojevic, Marko. 1989. "The Spratly and Paracel Islands Conflict." *Survival*, 31 (January-February): 70-78.

Miller, H. Lyman. 1993. "The Fourteenth Party Congress." *Washington Journal of Modern China* (spring).

Min, Byung O., Nelson, Daniel N. and Yang Zhong. 1990. "Foreign Policy Pragmatism and Domestic Reform: Linkages in the USSR and China." *Journal of Asian and African Affairs*, 2 July): 29-68.

Moeller, Kay. 1994. "Taiwan Between Annexation and Independence." *Aussenpolitik*, 45 (2): 199-208.

Morgan, Patrick M. 1991. *Assessing the Republic of China's Deterrence Situation.* Kaohsiung, Taiwan: Sun Yat-sen Center for Policy Studies, p. 23.

Morrison, Charles E., and Robert F. Dernberger, eds. 1989. *Focus: China in the Reform Era.* Honolulu, Hawaii, East-West Center.

Mosher, Stacy. 1992. "Hong Kong Straight Talk: Britain Toughens Stance on Colony's Future." *Far Eastern Economic Review*, 155 (July 2): 19.

——. 1990. "Most Favored Nation Status for China: Pro and Con." *International Economy*, 4 (August-September): 62-67.

——. 1993. "New Initiatives Across the Taiwan Straits." *Global Affairs*, 8 (spring): 136-153.

Muray, Leo. 1989. "China--The Puzzling Uncertainty." *Contemporary Review*, 225 (August): 63-67.

Murthy, P.A. Narasimha. 1991. "Japan and China in the Nineties: The Bumpy Road to Consolidation of Ties." *China Report*, 27 (October-December): 275-297.

Myers, Ramon Hawley. *1994. Thoughts on U.S. Foreign Policy Toward the People's Republic of China.* Stanford, CA: Hoover Institution on War, Revolution, and Peace, Stanford University.

Nathan, Andrew J. 1989. "The Effect of Taiwan's Political Reform on Taiwan-Mainland Relations." *Issues & Studies,* 25 (December): 14-30.

——. 1994. "Human Rights in Chinese Foreign Policy." *China Quarterly*, 139 (September): 622-643.

Newby, Laura. 1990. "Sino-Soviet Rapprochement and its Implications for China's Foreign Policy." *RUSI and Brassey's Defence Yearbook 1990* London: Brassey's Defence Publishers.

North, Robert C. 1969. *The Foreign Relations of China*. Belmont, CA: Dickenson Publishing Co.

Nguyen, Hung P. 1993. "Russia and China: The Genesis of an Eastern Rapallo." *Asian Survey*, 33 (March).

Niou, Emerson M.S., Ordeshook, Peter C. and Guofu Tan. 1992. "Taiwanese Investment in Mainland China as a Policy Tool." *Issues & Studies,* 28 (August): 14-31.

Oksenberg, Michel. 1991. "The China Problem." *Foreign Affairs*, 70 (summer): 1-16.

Overholt, William H. 1991. "China and British Hong Kong." *Current History*, 90 (September): 270-274.

——. 1991. "Hong Kong and China After 1997: The Real Issues." *Proceedings of the Academy of Political Science,* 38 (2): 30-52.

Perkins, Dwight. 1994. *Human Rights and the Annual Debate Over MFN for China.* P. 8. Washington: National Bureau of Asian Research.

Pi, Ying-hsien. 1992. "Peking's Foreign Relations in the New International Situation." *Issues & Studies*, 28 (May): 13-28.

——. 1990. "Peking-Moscow Relations as Seen from Li P'eng's Visit to the Soviet Union." *Issues & Studies*, 26 (September): 12-26.

Pikcunas, Diane D. 1993. *Nations at the Crossroads: Unification Policies for Germany, Korea and Chin,.* Washington: Council for Social and Economic Studies, p. 88.

Pikcunas, Diane D. and Donald J. Senese. 1989. *Can the Two Chinas Become One?* Washington: Council for Social and Economic Studies, p. 223.

Pollack, Jonathan D. 1984. *Security, Strategy, and the Logic of Chinese Foreign Policy*. Santa Monica: Rand Corp., p. 58.

———.1989. *The Sino-Soviet Summit: Implications for East Asia and U.S. Foreign Policy*. Washington: Asia Society, p. 28.

Powell, Bill. 1993. "The Coming Power Struggle." *Newsweek*, 122 (November): 40-41.

Rafferty, Kevin. 1991. "China's Grasp and Hong Kong's Golden Eggs." *Harvard Business Review*, 69 (May-June): 54-56, 60, 62-63, 66, 68-69.

"Relations Between the Chinese Mainland and Taiwan: Problems and Prospects for Reunification: Symposium." 1989. *Asian Affairs*, 16 (fall).

Ritcheson, Philip L. 1994. "China's Impact on Southeast Asian Security." *Military Review*, 74 (May): 44-57.

Rimmer, Peter J. 1992. *Hong Kong's Future as a Regional Transport Hub*. Canberra, Australia: Strategic and Defense Studies Centre, Australian National University, p. 110.

Robinson, Thomas W. 1993. "U.S. Policy Toward China." *American Enterprise*, 4 (March-April): 43-51.

Ross, Robert S. 1989. "Chinese Pacific Security Policy in the 1990s." *Evolving Pacific Basin Strategies*, Pp. 37-57.

———. 1989. "From Lin Biao to Deng Xiaoping: Elite Instability and China's U.S. Policy." *China Quarterly*, 118 (June): 265-299.

Roy, Denny. 1993. "Consequences of China's Economic Growth for Asia-Pacific Security." *Security Dialogue*, 24 (June): 181-191.

———. 1990. "The Triumph of Nationalism in Peking's Hong Kong Policy." *Issues & Studies*, 26 (April): 105-120.

Scalapino, Robert A. 1990. "Asia and the United States: The Challenges Ahead." *Foreign Affairs*, 69 (1): 89-115.

———. 1991. "China's Relations with its Neighbors." *Proceedings of the Academy of Political Science*, 38 (21): 65-74.

Schaller, Michael. 1990. *The United States and China in the Twentieth Century*. New York: Oxford University Press.

Schuster, Alice. 1990. "Communist China at a Critical Turning Point: Entering the 1990s." *Asian Thought and Society*, 15 (January): 47-58.

Segal, Gerald. 1994. "China After Deng." *Jane's Intelligence Review*, (November).

———. 1994. *China Changes Shape: Regionalism and Foreign Policy*. P. 72. London: Brassey's.

———. 1994. "China's Changing Shape: The Muddle Kingdom." *Foreign Affairs*, (May-June).

———. 1991. "North-East Asia: Common Security or A La Carte?" *International Affairs* (London), 67 (October): 755-767.

Shaffer, Bretigne. 1991. "Beijing, the West, and the Approaching Sack of Hong Kong." *Orbis*, 35 (summer): 327-343.

Shambaugh, David. 1994. "China's Fragile Future." *World Policy Journal*, 11 (fall): 41-45.

———. 1992. "China's Security Policy in the Post-Cold War Era." *Survival*, 34 (summer): 88-106.

———. 1994. "Growing Strong: China's Challenge to Asian Security." *Survival*, 36 (summer): 43-59.

———. 1993. "Losing Control: The Erosion of State Authority in China." *Current History*, (September).

Shao, Wenguang. 1990. "China's Relations with the Super-Powers: Strategic Shifts and Implications." *Survival*, 32 (March-April): 157-172.

Shen, Chun-chuan. 1989. "Peking's Relations with India and Pakistan." *Issues & Studies*, 25 (September): 119-129.

Shirk, Susan. 1990-1991. "The Domestic Roots of China's Post-Tiananmen Foreign Policy." *Harvard International Review*, 13 (winter): 32-34, 61.

Silk, Michael. 1994. "Cracking Down on Economic Crime." *China Business Review*, (May-June).

Silverberg, David. 1994. "China: The Paper Dragon." *Armed Forces Journal International*, (February).

Simone, Joseph T., Jr. 1993. "Damming the Counterfeit Tide." *China Business Review*, 20 (November-December): 52-58.

Sino-American Relations at a Time of Change. 1994. Washington: Asian Studies Program, CSIS; Taipei: Institute of International Relations, p. 274.

Smith, Esmond D., Jr. 1994. "China's Aspirations in the Spratly Islands." *Contemporary Southeast Asia*, 16 (December): 274-294.

Sobin, Julian M. 1991. "The China-Israel Connection: New Motivation for Rapprochement." *Fletcher Forum*, 15 (winter): 111-125.

"The South China Sea Territorial Disputes." 1994. *American Asian Review*, 12 (fall).

St. Amand, Gerard A. 1994. "Schizophrenic Sanctioning: A Failed U.S. Policy Toward China." *Essays on Strategy*; National Defense University, 12: 3-44.

Stanzel, Volker. 1994. "The Reshaping of Socialism in China." *Aussenpolitik*, 45 (4): 364-373.

Stokes, Bruce. 1992. "Challenging China." *National Journal*, 24 (September): 2106-2109.

"Strategic Developments in the Asia-Pacific." 1991. *Contemporary Southeast Asia*, 13 (June).

Sullivan, Roger W. 1992. "Discarding the China Card." *Foreign Policy*, 86 (spring): 2-23.

Suryadinata, Leo. 1990. "Indonesia-China Relations: A Recent Breakthrough." *Asian Survey*, 30 (July): 682-696.

Sutter, Robert G. 1990. "American Policy Toward Beijing, 1989-1990: The Role of President Bush and the White House Staff." *Journal of Northeast Asian Studies*, 9 (winter): 3-14.

———. 1990. "Changes in Eastern Europe and the Soviet Union: The Effects on China." *Journal of Northeast Asian Studies*, 9 (summer): 33-45.

———. 1991-1992. "The Crisis in U.S.-China Policy, 1991: The Role of Congress." *Journal of Northeast Asian Studies,* 10 (winter).

———. 1990. "Sino-American Relations in Adversity." *Current History*, 89 (September): 241-244, 271-273.

———. 1991. "Tiananmen's Lingering Fallout on Sino-American Relations." *Current History*, 90 (September): 247-250.

———. 1990. "U.S. Regional Policies: China and Taiwan." *American Asian Review*, 8 (winter): 68-115.

Swaine, Michael. 1992. *The Military and Political Succession in China.* Rand Corporation.

Tan, Qingshan. 1992. *The Making of U.S. China Policy: From Normalization to the Post-Cold War Era.* Boulder, Colo.: Lynne Rienner Publishers.

———. 1990. "The Politics of U.S. Most-Favored-Nation Treatment to China: The Cases of 1979 and 1990." *Journal of Northeast Asian Studies*, 9 (spring): 41-59.

Terrill, Ross. 1992. "Leaving Deng Behind." *World Monitor*, 5 (November): 50-54.

Trends of Future Sino-U.S. Relations and Policy Proposals. 1994. Beijing: Institute for International Studies, Beijing Academy of Social Sciences (September).

Thurston, Ann. 1994. "A Society at the Crossroads." *China Business Review* (May-June).

———. 1992. "The Dragon Stirs." *Wilson Quarterly* (spring).

Tsai, George W. 1991. "An Analysis of Current Relations Between Taiwan and Mainland China: A Political Perspective." *Issues & Studies,* 27 (September): 18-42.

Turack, Daniel C. 1994. "China's Human Rights Record Since Tiananmen 1989 and the recent mixed response of the United States." *Political Geography*, 13 (January): 507-527.

United States and China Relations at a Crossroads. 1995. Lanham, MD: University Press of America; Washington: Atlantic Council of the United States.

U.S. Central Intelligence Agency. 1993. *"China's Economy in 1992-1993: Grappling with the Risks of Rapid Growth* (July 30).

U.S. China Policy: Building a New Consensus. 1994. Washington: Center for Strategic and International Studies.

"U.S.-China Relations." 1993. *In Depth*, 3 (fall).

U.S. Library of Congress. Congressional Research Service. 1995. "China After Deng Xiaoping--Implications for the United States," by Robert Sutter and James Casey Sullivan. Washington: CRS Report 95-465S, April 7, p. 27.

——. 1993. "China and Congress in 1992," by Kerry Dumbaugh. Washington: CRS Report 93-894 F (October 12).

——. 1994. "China as a Security Concern in Asia: Perceptions, Assessment and U.S. Options," by Robert G. Sutter and Shirley Kan. Washington: CRS Report 95-46 S, (December 22), p. 28.

——. 1993. "China in Transition: Changing conditions and Implications for U.S. Interests," by Robert G. Sutter, Shirley Kan, and Kerry Dumbaugh. Washington: CRS Report 95-1061 S, (December 20), p. 23.

——. 1995. "China in World Affairs--U.S. Policy Choices," by Robert Sutter. Washington: CRS Report 95-265 S (January 31).

——. 1995. "China Policy." CRS report 95727-S (June 19).

——. 1995. "China-U.S. Relations," by Kerry Dumbaugh. Washington: CRS Issue Brief 94002 (December 1).

——. 1995. "China's Changing Conditions," by Robert Sutter, Shirley Kan, and Kerry Dumbaugh. Washington: CRS Issue Brief 93114 (December 1).

——. 1991. "China's Military: Roles and Implications for U.S. Policy Toward China," by Shirley Kan. Washington: CRS Report 91-731 F (October 3).

——. 1994. "Chinese Nuclear Weapons and Arms Control Policies: Implications and Options for the United States," by Robert G. Sutter. Washington: CRS Report 94-422 S (May 15).

——. 1994. "Sino-U.S. Relations: Status and Outlook--Views From Beijing." Washington: CRS Memorandum (August 15).

——. 1995. "Taiwan." CRS Issue Brief 94006 (December 1).

——. 1995. "Taiwan-Mainland China Relations." CRS report 95-968 S (September 8).

VanderKroef, Justus M. "Hesitant 'Normalization': Indonesia's Slow Boat to China." 1989. *Asian Affairs, An American Review*, 16 (spring): 23-44.

Vasey, Lloyd, 1993. "China's Growing Military Power and Implications for East Asia." *Pacific Forum,* CSIS (August).

Vause, W. Gary. 1989. "Tibet to Tienanmen: Chinese Human Rights and United States Foreign Policy." *Vanderbilt Law Review*, 42 (November).

Vohra, Ranbi. 1987. *China's Path to Modernization*. Englewood Cliffs, NJ: Prentice Hall, p. 24.

Voskressenski, Alexei D. 1994. "Current concepts of Sino-Russian Relations and Frontier Problems in Russia and China." *Central Asian Survey*, 1 (3): 361-381.

Wai, Ting. 1992. "The Regional and International Implications of the South China Economic Zone." *Issues & Studies*, 28 (December): 46-72.

——. 1992. "Hong Kong's Changing Political Order and Its Relations with Taiwan." *Issues & Studies*, 28 (August): 46-72.

Waldron, Arthur. 1995. "China's Coming Constitutional Changes." *Orbis* (winter).

——. 1992. "The Sino-American Scene." *Wall Street Journal* (May 22).

Walsh, J. Richard. 1993. "China and the New Geopolitics of Central Asia." *Asian Survey*, 33 (March): 272-284.

Wang, Chien-hsun. 1991. "Peking's Latin American Policy in 1980s." *Issues & Studies*, 27 (May): 103-118.

Wang, Guiguo. 1994. "China's Return to GATT: Legal and Economic Implications." *Journal of World Trade*, 28 (June): 51-65.

Wang, Guzngwu. 1993. "Greater China and the Chinese Overseas." *China Quarterly*, 136 (December): 926-948.

Wang, N. T. 1991. "Taiwan's Economic Relations with Mainland China." *Asian Affairs*, 18 (summer): 99-119.

Wesley-Smith, Peter, and Albert H. Y. Chen, eds. 1988. *The Basic Law and Hong Kong's Future*. Hong Kong: Butterworths, p. 389.

Whiting, Allen S. 1960. *China Crosses the Yalu*, p. 4-5. Macmillian.

——. 1992. "China's Foreign Relations." *Annals of the American Academy of Political and Social Science,* 159 (January).

——. 1990-1991. "Sino-Japanese Relations: Pragmatism and Passion." *World Policy Journal*, 8 (winter): 107-135.

Whiting, Allen S., and Robert F. Dernberger. 1977. *China's Future: Foreign Policy and Economic Development in the Post-Mao Era*, p. 41. New York: McGraw-Hill

Whyte, Martin King. 1992. "Prospects for Democratization in China." *Problems of Communism*, 41 (May-June): 58-70.

Wilborn, Thomas L. 1994. *Security Cooperation with China: Analysis and a Proposal*. U.S. Army War College, Strategic Studies Institute. p. 32.

Wilhelm, Alfred D., Jr. 1994. *The Chinese at the Negotiating Table*. Washington: National Defense University Press. p. 281.

Williams, Richard L. *U.S. Response to Changes in China*. Washington: U.S. Department of State, Bureau of Public Affairs, 1989. p. 3.

Wilson, Ian. 1991. *Power, the Gun and Foreign Policy in China Since the Tiananmen Incident*. Canberra: Strategic and Defence Studies Centre, Australian National University, p. 22.

Womack, Brantly. 1991. "China and Vietnam: Peace at Last?" *World Today*, 47 (October): 164-166.

——. 1994. "Sino-Vietnamese Border Trade: The Edge of Normalization." Asian Survey, 34 (June): 496-512.

Wortzel, Larry M. 1994. "China Pursues Traditional Great Power Status." *Orbis* (spring).

Wu, An-china. 1989. "Relations Between the Two Sides of the Taiwan Strait: Evaluation and Prospects." *Issues & Studies*, 25 (March): 80-99.

——. 1991. "The ROC's Mainland Policy in the 1990s." *Issues & Studies*, 27 (September): 1-17.

Wu, Jaushieh Joseph. 1992. "Lessons Learned From the Persian Gulf War: Taipei's Perspective." *Issues & Studies,* 28 (April): 83-103.

Xu, Zhixian. 1992. "Sino-Japanese Relations Continue Enhanced." *Beijing Review*, 35 (October 12-18): 19-21.

Yahuda, Michael. 1992. "Chinese Foreign Policy and the Collapse of Communism." *SAIS Review*, 12 (winter-spring): 125-137.

———. 1993. "The Foreign Relations of Greater China." *China Quarterly*, 136 (December): 687-710.

Yang, Jiemian. 1992. "Sino-U.S. Relations: Problems and Solutions." *American Asian Review*, 10 (spring): 62-71.

Yi, Xiaoxiong. 1994. "China's U.S. Policy Conundrum in the 1990s: Balancing Autonomy and Interdependence." *Asian Survey*, 34 (August): 675-691.

Yin, Jason Z. and Charles C. Yen. 1992. "An Assessment of the Economic Relations Between Taiwan and Mainland China." *American Asian Review*, 10 (winter): 53-78.

Yu, Peter Kien-Hong. 1990. "On Taipei's Rejoining the Asian Development Bank Subsequent to Beijing's Entry: One Country, Two Seats?" *Asian Affairs*, 17 (spring): 3-13.

Zhang, Ming. 1994. "China and Its Major Power Relations." *The Journal of Contemporary China* (fall).

Zhang, Yongjin. 1991. "China's Entry into International Society: Beyond the Standard of 'Civilization.'" *Review of International Studies*, 17 (January): 3-16.

Zhao, John Quansheng. 1989. "'Informal Pluralism' and Japanese Politics: Sino-Japanese Rapprochement Revisited." *Journal of Northeast Asian Studies*, 8 (summer): 65-83.

About the Book and Author

This book considers Chinese foreign policy and China's future role in world affairs in the context of the country's recent past. Robert Sutter shows that although it appears to be in U.S. interests for post-Mao leaders to continue moving toward international norms, a post-Deng leadership backed by growing economic and military power and reflecting profound changes in China's economy and society could move in markedly different directions.

Most foreign powers appear willing to accommodate China, avoiding actions that could prompt a sharp shift in Chinese foreign policy, but Sutter argues that current U.S. policy intrudes on so many issues that are particularly sensitive for Beijing and for China's future that it represents perhaps the most critical variable determining how China will position itself in world affairs. Concluding that there is no guarantee the United States will use this influence wisely, Sutter examines the uncertainty and unpredictability of U.S. foreign policy in the post–Cold War environment that work against the creation of an effective U.S. policy toward China.

Robert G. Sutter is a senior specialist in international politics with the Congressional Research Service and an adjunct professor of East Asian studies at Georgetown, George Washington, and Johns Hopkins Universities.

Index